The Microgrid Revolution

The Microgrid Revolution

Business Strategies for
Next-Generation Electricity

Mahesh P. Bhave

An Imprint of ABC-CLIO, LLC
Santa Barbara, California • Denver, Colorado

Library of Congress Cataloging-in-Publication Data
Names: Bhave, Mahesh P., 1957– author.
Title: The microgrid revolution : business strategies for next-generation
    electricity / Mahesh P. Bhave.
Description: Santa Barbara, California : Praeger, [2016] | Includes
    bibliographical references and index.
Identifiers: LCCN 2016024233 (print) | LCCN 2016036079 (ebook) |
    ISBN 9781440833151 (alk. paper) | ISBN 9781440833168 (ebook)
Subjects: LCSH: Electric utilities. | Microgrids (Smart power grids) |
    Electric power distribution—Environmental aspects. | Electric
    industries—Environmental aspects. | Renewable energy sources.
Classification: LCC HD9685.A2 B497 2016 (print) | LCC HD9685.A2 (ebook) |
    DDC 333.793/20684—dc23
LC record available at https://lccn.loc.gov/2016024233

ISBN: 978-1-4408-3315-1
EISBN: 978-1-4408-3316-8

20 19 18 17 16   1 2 3 4 5

This book is also available as an eBook.

Praeger
An Imprint of ABC-CLIO, LLC

ABC-CLIO, LLC
130 Cremona Drive, P.O. Box 1911
Santa Barbara, California 93116-1911
www.abc-clio.com

This book is printed on acid-free paper ∞

Manufactured in the United States of America

For our sons,
Vivek and Varun

In our era, the road to holiness necessarily passes through the world of action.
—Dag Hammarskjold

Contents

x   Contents

Preface

This is an accessible book meant for the concerned or interested layperson. It is aimed at policy makers wishing to encourage and foster the new energy industry anchored in renewables and progressively moving away from coal burning. It will also help entrepreneurs and prospective entrepreneurs and new business development and strategy professionals in existing companies. It draws upon my experiences in the telecom industry during and after the spectrum auction–led evolution of today's wireless business in the mid-1990s; I then worked at Citizens Utilities, Sprint, and Hughes Network Systems in strategy and new business development.

The book proposes that the topology of the grid of the future is a cluster of interworking and complementary microgrids of various sizes working synergistically—a federation of microgrids. This federation of microgrids will resemble the honeycomb-like structure used to describe the cellular network; some describe the topology of microgrid clusters as fractals.

The book makes comparisons between the telecommunications industry of about 20 years ago and the electricity business today. The parallels are striking, and the differences are notable too. Can the success—admittedly qualified, yet transformative and even revolutionary—of telecom be replicated in the creation of a new energy infrastructure? The book argues: yes, comparisons are apt, and policies are replicable, with suitable modifications.

Of course, the book has business, economics, public policy, technology, and climate change–related ideas, but they are presented in easy-to-understand terms. References at the end of the book may help the interested reader dive deeper.

In my time during the past 20 years, I have had the privilege to watch and participate in the emergence of two related revolutions worldwide: one, the telecommunications revolution, involving the transformation of landline telephones—wireline followed by wireless—and then the even broader and more fundamental Internet revolution and associated content explosion. The second, and related revolution, involves the wireless Internet and a plethora of applications blended on smartphones. The resulting personal empowerment has been mind-boggling.

I believe I am now a participant, as we all are, in a third related revolution—the blending of Transport and Electricity with ICT, and leading to the Enernet of Things (EoT), even greater in scope than the much hyped Internet of Things (IoT).

Now we are transforming traditional electricity toward the Enernet of things (EoT)—energy compounded with IoT, an equally momentous enterprise. Traditional electricity has jumped out of its skin to encompass, first, information and communications technologies, called ICT, and, second, transport, especially in the form of electric vehicles. I suggest calling the new unit of analysis ICTTE in the book—ICT plus transport and electricity. The point is, industry boundaries are breached. To the classic strategy question "What business are we in?," we have no easy answer.

It is altogether undeserved good fortune for me to now watch, and in some manner participate in, the evolving energy industry transformation already under way. What makes engagement with the electricity revolution urgent is that the stakes are high as the broader subject is energy, largely fossil fuel based and untenable; the cost of not managing this revolution right is human survival itself. It makes the successful pursuit of this revolution, by all of us, a timely and urgent necessity.

When the world was in the midst of the Cold War, I was too young to appreciate its implications. What was happening at that time was, as I now recognize, a fundamental threat to the planet itself and thus similar to what we now confront as a result of anthropogenic climate change. Had the Cold War become a real war, it might have been relatively quick in its consequences. With climate change, the global warming physics is straightforward, and the consequences will play out over decades.

What we have is a kind of a Cold War that has already begun, largely invisible as of now; the genie is out of the bottle and uncontrolled at this time. It is in fact more properly described as a Hot War, troubling, with only the possibility, though not the promise, of controlling the fallout. Unlike the Cold War of the USA v Soviet Union, the Hot War is all of us against all of us in that we are all responsible for emissions, and therefore global warming. Embedded in this grim prospect is the thrill of business, and the possibility of one winning outcome being a prosperous, equitable, and fulfilling future for all peoples, thanks to the magic of clean electricity, clean transport, and access to the bounty of the Internet.

Acknowledgments

I am grateful to Walt Patterson, who taught me to think in novel ways about the electricity business. It was thrilling to read his work on his website, almost nonstop until I was done. Nancy Wimmer visited IIM Kozhikode (IIMK) in 2015, and discussions with her helped me understand the ways of Grameen Shakti and its deployment of solar home systems in Bangladesh. Dr. Bibek Bandyopadhyay, head of the Solar Energy Centre (now NISE, National Institute of Solar Energy), showed me a variety of prototype solar deployments around his facilities outside New Delhi. Dr. S. Gomathinayagam, executive director, Centre for Wind Energy Technology, Chennai, now renamed National Institute of Wind Energy (NIWE), hosted me at his center.

I'm grateful to IIMK as an institution for encouraging my work in renewable energy and for providing me with forums for discussion through formal and informal seminars. My faculty colleagues Shahid Abdullah, Saji Gopinath, Keyoor Purani, Priya Nair Rajeev, Rudra Sensarma, Anubha Shekhar Sinha, and Directors Debashis Chatterjee and Kulbhushan Balooni, have been most supportive. K. T. Bose, the institute's electrical engineer, helped with tours of the campus's electricity infrastructure and shared load profile and cost data, which are helpful for modeling IIM's academic hill as a microgrid.

I discussed conceptual issues relating to the electricity industry structure—from regulated versus market driven to role of markets and institutions, and what constitutes the new public interest—with Milind Padalkar, a doctoral student and an experienced business executive. We also discussed the economics of intermicrogrid communications and resource sharing and the resulting improved economics of microgrid clusters when compared to stand-alone microgrids.

Jennifer Runyon, chief editor, *Renewable Energy World,* and Brian Hayden, CEO of Heatspring, suggested I conduct *MicrogridMBA* as an online course. I taught three sessions for approximately 75 students from across the world.

Nothing of the kind has been done before, so my classes have been experiments. I thank my students for their indulgence; they suffered through my freewheeling curriculum, online discussions, and the vagaries of an online platform. Many expected "truths" about microgrids, captured in implacable numbers in spreadsheets. Instead, I offered "conjectures" with assumptions and Excel analysis. Such is the field; microgrids are an evolving latent market.

I've enjoyed arguing about the state of the industry with Scott Anders, director, EPIC, University of San Diego. Terry Mohn offered operator-oriented insights into microgrids, and we have had wonderful discussions over coffee at Peet's in Carmel Valley.

Bob Lasseter, University of Wisconsin, a pioneer in microgrids, shared with me historical insights into their emergence. I remember asking Chris Marnay, Lawrence Berkeley Labs, also a microgrid champion: "Microgrids are not happening fast enough. Why is that?" He said, "Since the time I began, they have come a long way." We were at the 2015 Global Microgrid Summit at the University of California, Irvine.

In Washington, DC, I met Blair Levin, who had a role in conducting the Federal Communication Commission's (FCC) spectrum auctions in the mid-1990s. I asked, "Can similar auctions of markets, like MTAs and BTAs, be conducted in the electricity industry?" Also in the District of Columbia, I met Harvey Reiter, among the few whose scholarship and experience includes both electricity and telecom; his articles have been most helpful. Kiran Magiawala has been my informal guide since September 2012, when he responded to my article in the Hindu *Business Line,* "Solar Power on Every Rooftop." I continue to benefit from his scholarship and commitment to the cause of universal and clean electricity.

Mehul Rumde in Mumbai converted my PowerPoint diagrams into the vector format. My son Vivek has been a fine copy editor. He has an eye for detail and goes deep into the logic and structure of my arguments. He raised legitimate conceptual issues that I spent hours addressing after I thought I had completed the book. My teaching assistants Athulya Sadanand and M. P. Raseela have been helpful in numerous ways, from copying to formatting to research. Praeger's Hilary Claggett, Senior Editor, has been patient and persistent, cajoling me to finish on time, and guiding me through the publication process from day zero to the present; I thank her for her role. Leah Georgina, project manager and leader of the editing team, has been prompt with inputs, and equally prompt in converting my revisions into publication quality text. Michelle Scott, Production Editor at ABC-CLIO, manages the production schedule and interfaces with Leah. Among Leah, Michelle, the copy editor and me, we have managed deadlines smoothly and well. It has been my pleasure working with the entire Praeger and ABC-CLIO team.

Professor Aravind, TU Delft, an expert in fuel cells, and my partner in brainstorming on all matters energy, introduced me to energy-related work at his university in The Netherlands. I toured several of their labs and presented my early finding at the university's energy club. He has generated interest in microgrids among his students, several of whom have worked on internship projects with me at IIM K.

San Diego; Kozhikode; Mumbai; Pune; Washington, DC; and airport lounges have been my offices while I worked on this project. My IIM K apartment, overlooking valleys, and deep green and sometimes misty, layered hills, is a sacred place conducive to reflection. Many mornings, the clouds are below my eye level, and the peace is augmented by the sounds of birds. It is here that the core idea of the book struck me: divide up the market into small, interlinked service territories for clean, green, and universal electricity.

For all the help I have received, I am grateful. For whatever faults remain, I am responsible.

Introduction

*You never change things by fighting the existing reality. To change some-
thing, build a new model that makes the existing model obsolete.*

— R. Buckminster Fuller

When faced with a formidable and daunting adversary, it is best to not attack
head-on. Rather find a niche that can be leveraged for continuous and progressively larger gains. This is Sun Tsu—*Art of War*. There is simply too much inertial
momentum favoring the existing oil and electricity industries. What we need to
create a clean, nonpolluting world is a substitute on a different trajectory, complementary yet intersecting with the existing industry.

Consider pagers. Hardly anyone uses them anymore. Superior pagers did not
supplant existing pagers. They were rendered obsolete by screens and SMS mes-
sages and Whatsapp on cell phones, the cellular infrastructure being completely
independent of the paging network. In my MBA classes, I distribute to students
the old numeric-only, one-way pager and the bulkier two-way, alphanumeric,
ASCII keypad–based pager, with a clip for the belt, which I used when I worked
for Citizens Utilities between 1991 and 1995. It makes for a quaint comparison
with the smartphones my students have.

The message: this too shall pass; "time and chance happeneth to them all." The
gale forces of Schumpeterian creative destruction will incessantly overturn, from
within the industry and from without, what looks imperishable and permanent.
Such a fate awaits the electricity industry of today, though I cannot distribute any
token of the industry as pithy as a pager in class.

Can the experience of auctioning spectrum for mobile telecom services in specific geographies be replicated in the case of next-generation electricity? It is the
thesis of this book that it can be, and it should be tried. This book proposes a path.

The challenge is to transform the existing oil–electricity (OE) complex over the next 20 years to curtail carbon dioxide (CO_2) emissions. The good news is that what needs to happen is clear. Most educated people are aware of the dangers of anthropogenic climate change, thanks to the efforts of scientists and of the United Nations and its affiliates.

THE THESIS

I believe that we are on the cusp of a new curve in industrial organization. Under threat from this transformation is among the largest industries in the world—the energy industry, both oil related and electricity. Its strength may appear overwhelming, yet gigantic structures routinely crumble when confronted with changes resulting from the organization and conduct of timely and specific new activity.

As Victor Hugo noted, "All the forces in the world are not so powerful as an idea whose time has come." It is also true that the industry is such a giant that the edifice, to paraphrase David Hume's words (that he applied to *liberty*), will not be "lost all at once." Yet in the case of electricity, Schumpeter's "crumbling walls" are already visible—lower costs and better sunlight-to-electricity conversion for solar panels, superior batteries, demand loss for traditional electricity, more efficient home appliances, and people's willingness to deploy new solutions.

Climate change may appear as the driver, and, certainly, its dangers are cause enough for impelling this industrial evolution forward. Yet philanthropic concern for the environment is not the principal causal force driving the new industrial organization. I believe the more fundamental driver is the age-old driver of all economic activity—opportunity and its pursuit. As Rhett Butler observed in Margaret Mitchell's *Gone with the Wind*, "There is just as much money to be made out of the wreckage of a civilization as from the upbuilding of one."

Public policy may well recognize and state a need, yet its role is largely reactive, supportive, and enabling. Unless an opportunity passes the check of entrepreneurial evaluation, there can be no successful new business. Although installing solar panels will, for instance, reduce greenhouse gas (GHG) emissions and help in mitigating climate change impacts, the panel installation companies have to meet strict business criteria of financial viability. There has to be timely demand for their services. The entrepreneur starting the panel installation and services company, or a microgrid company, or a solar panel company, is mostly focused on business opportunity and its pursuit, not climate change. It is worth mentioning this seemingly obvious fact to place in perspective the work of climate policy makers in Paris at COP 21 and in national capitals around the world.

What the traditional energy industry has to confront is this entrepreneurial recognition of opportunity and entrepreneurial willingness to pursue it with commitment. Such entrepreneurial initiatives may be among the critical gating factors holding back the new energy economy. Quantity or volume of entrepreneurial activity matters less than the presence of a critical mass of willing entrepreneurs and the quality of their conceptualizations and visualizations of their new businesses. No doubt false starts—often wrongly called *failures*—will occur in the entrepreneurial ecosystem.

How powerful can entrepreneurial initiatives be? Very influential, when one considers that between them, Jack Goeken and Bill McGowan and their company, Microwave Communications, Inc., later famous as MCI, brought down the entire, gigantic AT&T of old. It is a truism that entrepreneurs routinely run circles around incumbents, however large.

In my office at IIM Kozhikode, every few weeks, students wishing to start new businesses visit me. Whereas in the past, the opportunities they sought to pursue usually related to IT applications or networking, the new prospective entrepreneurs wish to pursue something in energy. For example, no sooner did I mention microgrids, and describe how they may be deployed on campuses, than half a dozen students from my executive MBA class of about 100, mostly all engineers working for global electricity equipment multinationals, offered to design and build a microgrid for our campus, both technically and with financial analysis. This *zeitgeist* is a potent new transformative force.

I believe entrepreneurial efforts will lead to a new partly parallel and partly complementary energy infrastructure that will give rise to new services, innovation, and environment-friendly economic growth, worldwide. Having already unshackled entrepreneurial imagination, their initiatives will launch a new growth trajectory—a new S curve in business school jargon—along a path now in a latent phase. The existing infrastructure will be absorbed into the new one, and the damage from the transformation—for the existing electricity model will first stall and then decline, and the existing transport model will also later be transformed—will be outweighed by the economic benefits from it. Many employees of the present electricity and transport model will be in demand for the new one. The employment impact in the aggregate could be positive.

LESSONS FROM THE TELECOM EXPERIMENT

In the mid-1990s, the United States decided to introduce a new kind of wireless telephone service called PCS (personal communications services). It allocated the 2-GHz band spectrum band for use, in markets defined by and divided into over 500 BTAs (basic trading areas) and about 50 MTA (major trading areas), using the Rand McNally geographical classifications. It then opened up the spectrum for bidding to both incumbent telecommunications operators and new entrants. The draft guidelines for bidding were written in Federal Communication Commission (FCC) dockets and commented upon by those interested. Final bidding rules were eventually formulated. The auctions took place, the bidding was successful, and numerous service providers began offering this next-generation cellular service.

I worked for Citizens Utilities at that time and developed the business model and *pro forma* financials for my company's bids in the auction. Citizens Utilities bid for certain markets and won the rights to service some of them. The company built the systems in its geography and eventually sold the network to a larger operator. By that time, I had joined Sprint, which had won the rights to serve the entire continental United States.

With some variations, India developed a similar system for dividing up the nation's geography into service areas and sought bids from the private-sector companies for implementing wireless services. In India, the auctions were successful; the investments that followed have led to a spectacular growth and unbelievable penetration of mobile telephony access, at unimaginably low prices, and to the proliferation of smartphones with Internet browsing and applications, including GPS-based navigation, online purchases, and Uber service.

In contrast, the classical wireline telephone service remains primitive. Both the instruments and the network appear comparatively feature poor and antiquated, even though the underlying network has transformed materially from a hub-and-spoke circuit-switched topology to a more distributed topology of routers. By no means is this experiment in public policy and private-sector initiative complete, even though the market worldwide for mobile telephone service now has largely matured.

AS TELECOM, SO ELECTRICITY—WITH DIFFERENCES

It is the hypothesis of this book that a similar revolution in electricity—infrastructure upgrade, substitution, and the rise of new applications, on a distinct yet intersecting trajectory—is inevitable, if aided by enlightened public policy. Just like in telephone services in the 1990s, ambiguity toward the emerging transformation, and some active resistance to this emergent future by incumbent service providers, is also palpable in the electricity industry. This is to be expected. But the inexorable ocean tide of the new transformative forces cannot be held in check. The monolith has begun to crumble; its centripetal forces today no longer pull as strongly as once they did.

DIVIDING GEOGRAPHY FOR ELECTRICITY 2.0

Even after the principle of geographical division of electricity markets into smaller chunks is accepted, numerous questions remain. For instance, is it appropriate to divide up the geography of a nation among basic and major trading areas, BTAs and MTAs or equivalent, for electricity as was done with personal communications services? In electricity, do we need the equivalents of MTAs at all? Why should we not focus only on sub-BTAs, however defined, and let the market and the service providers decide how they wish to combine them to form larger service areas?

Many questions arise: in next-generation electricity, are contiguous service areas better than separated service areas or even necessary? Would it be appropriate to require the division of geographies such that all metropolitan areas be linked or associated with a corresponding rural area, where the rural area enables the electricity service providers the space to generate electricity to service the urban areas? Would the value of an urban BTA be more if it was combined with a neighboring rural area? Can energy be traded across BTA equivalents, and across service providers, giving rise to, say, "roaming electricity"?

Given the trend toward community-based electricity solutions and municipalization, more questions need to be addressed. Should municipalities self-define neighborhoods, say, of areas as small as 1 to 3 square kilometers? Can a gated community, specialized enterprise zone, school or college campus, a high school, and so on be the electricity unit of service? Is a national policy for such geography division better than the decision to do so at the state level or city level? Should today's IOUs themselves make such divisions, say, based on the service territories associated with each substation?

As the microgeographical service areas are defined, and infrastructure on them is built, what will be the role of the existing electric utility? Will it be a supplier of last resort? Will it be an insurance provider? Surely, such newly defined geographical service areas will conflict with historical franchise jurisdictions; should the new geographical divisions be a competing overlay on what exists today? Will different nations define service territories differently?

MAIN DIFFERENCE BETWEEN TELECOM AND ENERGY

The value of telecom or the Internet infrastructure directly depends on the so-called network externalities. Give a person in a remote, rural, unelectrified area a telephone, and however poor or illiterate, his access and reachability includes someone as remote and exalted as Barack Obama, Xi Jinping, Angela Merkel, Narendra Modi, or Ban Ki-moon, or Warren Buffett, Bill Gates, and Mark Zuckerberg. My point being the value of telephone service, or the value of the Internet, depends on the number of other people and nodes on the network.

But it is otherwise with electricity. My self-generated local electricity is as good as networked electricity—the electrons can originate as easily on my rooftop as in an Ultra Mega Power Plant, and my microwave oven or refrigerator would not know the difference. I need telecommunications for linking across distance, but electricity can be hyperlocal.

PUBLIC POLICY: INSTITUTIONAL MEMORY AND THE NEW PUBLIC INTEREST

It has only been some 20 years since the last major policy and regulatory restructuring of the telecom industry. In countries other than the United States, the time has been even shorter. Expertise exists within the public policy establishment to help the electricity transformation along. For example, the FCC may work with the Federal Energy Regulatory Commission (FERC) and the state public utilities or service commissions to help with the transformation.

Tokens of transformative change are everywhere—from NRG Energy's automobile charging stations to Tesla Motor's electric vehicles, and the hundreds of solar installation companies cropping up around the world. How can the context for them be made more favorable? Beyond subsidies, I believe a new conceptualization of what constitutes the *highest public interest* needs to be explicitly stated.

"Competition" has to be up there besides the traditional operating measures of reliability, stability, resilience, and security. And competition surely means new market entry and therefore entrepreneurs. Is the climate favorable for start-ups and new business development initiatives of existing players? Steve Pullins, formerly of Horizon Energy: "When we propose a microgrid, we consider four business case scenarios. We consider maximum savings, maximum renewables, grid independence, and maximum diversity. The difference in cost between the maximum savings and grid independence scenarios isn't very large."[1]

NATURAL MONOPOLIES, NATURAL NETWORKS

Whereas telecommunications is a natural network, electricity need not be. The *control* of an electricity infrastructure benefits from the telecom network which helps optimize its operations, say, through the smart grid. To the extent we can leverage the existing ICT (Information and Communications Technologies) infrastructure, we can have pockets of stand-alone electricity assets, islands of electricity generation and consumption, operate with great efficiency. Historically, some businesses have been regarded as natural monopolies, and they have been regulated accordingly. With technological change, the natural monopoly status of the electricity industry no longer holds—barriers for electricity provision have fallen and are falling, and unit costs of electricity no longer depend on gigantic scale generation—small is beautiful, clean, and economical.

INCUMBENT ELECTRICITY PROVIDERS WIN

What happened to Bell Atlantic, NYNEX, Bell South, Southwestern Bell, Pacific Bell, and the independent telecommunications providers of not too long ago? What happened to MCI, Sprint, and AT&T as long-distance providers? They survive under different names or have transformed their character. In a sense, they survive; their infrastructure and employees remain. They simply got absorbed into a large and different infrastructure. This will happen to today's utilities too. "The utility could offer microgrids as a service, but as far as I know no utility does," Guy Warner, CEO of Pareto Energy, says. "I don't understand why."[2]

ROLE OF MICROGRIDS—WORLD BANK AND RURAL DEPLOYMENTS

Microgrids in rural, developing economy deployments differ from those for economically developed regions. The former deployments are concerned with *access,* the latter with *reliability.* While the underlying technology will be similar, the problems being solved, or the needs being met, are distinct. A product manager has to treat them as distinct segments for marketing. Whereas the grid solutions are developed and maturing for the developed nations, there is recognition that the needs of the 1.5 billion rural unelectrified customers and others who have unreliable electricity are not being met.

The World Bank recognizes the benefits of microgrids and hosted an online forum to discuss their role in 2014. The bank recognizes the role for anchor tenants, say, a cell phone tower or a school, as part of the economic justification for a stand-alone microgrid. Typically, such microgrids are small—about 0.5 to 3 MW. In contrast, microgrids for diesel substitution in military bases, remote mining towns, and islands or for *captive capacity* for reliability in industrial manufacturing factories are larger, greater than 5 MW. Companies like ABB historically focus on the latter. The technical issues involved in the large-scale deployment of microgrids smaller than 500 kW, and, to an even greater extent, the interaction of several microgrids in a cluster, are largely unaddressed today.

Technically speaking, one could regard Solar Home Systems as microgrids too, and this is often done. For instance, in June 2016, India's Ministry of New and Renewable Energy put out a draft policy document on mini- and microgrids. In that document, even 10 kW systems are regarded as mini-grids. Such systems typically address the need for illumination, fans, phone charging, and television. The world is now better off—relatively inexpensive solutions for this level of access are now available, though not yet well distributed. Many government organizations and NGOs are engaged in the distribution of such solutions, typically for remote populations of relatively low densities in difficult geographies where affordability is an issue.

For this book, microgrids are technologically sophisticated systems, involving monitoring and control, supply optimization among a number of generation sources, and demand-side management. They support all typical home-use appliances, including refrigerators, induction and microwave cookstoves, washers, dryers, clothes irons, hair-dryers, and air-conditioners. They can be deployed easily in urban settings in grid electricity environments, easily and equally in rural settings. Microgrids as described in this book are fully competitive with the traditional grid—the macrogrid or megagrid—and also complementary to it.

ROOFTOP SOLAR AS A SATURATED SALT SOLUTION

Rooftop solar installations with feed-in tariffs or net electricity metering may be regarded as nuclei in a beaker of a not-quite-saturated salt solution. A whole new infrastructure can crystallize quickly under the right context, and should such a context occur reasonably soon in any country, its extension to the rest of the world will be rapid. The transformative impact of rooftop solar or solar home systems in a relatively short time cannot be underestimated. For all the solar hype, however, I do believe the renewables industry is still to the left of Geoffrey Moore's "chasm," that is, at the latent market stage. There will be hiccups before take-off.

Who will take the lead? I discuss whether emerging economies or the developed markets will be leaders in the book, depending on whether maturity of institutions and history, or sheer need, drive the transformation. In both instances, vision and leadership matter.

CLUSTER OF BUBBLES, NOT A CLOUD

Images matter. A cloud conjures an image of a soft, benign, cuddly, friendly, and a benevolent entity—it delivers rain. And yet, the cloud in cloud computing, for instance, and even today's grid as a megacloud, while efficient in delivering services, can be anything but benevolent in the wrong hands. Further, the greater its size, the more vulnerable it is to either cyberattacks or catastrophic failures.

The emerging electricity infrastructure may be visualized not as a grid or a cloud with hubs and spokes linked to form a whole but more like a cluster of bubbles linked to each other. Ideally, each bubble should be independent and yet cooperate with other bubbles when needed. How small can the smallest bubble be? Should it be the size of a municipality? A community? A homeowners' association?

Urban areas may not offer sufficient rooftop space for needed power generation. And yet, within any given geography, sufficiently large, there would be enough open spaces for next-generation power when a community, or a municipality, is the unit of analysis. Can New York City draw upon the open spaces of New Jersey or Connecticut for its electricity?

SCALE OF OPERATIONS WITHOUT GEOGRAPHICAL CONTIGUITY

As I argued in a series of articles in *Renewable Energy World*,[3] with silicon-based solar panels and no moving parts, electricity networking parallels Internet networking. Solar panels are merely another "desktop" managed on the Ethernet, from home or from a remote station. All IT companies, therefore, are tomorrow's electricity companies. In fact, all companies may buy the needed components for becoming their own power source.

With the Internet as a wide area network, which may be visualized as a control and communications bus, it is not difficult to manage disparate power-generating assets, separated by distance, from any Internet terminal or mobile phone, anywhere in the world. An operator or service provider can establish economies of scale without geographical contiguity.

RENEWABLES AS INFRASTRUCTURE ELECTRICITY

Electricity of the future is no different than buying a microwave oven or a refrigerator and plugging into a power outlet; except in the new instance, it generates rather than consumes electricity. Walt Patterson, Chatham House, prefers to call next-generation electricity, what the rest of us call renewables, infrastructure power. Electricity of the future is more like hardware than a flow of electrons for payment based on hours of use, or time of day based charges. It is like furniture—use it all you want, nothing metered or measured or billed.

It is worth speculating about what humanity might have done if oil had not been discovered or exploited as it is today, or if the alternator had not been invented for electricity, or if the internal combustion engine had not been invented for locomotion. What would have happened if there was no effective, portable, and safe storage for electricity beyond batteries? The civilization path has delivered us to the present by a series of happy accidents. Would some micro, nano, and pico technology deliver us from fossil-based electricity and transport?

SMART GRIDS: BAND-AID FOR THE MORIBUND

The national grid as it exists is a part of the problem today—too large to be secure and unclean because of coal-based generation. True, the grid infrastructure is antiquated and needs to change. But is smartening the grid infrastructure the best way to bring the grid in phase or alignment with market conditions? Why should we shore up this old infrastructure when a new one is better? Thus the smart grid developments appear to fix what ought to die or at least have a secondary place in the overall electricity infrastructure of the future. We rather need new smarter grids—microgrids—resilient, reliable, secure, clean, with local control, and stand-alone when necessary— tied to other microgrids or the megagrid when necessary, for managing electricity needs of the future.

OVERVIEW OF THE BOOK BY CHAPTER

In Chapter 1, Centrifugal Revolution: Strategies for Next-Generation Electricity, I propose that the microgrid revolution underway results from centrifugal forces, primarily technological, including and especially advances in solar photovoltaics and batteries. Solar panels and batteries have both become progressively cheaper, and we can conceive of "edge" solutions not possible before. As a result of the edge forces, the traditional way of organizing the electricity industry no longer works. New business strategies are necessary, as well as new regulations and public policy.

I identify 10 major strategies and further classify them into three categories for distinct sets of players: (1) new product or business strategies for existing companies and also for entrepreneurs, (2) supportive, impeding, or breakthrough strategies for incumbent electric utilities, and (3) strategies and public policies at the industry structure level.

In Chapter 2, Microgrids for Autonomy: Local Generation, Local Consumption, I describe a variety of microgrids, and suggest that off-grid microgrids supporting all of today's applications represent the toughest business case to make. How does microgrid economics compare with the economics of traditional fossil fuel–based power?

I also argue that entrepreneurial start-ups in the microgrid space are in the public interest, though historically absent in the monopolistic organization of the industry, and that electricity entrepreneurs are stakeholders in Electricity 2.0.

Chapter 3, Toward Off-Grid Campuses: The Design Challenge, is devoted to comparing microgrid economics for a standalone off-grid microgrid with the economics of traditional power supplied by a distribution utility. I describe our efforts to model a ~1-MW microgrid for a college campus, IIM Kozhikode, and a comparably sized microgrid for a homeowners' association in California. Our results suggest that microgrids will soon be economical and compete with traditional power, initially in some places, and more broadly later.

In Chapter 4, Microgrids: Common Intersection between Developed and Emerging Economies, I explore how the electricity infrastructure compares to the telecom network, and to other delivery networks like those for natural gas and water. In what ways do emerging markets differ from developed ones? Whereas the reasons for developing microgrids differ, the *technology* of microgrids can largely be the same. No one has adequately addressed how microgrid developments might lead to clean, biomass- or fossil fuel–free cooking, even though much work has been done in designing clean-burning cookstoves.

I further show how the maturing of microgrids leads to a new topology for the electricity distribution infrastructure of the future. The topology comprises the traditional grid, solar home systems (SHS), and sophisticated microgrids in both rural and urban deployments.

Chapters 5 and 6 emphasize what electric utilities might do as strategy; they may be read together. I show how macro forces impacting the industry leave utilities no choice but to face up to difficult alternatives.

In Chapter 5, Divest and Fractionate for Value, I propose *fractionate* as strategy with two components. (1) Breakup of the service territory into smaller geographical units that are serviced by microgrids; that is, the macrogrid functionality rendered small. (2) Reorganize—or encourage the reorganization of—the electricity industry by splitting it up into *product-markets*. Who should own such businesses? One option might be to sell off the fractions to companies interested in them—*divest*. It might work equally well if the incumbent utilities themselves reorganize to offer services for the fractions, through microgrids and *product-markets*. Analogous initiatives have been implemented in the past. For instance, the split of geography into basic trading areas (BTAs) for telecom in the United States as described in Chapter 4. Similarly, can the roughly 250,000 *panchayats* in India, local government units typically at the village level, be a unit of analysis each, for electricity services?

Also in Chapter 5, I propose that the market value of today's electricity business is greater when it is split into *product-markets*, and then added up, than the aggregate valuation of today. Equally, the market value of today's electricity business is greater when the market is split into microgrids, and the valuations of individual microgrids added up (see Figures 5.3 and 5.4). More research is needed to examine the truth of these propositions.

Of course, *product-markets* may also be parsed into *technology-markets*, or *location-markets*. When regulated *natural monopoly* as an organizing principle for the industry no longer holds, and when *barriers to entry* are low for starting electricity businesses, having the industry organized the way it has been for a hundred years no longer makes sense. It is mostly a matter of time before the splintering begins. "If you are falling, dive" said Joseph Campbell, and that might be a valid strategy for investor owned utilities, and for distribution companies in general.

Chapter 6, Define and Auction Market Blocks, focuses on one particular way of organizing next generation electricity markets, namely, by *splitting geography* into small blocks or parcels of service territory, and then *auctioning them off*. The United States was divided into BTAs in telecom, and auctions held for licensing them. It is clear that gigantic and costly generation and large service territories are no longer needed for economically viable electricity service. However, we do not know how small microgrids can be, for both operational efficiency and aggregate economics. One benefit of auctions—*divesting*—is that we let the markets determine the size and value of the service territories.

Deciding upon an optimal size of a market unit is complicated, for both electricity generation potential, that is, "supply," and revenue potential have to be understood simultaneously for each newly defined market unit. One logical way to divide geography might be to locate the hub of the new service company at each substation.

Should small service territories—constituted as microgrids—interact with each other for superior economics and operational independence from the macrogrid? Who should initiate the geographical split of the service territory of an investor owned utility? Should it be regulators, or the companies themselves? Maybe, an investor owned utility with the regulators in particular states might use a "laboratories of democracy" approach. The CEO of a utility may initiate the change, or the chief minister of a state in India, or a governor in the United States.

Chapter 7, Entrepreneurial Opportunities in Electricity 2.0, addresses *entrepreneurial opportunities* resulting from technological advance, and the resulting reorganization of the historically uniform, commoditized electricity product. For instance, I show how franchise boundaries are no longer meaningful when an entrepreneurial company decides to focus on lighting solutions—for municipalities, campuses, office buildings, and more—across the world. Or when some entrepreneurs organize around solar-powered water pumps, again worldwide. Scale now is associated less with gigantic generation and more with market reach—*extensive* strategy. And market reach is not defined by regulations and franchises, but rather by the *strategic intent*, and by the resources and capabilities of the services company.

A market may also be defined by specialization, say, electricity for police sta-tions in a region, or traffic lights, or supermarkets, or malls. Equally, a strategy might be to focus on *intensive* services, concentrated on certain geography, say a city, and offer customers multiple services in that city. The reorganization of the industry either into microgrids or into *product-markets* is already discussed in Chapter 5; *intensive* or *extensive* organization of electricity businesses represents an overlay on that basic organization.

Chapter 8, Electricity Most Glamorous: The Enernet of Things (EoT), addresses *industry structure* issues, in particular the impact of technological advance on industry boundaries. In the case of electricity, the boundaries are well established for over a hundred years. This has created well-established processes, procedures, habits of mind, business approaches, and regulatory instincts that are becoming obsolete today. For instance, electric utilities are getting into the ISP business, and IT companies can get into the electricity business. Municipalities too are exploring entry into both electricity and ISP services. And every hospital or office building or mall or neighborhood can act as its own power plant; how do we accommodate such happenings with the ways of the past?

Chapter 9, Functional, Therefore Dysfunctional, Business Schools, addresses the relative absence of topics related to renewable energy in business schools. I argue that whereas climate change due to the use of fossil fuels for electricity and transport is reflected in public policy and regulations, and whereas engineering and sciences programs in universities study it, it is astonishingly absent in business schools. "Sustainability" as a topic is covered in certain classes, and that is about all. There are not sufficient numbers of cases, or centers for the study of renewa-ble energy and its business implications, in business schools. For instance, indus-try structure changes brought about due to new technologies, or new business development options emerging at the inflection point of the evolving electricity industry, are seldom discussed in classes. Such critical questions as: What might utilities do? What might entrepreneurs do? Would non-traditional players enter the electricity industry, and in turn, electric utilities enter new businesses?, are unexplored in business schools. This situation obtains despite the fact that busi-nesses are the key drivers for mitigating the effects of climate change.

Chapter 10, Wrapping Up: Microgrids Everywhere, suggests that a global change in consciousness is needed to recognize that climate change is a "Hot War," similar to the Cold War of the 1960s and 1970s. Whereas the Cold War would have destroyed civilization in a short time had it become a real war, the Hot War has begun, though the changes wrought by it play out over decades.

In Appendix I, I address the need for policy advocacy on behalf of microgrids. I suggest that the International Solar Alliance be leveraged as a platform for spreading the word about the benefits of microgrids.

In Appendix II, I have a sample course outline for an MBA-level course, "Stra-tegic Management of (Renewable) Energy Systems" in which microgrids are addressed as among the topics. Though listed as a 3-credit course, the contents can be easily split into two 3-credit courses, one giving an overview of the subject, and the second focused on student projects. However, the material can also be addressed at a higher level for an executive Management Development Program (MDP) too followed by courses in specialized topics, especially for representatives of the countries of the International Solar Alliance.

In Appendix III, I list select microgrid-related articles I have written over the recent past. Those interested may review them as complementary material to what is covered in the book.

Abbreviations

BAU	Business As Usual
BOS	Balance Of System
BTA	Basic Trading Areas
CA	California
CCA	Community Choice Aggregation
CEED	Centre for Environment and Energy Development
CERC	Central Electricity Regulatory Commission
CERTS	Consortium for Electric Reliability Technology Solutions
CO	Central Office
CPUC	California Public Utilities Commission
DC	Direct Current
DER	Distributed Energy Resources
DG	Distributed Generation
DSL	Digital Subscriber Line
DSPP	Distributed Services Platform Provider
EDF	Environmental Defense Fund
EEI	Edison Electric Institute
EoT	Enernet of Things
EPB	Electric Power Board
EPRI	Electric Power Research Institute
ET&P	Entrepreneurship Theory And Practice
FCC	Federal Communication Commission
FERC	Federal Energy Regulatory Commission
HOA	Homeowners' Association
ICA	Information And Communications Applications

ICATE	Information And Communications Applications Transport and Electricity
ICS	Information and Communication Services
ICT	Information And Communications Technologies
ICU	Information And Communication Uses
IEEE	Institute of Electrical and Electronics Engineers
IIMK	Indian Institute Of Management Kozhikode
IOT	Internet Of Things
IOU	Investor Owned Utility
IPP	Independent Power Producers
ISP	Internet Service Provider
IT	Information Technology
ITU	International Telecommunication Union
KSEB	Kerala State Electricity Board
LAN	Lamp Area Network
LAWN	Local Area Water Network
LED	Light Emitting Diode
LEED	Leadership in Energy and Environmental Design
LEVA	Light Electric Vehicle Association
LPG	Liquefied Petroleum Gas
M2M	Machine-To-Machine
MBA	Master of Business Administration
MDP	Management Development Programs
MTA	Metropolitan Trading Areas
NYSERDA	New York State Energy Research and Development Authority
OSI	Open System Interconnection
PCS	Personal Communication Service
POTS	Plain Old Telephone Service
PPA	Power Purchase Agreement
PSEDC	Punjab State Electricity Distribution Company
PUC	Public Utilities Commissions
REV	Reforming the EnergyVision
RPS	Renewable PortfolioStandard
SCADA	Supervisory Control and Data Acquisition
SDG&E	San Diego Gas & Electric
SHS	Solar Home System
UPS	Uninterruptible Power Supply
USA	United States of America
USB	Universal Serial Bus
VEC	Village Electrification Committee

ONE

Centrifugal Revolution: Strategies for Next-Generation Electricity

Turning and turning in the widening gyre
The falcon cannot hear the falconer;
Things fall apart; the centre cannot hold

—William Butler Yeats

CENTRIFUGAL SOCIAL REVOLUTION

Typically, when we consider a centrifugal force, we expect its intensity to diminish as it reaches the periphery of the circle of influence it defines. The force is strongest at the center and weakest at the edge. I would like to describe what is happening in the electricity industry as a centrifugal revolution—where the "center does not hold"—but with a difference. The centrifugal forces, represented by start-ups, instead of diminishing in intensity as they radiate outward, gain in strength at the rim of the circle. Next-generation electricity is strongest at the edges.

What analogy describes this condition? Social revolutions have this character-istic. People power militates against central authority. Sometimes democracies are born. This happened during the French Revolution in 1789,[1] the American Revolutionary War in 1775–1783, and the Indian Independence struggle in 1947. I believe the electricity revolution is principally a social revolution, though cer-tainly a technological one. Market forces will soon accommodate the forces of this revolution.

Unlike the electricity revolution, the mobile phone and Internet revolution retains its centripetal characteristics, though it is social too (note the impact of social media) and comparably empowering for people. Arguably, even as a host of applications enrich our lives, the underlying organization of the Internet and the telecommunications infrastructure remains centralized and even undemocratic. Power aggregates at the center—and literally at the data centers of hosting and media companies—so much so that Hillary Clinton, when she installed a mail server at her home, expressing a perfectly reasonable need to retain her privacy and control over her content, has been chastised in the media.

In fact, we all ought to have our personal mail and web servers, define our circles, and communicate within and outside of them, without Big Brother, be it a government authority or Google, Yahoo!, Facebook, or anyone else as intermediaries. Hillary Clinton could have made this argument, but she did not. Of course, Hillary Clinton was conducting official work on a personal machine and not personal work on a personal machine. But then, do we not use phones for personal and official purposes without a thought of exposing ourselves to the criticism leveled at the former first lady? But that is another story beyond the scope of this book.

EMERGING EDGE FORCES

An expansionist force, represented by solar- and battery-based start-ups, arising at the network edge, challenges the historical power of the incumbents. At one level, it is easy to explain what is happening. The forces at the edge are qualitatively different from the traditional, centripetal, gravitation-like forces that define the electricity industry. Although both lead to electricity services, the traditional forces typically represent thermal or hydroelectric power derived from rotating turbines and generators. The edge technologies like solar and batteries involve no moving parts, no rotating magnets, no steam, and no rush of water. They are a different species of electricity in that the method of generation is novel. No matter, they address the *same* market.

So strong are the edge forces that they are poised to upset the historically strong, monolithic electricity industry, as we know it. Three illustrations will make my point:

1. A building of 30 apartments[2] in Bangalore decided to be independent of the local distribution company. Its owners installed solar panels, batteries, and a diesel generator and effectively went off grid. They maintained the connection with the grid "just in case." This is an example of a *microgrid—all* existing services, from lighting to refrigeration to electric cooking, needed by the apartment dwellers, are now provided by this new solution. The builder initiated the proposal to do this and implemented it.

2. The Indian Institute of Management Kozhikode (IIMK) campus decided to manage its streetlights and corridor lights by a solar plus battery solution. The panels and batteries were placed at the junction where all the lighting cables came together. As a result, the common lighting went off grid, while the other services remained on the grid. This is an example of a select *product-market* now addressed by a renewable energy solution.

3. In June in 2015, I met a reseller of submersible water pumps, who told me that his customers constantly ask him: "Could you power your pumps using solar?" He did not know how to do so. When he heard I worked in "solar"—often a synonym for renewable energy—he offered to introduce me to the pump manufacturer and also offered to distribute such pumps in the market he knew so well. Could we partner? Would I solve this problem? I could easily help design the solar and battery requirements for various sizes of pumps. I also offered, "In phase two, the pumps can be networked, and remotely managed, using existing wireless technologies." Further, I said, "We could build an app for farmers' smartphones to manage the pumps remotely."

All three are *edge* solutions, outcomes of centrifugal forces nibbling at the traditional grid services. The use of such applications, *product-markets*, will only increase with time. Their economics will improve, as the barriers to entry for such services are negligible. This will result in demand loss, and therefore revenue loss, for the traditional electricity companies.

All three are also entrepreneurial solutions, and the incumbent electricity provider is not involved, though little stops the incumbents from offering similar and other services. There are more illustrations in the book.

CREATE AND RELEASE LOCKED-UP VALUE

In the past,[3] I have called this process of creating small yet economically viable services—the splintering of a monolithic market, the peeling off of market segments, the formation of microgrids, and so forth—fractionation.

From a marketing perspective, the relatively undifferentiated, commodity-like, product that is today's electricity, appears almost anachronistic and quaint. There is little or primitive packaging, almost no branding, practically no customization, and the most basic pricing by kilowatt-hours, unrelated to and independent of benefits supplied. Years hence, people will wonder: How did such a situation exist for over a hundred years without competitive challenge? Where has all the business creativity disappeared?

At least three consequences of the emerging electricity paradigm are clear: one, within the next decade, practically everyone everywhere in the world will have access to electricity, thanks to decentralized, inexpensive, and economical technical solutions. For this reason alone, the revolution has to be encouraged. Two, the electricity generated will be cleaner than what is obtained today and thus better for the planet. This is also a reason enough to encourage the revolution. Three, fossil fuel–based transport—the second-largest contributor to emissions after electricity—will be affected by this edge electricity revolution, too. The rise of the electric car, electric motorbike, and electric scooter complements, augments, and intermingles with the edge electricity revolution. We can have rooftop-based, ubiquitous charging for nearly emission-free transport. Although transport is beyond the scope of the book, it is also a reason to encourage the edge electricity revolution.

Traditional electricity industry walls are crumbling. The old electricity business model, rate of return–based regulated prices is breaking down. What business strategies will accelerate this trend? What might new entrants do? What might incumbents do? What policy choices—positive and reactive—accommodate such a revolution? Eventually, how will the electricity infrastructure of the future look like? This book attempts to answer such questions.

BUSINESS STRATEGIES FOR NEXT-GENERATION ELECTRICITY

If you have electric cars and a coal-fired plant producing the electricity, you gain nothing.

—*New York Times*, September 25, 2015[4]

Like telecommunications in the late twentieth century, electricity is a monolithic, regulated, and monopolistic industry in the throes of transformation. The largely "one-size-fits-all" electricity of today—AC, 220 or 110 V, 50 or 60 Hz, one- or three-phase supply—faces challenges from newer generation, newer storage, newer topology, and new business models. The regulated monopoly is giving way to a "free-for-all" electricity market, driven by technical possibilities.

What business strategies are driving and will drive the electricity industry transformation? Given here briefly, and discussed in greater depth in the book, are 10 generic business strategies different companies and policy makers might adopt to adapt to Electricity 2.0. The strategies may be classified further, as I will in the later part of this chapter, into:

a. New product or new business strategies deriving from technological advance, often entrepreneurial

b. Corporate strategies supporting or impeding the emerging ecosystem—active or defensive by incumbents as they adapt to the changing environment

c. New ecosystem creation strategies, including active public policies, to accommodate the transformative forces in the industry

However wrenching the transformation, one thing is clear: this process is creating better electricity, new employment, new capabilities, and a greener planet. The classic Schumpeterian drama of creative destruction is at work, awe inspiring, and a privilege to behold.

1. ***Miniaturize—the same solution or product as today, writ small.*** The so-called captive power plants built by certain industries that need an assured power supply are instances of this. The industries that cannot rely on power supplied by utilities typically build their own power plants, using either coal or diesel. Microgrids may

be regarded as a newer incarnation of captive power plants, except that instead of industries, even homes, office buildings, and businesses, large and small, are generators of their own power.

When microgrids proliferate, one consequence will be intermicrogrid trading. The motivation may include not only local control and autonomy, or local empowerment, but also the superior economics resulting from multiple microgrids interacting with each other for optimum use of resources, lower prices, and environmentally superior mixtures of renewable generation sources and some traditional fuels.

2. *Fractionate—into product-markets, and by creating parallel and overlay networks.* Affordable solar panels have made possible distributed generation and, therefore, allowed entrepreneurs to provide a variety of edge electricity services. Solar home systems are a distinct *product-market*, in urban and rural locations. So are solar-powered agricultural water pumps and solar-powered street lights in locations such as campuses, towns, or building corridors. The sprinkler system in a home may have its own stand-alone power supply using solar plus batteries. Each of these can be an entrepreneurial business, independent of the grid.

A home may use solar plus batteries to create a DC network within the home for electronics and computer networking. This would be similar to an office using uninterrupted power supply (UPS) based on batteries for its computer networking. Instead of charging using the mains, however, the home may use sunlight. When Hurricane Sandy disrupted electricity supply in the United States, homes with overlay DC power would have delivered services—lighting, fans, TV and other home electronics, phone charging—thanks to solar plus battery systems. Similarly, when northern India sank into darkness in 2013, had people had a microgrid solution, or DC power overlay, basic services would have continued.

3. *Divest—find a way to sell off service territories to willing and able bidders.* An investor-owned utility (IOU) facing small increases in demand, or falling demand, due to efficient appliances and the spread of solar-based systems, may decide that divestment is an ideal strategy, especially since the long-term valuation of utilities will likely fall. This is the opposite of *municipalization*, where a municipality seeks to wrest control of a service territory upon expiration of franchise agreements. The phenomenon is similar; only the approach is the opposite. The problem with municipalization, or divesting service geography, is that the optimal or smallest autonomous size of the service territory is unknown. Why should a historically defined administrative territory be the unit for electricity services? The optimum service territory can be smaller. Or a combination of small service territories, under one management, may be a superior answer. With *divest* as strategy, the onus for fair-value determination is on the seller and buyer—market forces—and not on an administrative entity like a municipality. In India, the municipalities are divided into *wards*, and a ward may well have its own electricity company.

4. *Consolidate—a defensive and reactive strategy indicating the maturity and decline of the traditional business.* As traditional electricity is a mature business,

and as the operations of electricity companies are similar, consolidation can generally yield some benefits—cost savings, typically. The takeover of Pepco by Exelon belongs to this category. Whatever the regulatory challenges, as strategy, this is the basic business school case study material. When viewed from the perspective of industry structure change, driven by new technological forces, such consolidation is not sufficient to address the issues created by the industry structure change.

In telecom, the Baby Bells—the wireline companies formed from the breakup of the old AT&T—began consolidating and gave birth to today's new AT&T. This strategy made sense, for common staff resources could be leveraged across a large service area and over a larger customer base. As long as the costs of coordination were low, this did yield benefits.

Of course, more fundamental forces overran the wireline business—the rise of broadband Internet and mobile telephones. The proposed merger may be regarded as analogous to the consolidation of the Baby Bells; it will yield some benefits, provided the regulators approve the deal. But, like these changes in telecom, the rise of distributed generation is a more fundamental force that may likely overshadow the benefits of consolidation. In electricity, consolidation can at best be an interim strategy. The larger—even heroic—strategic challenge is to understand, anticipate the changes in, and actively address the implications of the distributed generation revolution.

5. *Privatize—seeks explicitly to eliminate the state's role in electricity services, except for some regulation.* It may be regarded as a special instance of *divest* in that options such as municipalization, or the forming of cooperatives as organizational forms, may be separated out as a distinct category, in the private or quasipublic sector.

6. *Auction—the geography of a nation may be divided into optimal territories and auctioned off for services.* When trying to fairly distribute scarce public resources, such as spectrum, governments often resort to auctions. Consider the 2-GHz band auctions conducted in the United States in the mid-1990s, where the nation's geography was divided into major trading areas (MTAs) and basic trading areas (BTAs), and bids were sought through auctions and the spectrum was allocated to the highest-qualified bidders. India allocated mining coal using auctions.

7. *Diversify into new network services.* Electricity distribution companies have access to customers, just as wireline phone companies and cable companies. Why should not the electric utilities enter into the Internet service provider (ISP) business or even the entertainment business using the Internet? Electric Power Board (EPB) in Chattanooga, Tennessee became an ISP business. So might other electric utilities. Faced with declining demand, and even grid defection, an electric utility may choose to diversify into ISP and entertainment services.

8. *Extend geographically with specialization.* This approach seeks scale and, therefore, lower costs, and also the benefits of becoming a possible national brand or global brand, through focus and specialization. For instance, a company may

specialize in solar-powered water pumps for agricultural applications across an entire nation and attain economies of scale. Another may specialize in traffic lights. Yet others may specialize in street lights on campuses, or on city streets, and create a national brand for such lighting. Even GE or Philips, who traditionally sells lamps, may enter such businesses.

9. *Grow intensively by region—omnibus or a rich menu of services.* A general contractor, focused on a city, for instance, may offer customers a host of electricity services. The contractor may not specialize in any one *product-market*, say, street lighting. The emphasis would be on a broad scope of services, and less scale in any one service. Many electricians have entered the solar installation and maintenance business in their particular cities. They may further expand their service portfolio to include energy audits, value-added in-premise services, LEED certification, and DC overlay infrastructure. They may expand into facilities management too, for office buildings and school and college campuses, since electricity services may be regarded as an extension of facilities management.

10. *Organize differently—as cooperatives or as franchises.* In an article in Nov 2012,[5] I argued for *cooperatives* as an optimum form of organization for rural electricity and suggested that India's milk cooperatives diversify and enter into the electricity production and distribution business. Just as they source milk from farmers, the cooperative may source agricultural "waste" for electricity production. Should this happen, it would give an expanded, new, and richer meaning to the word *green revolution*.

When it is clear that the existing grid may not be economically extended to remote villages and population clusters, what might public policy do? Distribution companies in India attempted the creation of franchises. Not unsurprisingly, this does not work. One may not have businesses by fiat, as a command performance.

The order in which these strategies will play out, or the combinations of strategies that will be adopted, remain interesting open questions. What should public policy's role be—accommodative and reactive, or positive? And what country is in the best position to, or has the need to, pursue positive policy, and drive the transformation?

As already indicated, the strategies previously listed may be further classified into three broad categories:

a. *New product or new business strategies deriving from technological advance, often entrepreneurial*

When solar panels with falling costs—due to economies of scale in manufacture— and greater conversion efficiencies begin to generate new possibilities, we have new strategies by entrepreneurs addressing specific markets, for example, rooftop solar or solar table lamps. This splitting of an existing market can be described as fractionation (strategy 2 on the list) into *product-markets* or even, when solar home systems or microgrids are created, as miniaturization (strategy 1 on the list).

This is the approach for deprived communities in emerging markets; only capital costs are involved in the purchase of such appliances, no monthly charges.

While roaming around Rajiv Gandhi Plaza, formerly called Connaught Place, in New Delhi, I saw street vendors with panels of LED lights hoisted on a pole, powered with car batteries. Now the car batteries were likely charged on mains, but they could have been charged with solar panels. This is one kind of new business—a stand-alone, solar-powered, point solution for lighting.

Even in mature markets, if 80 percent of all lighting in a home "goes solar," parsed out from other demands, it would affect the incumbent electric distribution company. And fragmenting the demand in a home can be a business strategy for a new entrant. Beyond lighting, all home electronics—stereo systems, phone charging, laptop charging—can also be solar and battery powered, and independent of the grid, perhaps as an expansion strategy for the lighting company.

Many more examples of technological advance creating new business approaches can be given. For instance, flywheels may complement or replace batteries and therefore yield superior economics. Similarly, the solar panel plus battery combination can power agricultural water pumps. Control technologies for managing multiple generation technologies to work harmoniously as one optimized system can allow the creation of cost-efficient microgrids. Topological attributes of next-generation microgrids—organized as, say, fractals or honeycombs—can give rise to a whole set of intermicrogrid information and power transactions and flows, and therefore business strategies.

> *b. Corporate strategies supporting or impeding the emerging ecosystem—active or defensive by incumbents as they adapt to the changing environment*

It cannot be easy to be the CEO of an incumbent electric utility. There is a threat to "demand" through efficiency and next-generation appliances, plus a fundamental business model challenge. The old ways of measuring, charging, and cost recovery through the regulatory process are all now threatened.

What might be the new sources of revenue? What assets may be leveraged for such revenue? How does the existing organizational culture help or hinder?

One strategy is to diversify (strategy 7 in the list): offer broadband for new revenue, by monetizing the network and the utility's "right of way." Ensure that in so doing, the company both creates customer value beyond what today's broadband carriers offer and serves the public interest in the process. EPB in Chattanooga, Tennessee did just that.

Are broadband services ancillary, complementary, or fundamental to the core business of the electric distribution utility of the future? This remains a fundamental question. The strategic intent of a company will determine the answer as much as its assets and their value.

Another almost classic and textbook strategy is to consolidate (strategy 4 in the list) by merging with other companies to reduce costs, as Pepco and Exelon

Table 1.1 Strategies

	Strategy	Who	Illustration	Industry Structure Impact
1	Miniaturize	Utility and new entrants	The same functionality, only smaller sized	New entrants—competition
2	Fractionate	Utility and new entrants	Divide the market into distinct *product-markets*, each a business	New entrants—competition
3	Divest	Utility with policy support	Break up the service territory and sell off to municipalities, cooperatives, city governments	End of electricity services companies as regulated, quasimonopolistic companies
4	Consolidate	Utility with policy support	Mergers among utilities, for instance, between Exelon and PEPCO	Interim strategy; scale benefit and lower-cost operations. Challenge of addressing distributed generation remains
5	Privatize	Utility with policy support	Break up the service territory and sell to private suppliers	End of electricity services companies as regulated, quasimonopolistic companies
6	Auction	Utility with policy support	Break up the service territory and auction off the geography	End of electricity services companies as regulated, quasimonopolistic companies
7	Diversify into new network services	Utility with policy support	Electric utilities diversify into the broadband ISP business, and vice versa, IT companies into electricity services business	Merging industries; new revenue streams for existing electricity services companies
8	Extend geographically with specialization	New entrants	Hardware or traditional suppliers extending into service companies	New business growth as distinct *product-markets*
9	Grow intensively by region	New entrants	Electrical contractors expanding the scope of their business with value-added services	New business and services growth in geographically focused markets
10	Organize differently	Utility, new entrants with policy support	Cooperatives or homeowners' association as electricity services company	Newer organizational forms; empowered existing organizational forms

did. I consider this a largely defensive interim strategy. Another defensive strategy, though not explicitly numbered in the list, may be described as "delay through friction"; this involves creating barriers to the operations of competitors, by lobbying regulators, or by other means. For instance, limit the amount of distributed generation that can be deployed on the grid, challenge feed-in tariffs, and claim threats to the operations of the existing grid due to distributed generation.

An offensive strategy, a variant of diversify (strategy 7 in the list), is to acknowledge the new reality of distributed generation, and do that yourself. Many school parking lots are now covered by solar panels. Typically, the contractors for such deployment are solar installation companies. But existing distribution companies can get into that business, too. Further, incumbent distribution companies understand end user customers and their electricity usage well. They could leverage that knowledge into services that create additional revenue, say, security services, demand-side management, energy audits, and maintenance contracts, on the other side of the meter, on customer premises.

Despite such actions, the distribution utilities may not survive the onslaught of new players, unless they embrace the new paradigm themselves. How to carve a place for oneself in the emerging new ecosystem? This is a formidable challenge facing incumbents.

  c. *New ecosystem creation strategies, including active public policies, to accommodate the metamorphic forces in the industry.*

The rise of prosumers, both homeowners and businesses, is an extraordinary development. The historically passive electricity consumer, having no choice really, except to be at the receiving end of an elaborate electricity infrastructure, has now become an active consumer–supplier, who monetizes his or her space, to gain progressive independence from the grid. The proportion of electricity produced by consumers will only continue to increase.

The implications of the supply of 20 percent of all electricity through renewable, especially renewables based on distributed generation, may not be fully expressed in kilowatt-hours, because the social, economic, and political changes accompanying it are enormous, with secondary and tertiary effects, with implications for public policy. For instance, broad-based entrepreneurial contributions to that number are significant—the emissions reduction it represents, the employment generated, the local control and autonomy allowed, and in general the public good created are disproportionate to the percentage number.

It would be fair to say that the implications of the metamorphic transformations the new electricity ecosystem represents may yet be incomprehensible to an observer today. We may build scenarios and speculate, yet there is no alternative but to watch, and participate, in the unfolding industry.

In Table 1.1, strategies 1, 2, 3 (miniaturize, fractionate, divest); 8 (extend geographically with specialization), 9 (grow intensively by region), and 10 (organize differently, as cooperatives, for instance) belong to ecosystem transformation. All these strategies may be initiated and implemented by private players.

Auction (strategy 6 in the list), while contributing to ecosystem transformation, belongs to the policy-making domain. The initiative has to be with governments, as was the case when the Federal Communications Commission (FCC) auctioned 2-GHz spectrum for Personal Communications Service (PCS) in the mid-1990s, launching the mobile telephone revolution.

New York State's REV—reforming the energy vision—certainly belongs to (c)—fostering a new ecosystem. REV also encourages distributed generation, in that its scope supports the emergence of technology-enabled, entrepreneurial new start-ups, and thus strategies under (a). But that is not all. REV seeks to include the incumbents in the evolution of the grid and assigns them a role as DSPP—distributed services platform provider. The New York State initiative's scope is thus vast—it straddles all three broad strategy categories.

While comparisons are difficult and this is a state-level initiative, and not national in scope, I am of the opinion that we are witnessing changes, at business and policy levels, at least as significant as when AT&T was broken up in the 1980s.

TWO

Microgrids for Autonomy: Local Generation, Local Consumption

The most impactful way is to develop a large number of 100-kilowatt, half-a-megawatt projects that are distributed across the country, close to rural loads.

—Anshu Bharadwaj[1]

Whenever I am driving or in a taxi in any city, I look at shopping malls, office buildings, and residential streets with homes and say to myself: a savvy solar installation company can install microgrids and take them off grid, either in one shot or in phases, say 25 percent or 50 percent, or more of their load over time. How might the solar installers do this? Essentially, they would augment their business to include microgrid-based solutions. Instead of selling to individual households, the service provider would focus on groups of homes, neighborhoods, campuses, hospitals, or equivalents and deploy microgrids.

Let us assume variable pricing, that is, peak electricity rates higher than rates at other times, or tiered pricing, that is, higher-usage tiers much more costly than lower-usage tiers. Let us chop off the peak load, or higher-priced tiers, using solar panels and some batteries. Customers obtain immediate cost savings. Upfront capital costs, in part, substitute for monthly costs. We may finance the capital investment through a loan—given to an installer, the homeowner, or a third party—and still be able to offer a lower overall bill to the end customer. Essentially, this is what solar installation companies do. Their representatives call potential customers and ask what the monthly bill is. If it is above a certain threshold, they realize the customer is hitting a high-priced usage tier. They then know that a solar system will get the customer off that high-priced tier and thereby reduce the overall bill.

Not that the customer will always sign up and say "Yes" to an installer's offer merely because it saves money. The savings may not be worth the hassles of installation, and some customers will find the appearance of solar panels on their rooftop aesthetically unappealing. The installer's offer may have to be good for reasons besides cost savings and include new benefits or services.

What might be some additional, value-added services a provider may bundle with lower costs? Will there be regulatory incentives, such as tax deductions or write-offs, as part of the fight against global warming? Will there be new services for customers on the other side of the meter? Will there be bundled offers with nontraditional, nonelectricity products, for instance, entertainment or broadband?

Over time, progressively, the installer may take the customer's entire load off-grid as the economics of the solar plus battery solution improves. This may be expected because, after all, the solar panels are, technically speaking, value-added silicon—painted or coated sand—sand on land or sand on roof and costs can be lowered with scale manufacturing and continuous, incremental technical advances.

An installer may do more, for instance, create a DC (direct current) overlay solution for lighting, electronics, and appliance charging, or for solar-based UPS for a building's Ethernet networks, especially in new construction. It is surprising that this has not been explored in new housing developments or in office buildings. The DC electricity load might not be high, and can be off grid, using solar panels in the backyard or parking lots plus batteries in the garage or equivalent.

Some newer power outlets already have USB ports built into them; IKEA sells an adapter that, when inserted into a regular 110-V/220-V wall outlet, gives us several USB ports. The addition proposed here is that the supply of power to the outlets will be DC—no inverters are needed.

In effect, the SHSs (solar home systems) distributed in rural areas in emerging markets use DC directly and involve no inverters. Nancy Wimmer's 2012 study of rural electrification in Bangladesh, *Green Energy for a Billion Poor: How Grameen Shakti Created a Winning Model for Social Business*, describes such non-inverter-based solutions. In rural applications in un-electrified villages, DC power is sufficient for light, phone charging, fans, and TVs, though not for electric cooking or air-conditioning. The overall proposition is "local generation, local consumption, and local autonomous solution," in phases.

Instead of one rooftop at a time, microgrid service providers can deploy for, say, 30 to 50 apartments, or 20 stand-alone homes, or a strip mall, or an office building or a hospital at a time. The thesis is: It is better to have a microgrid solution in steps of, let us say 0.5 MW, and professionally managed by a local service provider—an entrepreneur—than selling to individual homeowners.

An entrepreneur as microgrid service provider may deploy and manage several contiguous microgrids of different sizes with relative advantages among them, some with daytime peak loads, and others with evening peak loads, some

Figure 2.1   Rooftop Solar Growth: Will It Confront the Chasm?

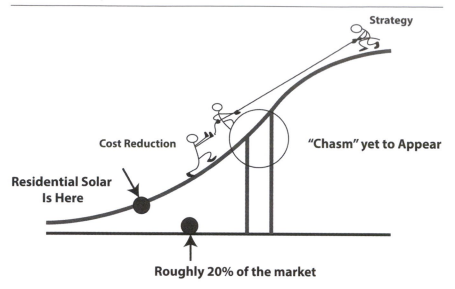

with advantages with one kind of generation, others with different kinds of generation, and all complementing each other.

The famous Geoffrey Moore chasm[2] is an additional reason for not selling to one home at a time. It is possible that many of today's home roof installations are by the technically savvy early adopters, and their share of the total population is typically around 15 to 20% percent.

This is shown in Figure 2.1, which shows that with "strategy" or public policy pull and "cost reduction," "supply side" subsidies, and installer push, solar rooftop deployments are increasing in number. Nevertheless, the growth is within the early adopter segment. What happens when that segment approaches saturation? Will the rooftop solar installation industry, especially in industrialized countries, level out for a while or fall into the chasm?

MICROGRID VARIETY AND HIERARCHY

Given in the following list is a hierarchy of microgrid economics, the most economical deployment to the most challenging. In every case, the incumbent distribution utility loses demand, and therefore revenue, except in the case where there is no grid

1. *Chopping off-peak load using solar, demand response, and some batteries*—
    likely most profitable deployment of microgrid in the short run. A company such as Advanced Microgrid Solutions[3] belongs to this category.

2. *DC microgrids as overlay for electronic equipment* such as TV, music systems, phone charging, and clocks using solar and battery systems. Eventually, a good fraction of home lighting can also be on such a DC overlay microgrid, which can be readily deployed. Why has this solution not become commonplace? Perhaps the savings are not large enough and the load offset is too small.

3. *Grid-tied buildings with some batteries* simply substituting today's electricity in its entirety, except that the grid serves as a backup, "just in case." This would be a full-fledged microgrid, with economics likely already better than grid parity, in many markets.

4. *Product-markets as microgrid* refers to the cases where solar- and battery-powered irrigation pumps, street lighting, traffic lights, corridor lights, and so forth work as application-specific independent systems.

5. *Off-grid full-fledged microgrid supporting all of today's electricity applications* in the home, likely the most expensive and still not cost competitive with today's grid pricing, principally because of the cost of batteries needed to compensate for the absence of the macrogrid. With microgrids, we may not compare with gas pricing, because the alternative is not grid electricity but the use of diesel generators or kerosene burning, both of which are far more expensive and less healthy than microgrid power. Over the next five years, however, even the stand-alone microgrid solution may attain and surpass grid parity in dollars per unit.

In general, this fifth option ought to be the solution for rural unelectrified populations. SHSs are a primitive version of this, in that not all home applications are supported. A microgrid deployed by Greenpeace in Dharnai village, Bihar, India was of this kind—it did not support all household loads. That cost Greenpeace some of its reputation, despite its pioneering work, and generated complaints that this was not "real" electricity. I describe the Dharnai microgrid–related issues in Chapter Four, and in an article in *Renewable Energy World*.[4] The Dharnai project has been a useful lesson in user-expectation management in the emerging microgrid space.

Chapter 3 describes a model for a microgrid that would cover all campus loads, including air-conditioning and electric cooking, at the Indian Institute of Management Kozhikode (IIMK). This worst-case scenario, that is, the toughest from an economic feasibility perspective, nevertheless gave optimistic results at approximately $0.15/unit and, for me, strengthened the case for microgrids.

Most of the time, when we speak of microgrids, we refer to situations 3 and 4, that is, the grid-tied solution, or electricity market segmentation through identifying and pursuing *product-markets*. The question arises: Where should we focus: on microgrids as instances of the macrogrid rendered small, or on segments represented by *product-markets*? In brief, the answer is, both.

Due to lower barriers to entry, and lower costs per unit of electricity produced without economies of scale in generation, that is, ever-larger plant sizes, and aided by new technologies, we have a revolution in the making. Entrepreneurs and new entrants in the electricity business are poised to erode the market of incumbent utilities through the deployment of microgrids. Even as they do so, it might be in the utilities' best interest to enter the microgrids business themselves.

It is inappropriate to assume that all microgrids will necessarily connect with the macrogrid as shown in Figure 2.2. The world of next-generation electricity may not be viewed from today's grid-centric lenses. Indeed, in many instances of rural deployment in emerging economies, there will be no nearby macrogrid to connect to and no need to necessarily seek such a connection either. Why should microgrids not interact with each other preferentially, in addition to interacting with the macrogrid, where possible?

Rather, the "edge" is the new center, and the public interest represented by the "edge" needs to be explored and understood, and public policies favoring it need to be defined and encouraged. *Distributed generation*, the buzzword du jour, does not begin to capture the profound implications of what this edge revolution is poised to deliver.

Having argued that microgrids are better than solar on rooftops for a number of reasons, and having identified a variety of microgrid solutions from stand-alone to grid-tied, and DC overlays to *product-market* segments, I now propose that microgrids are also in the public interest for the benefits they offer and, above all, because they make possible new market entry, by entrepreneurs and through business development by existing companies.

Figure 2.2   The Presumed Default Connectivity: Microgrids Tied to the Macrogrid

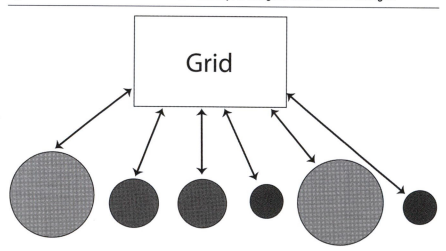

PUBLIC INTEREST AND MICROGRIDS

What is the *public interest* as it relates to microgrids?

1. The traditional argument for microgrids is that the region being served—remote geographies, islands, mining towns, and military bases, for instance—cannot be served any other way. In the unelectrified remote regions, electricity access is the overwhelming public interest. The effective cost of electricity's absence (and therefore kerosene or diesel burning) is high for the rural poor; microgrids make sense even at relatively high cost, though affordability for the population served is an issue. As mentioned before, the solution may not be "full service" right from the start. As long as light, fans, and phone charging are available, cooking using electricity, refrigeration, and air-conditioning can wait—at least for a while. SHSs and stand-alone, off-grid microgrids are the way to deliver the services. *Grid extension* will be uneconomical as shown in Figure 2.3, where even a modest population cluster, 15 km away from the presence of the grid, cannot get economical electricity through grid extension. For such a population, SHS are an immediate option, although with limited applications.

   Clearly, limited applications are not a longer-term viable option; full service infrastructure is a must that stand-alone microgrids should deliver. Today, such stand-alone microgrids are deployed on islands, in mining towns, and on military bases. With advances in technologies—photovoltaics and batteries—there is every reason to deploy such microgrids, affordably, in unelectrified villages, the least you already talked about some of these applications earlier in the paragraph and in the chapter.

Figure 2.3   Grid Extension vs. Fully Functional Stand-Alone Microgrids

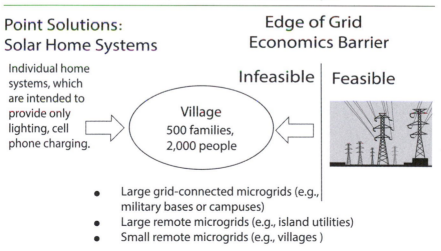

Point Solutions: Solar Home Systems

Edge of Grid Economics Barrier

Individual home systems, which are intended to provide only lighting, cell phone charging.

Infeasible | Feasible

Village
500 families,
2,000 people

- Large grid-connected microgrids (e.g., military bases or campuses)
- Large remote microgrids (e.g., island utilities)
- Small remote microgrids (e.g., villages)

At a distance of just 15 km from the grid, coal power is no longer competitive with solar PV, if one includes the infrastructure, maintenance, and distribution costs.

2. A recent concern raised in the northeastern United States is resilience of power supply during emergencies, such as during the next equivalent of Hurricane Sandy. The argument is: some basic services have to continue, at more or less any cost, and therefore microgrids. The Sendai microgrid in Japan continued to work for a while following the Fukushima earthquake and the resulting tsunami.

3. (a) "Clean" energy has now become a major public priority worldwide. Since microgrids include solar photovoltaics, wind, and batteries, they are likely to be cleaner than traditional electricity generation. And since microgrids involve local generation and local consumption, they eliminate the need for costly transmission infrastructure and the consequent losses in electricity's transit.

(b) But how does one translate the *pursuit of clean energy* or *emissions reduction* into a business driver? The fact of *global warming* from emissions is high school science, well known. What are we going to do about it? Regulatory fiat appears unappealing as a business driver—renewable portfolio standard (RPS) in California, for instance. The utilities agree to such standards publicly while fighting them behind closed doors.

(c) Here is what *Utility Dive* had to say in October 2015: "State Sen. Ben Hueso (D), chair of the energy and utilities committee in the California Senate, ushered SB 350, the bill that set the state's 50 percent RPS . . . this year. He said during a news conference that the utilities have always fought hard against any mandates behind closed doors, whether it was SB 350 or earlier efforts. In this last legislative session, he said, the power sector alone 'spent millions' to influence the system. 'It's about the survival of their industries. But for us, it's the survival of our planet.'"

4 (a) Microgrids represent competitive new market entry, and this is perhaps the most important public interest benefit of microgrids. India's Central Electricity Regulatory Commission's (CERC)[5] website notes, "Since the enactment of the Electricity Act 2003 the power sector has undergone major structural changes. The Act is based on the philosophy that consumers should benefit from growth of competitive markets. The Act has de-licensed generation, encouraged captive power by allowing them to sell almost half of the generation without any license requirements. *Multiple players are required for competitive markets.* This is done by allowing multiple licensees in the same area and also allowing 'Open Access'. The trading platform of Exchanges has already been started. Traders are also in existence in the power market." [italics added]

(b) In the United States, Europe, and other countries used to relatively reliable electricity, left to themselves, the incumbent utilities will always say that the public interest consists of "Resilience, Reliability, Cybersecurity, Customer Care, Affordability." Their regulators will agree with them, given the history of mutual quasicollaboration.

(c) Despite the stated intent and rhetoric, seldom do we hear anyone from a policy perspective say, "Let us have competition through startups." The benefit represented by *new market entry*, that is, *competition* in electricity services provision, is discounted. Surely, microgrid service providers, some who have graduated to this role after being solar installers, and new *product-market*–based businesses are a part of such competition. Such service providers, entrepreneurial risk takers, serve the public interest— though few explicitly say so, even in the United States.

How does one create multiple players for competition, and how does one implement multiple licenses in the same area? Policy makers in the telephone industry divided geography into market-sized chunks and auctioned them off to new service providers, with rules governing how the new licensees would behave.

WHO GOES FIRST: EMERGING MARKETS OR DEVELOPED ONES?

Microgrids are both (a) substitutes for and (b) complementary to the grid, particularly in unelectrified markets. Where will microgrids be first deployed? If we needed to make business decisions—investments—where would we rather put the money?

A student in my Microgrid MBA class said: "My opinion is that un-electrified markets will develop microgrids first. The closest analogies are to telephone networks. Developed countries (such as the USA) with well-established, reliable landlines took the longest to invest in and develop cellular GSM infrastructure. Even then, technology upgrades to that infrastructure were lagging behind Europe or Japan. It appears that the approach of carriers was 'if it ain't broke, don't fix it,' meaning that fairly reliable (even if not the most modern) infrastructure can stay in place for years."

"Developing countries, on the contrary, adopted and developed cellular networks in sometimes years, not decades. Every villager has a cellphone, but there may not be a landline within miles. By the same token, once an affordable and scalable solution is available, it will go viral in un-electrified markets."

"Developed countries will follow, but maybe as late as a decade later, because there is no real incentive—neither economical, technological or market demand. Isolated areas that are prone to natural disasters and suffer from grid failures or insufficient capacity, such as the US northeast and California, or have strong local government incentives, such as NYSERDA in NY, will lead in the US."

"One scenario is that the rush of microgrids in developing markets will increase supply of technology—PV, energy storage, energy management systems—and drive the cost of capital investment to a level where microgrid economics can strongly compete with grid utilities."

To this thoughtful argument, I replied: "My view is that the US always surprises me with initiatives one would never expect. For instance, who would have thought it possible that a lawsuit by Bill McGowan and Jack Goeken challenging AT&T's monopoly would give rise to MCI, and eventually lead to the breakup of the Bell System and the emergence of the Baby Bells? Who would have thought the FCC would auction 2 GHz band spectrum to launch PCS services in the mid-1990s?"

"That Universal Service in telephony is a public good of immense value, and it is therefore worth cross subsidies—this was remarkable insight, and implemented as a solution through foresightful public policy in the US. This benefit of 'network effects' of the telephone as an instrument, not merely of convenience and small transactions but as a tool for economic organization—this was lost on newly independent countries like India where telephone service was regarded as a luxury even into the 1980s. Rural electrification too was regarded as a public good in the US, and fostered through active public policy. Again, this benefit was not universally recognized in the 1950s by newly independent countries."

"NY State's REV initiative by the state's leadership has given a boost to the microgrid market, among other innovative themes. Similarly, the CA state legislators' decision to mandate 50 percent renewables in the energy mix may create incentives for start-ups, and for today's IOUs to enter into the microgrid market. True, unlike the United States, the need is real in emerging economies, and they ought to show initiative. But will they? Does the institutional inheritance, public policy, and business structure permit innovations, foster entrepreneurship? What should India do? What should Africa do?"

Which nation, or state within a nation, first deploys microgrids commercially in a big way remains an open question. Policy and business leadership is the key, less technology. There are, however, technical missing pieces in the overall microgrid puzzle that require focused lab and university-level research, some of which are described briefly below. The absence of credible, commercial grade solutions likely holds back the growth of microgrids, even if they are not showstoppers. The emerging economies are not up to the task of addressing these challenges. Today's multinationals and national energy research labs must engage in this work. They are likely not doing enough.

It is interesting in this context to ask: Who is best in a position to give a boost to this industry and take it a level higher? Will the state Public Utilities Commissions (PUC) in the United States show leadership? Federal agencies, say, FERC? The Department of Energy? A progressive governor? The Ministry of Power or New and Renewable Energy in India, or a state-level chief minister? The chief minister of Meghalaya in northeastern India has announced his interest in microgrids—he wants to have microgrids for villages and use the existing electricity grid for industrial applications.[6] New York State's bold effort, REV (Reforming the Energy Vision), initiated by Commissioner Audrey Zibelman, may deliver solutions of global applicability. The United Nations' SE4All[7] initiative until now, and the activities of the many NGOs and small, well-intentioned start-ups focused on basic electricity in rural India and Africa suggests that groundswell, economic drivers, particularly as regards microgrids, are missing in the rural electrification space.

MISSING PIECES, TECHNOFINANCIAL ANALYSIS
MOST CRITICAL

At least three critical missing pieces ought to be addressed as part of a comprehensive microgrid research agenda; it is unclear who is addressing them.

1. *Capacity planning for capital budget minimization at launch.* How much of each of solar, batteries, wind, and gas/diesel generators are needed in an optimum combination for minimizing first capital costs? If further cost reduction is needed, how may we incorporate *demand-side* management in the design? This is a stochastic, nonlinear optimization problem that has been neither adequately formulated nor solved.

2. *Dynamic control of generation sources and "demand management"* to realize lowest operating costs (or an equivalent operating objective). At least some papers (e.g., Zakariazadeh, Alireza, et al., http://dx.doi.org/10.1016/j.ijepes.2014.06.037) in the bibliography address this problem, but not to the extent needed. There appears to be no testing in the field, with a variety of microgrids of different capacities, load profiles, and uses or applications.

3. *Intermicrogrid collaboration including information and power flow.* Neither the business opportunities nor the technical challenges of intermicrogrid collaboration have been well defined as yet. The Institute of Electrical and Electronics Engineers (IEEE) might work on this, but it has not gone past microgrid–macrogrid interconnection. No one knows the synergies when clusters of microgrids work together as one or work with a macrogrid. It would appear that complementary microgrids would reduce overall capital costs, enable resource sharing, and enhance reliability, but we do not know what the financial and technological unknowns are.

More broadly, at least three levels of optimization and communication are involved: (a) power flows, (b) information flows, and (c) money flows, and all in multiple directions. The complexity involved appears daunting, but we have solved comparable problems in many other fields, for instance, mobile communications.

Why have these problems not been solved by the electricity industry and electrical engineering departments in academia? My conjectures are: to work on these problems, we require many typically isolated, though complementary, academic disciplines to come together. The incentive structures and the processes of doctoral research in academia (e.g., tenure, funding sources, history, path dependence) do not encourage such interdisciplinary work. Further, when technical analysis has to combine with business (strategy, industry structure, opportunity assessment, etc.) and financial analysis, the pool of problem definers and problem solvers shrinks even more.

Institutions such as the Rocky Mountain Institute, perhaps EPRI (Electric Power Research Institute) or EEI (Edison Electric Institute), can help, but they are not quite focused on comprehensive business, policy, and technical challenges simultaneously.

Universities typically create *centers* for the study of interdisciplinary problems. But I know of no center for the study of microgrids, certainly none in business schools, worldwide. See also Chapter 9, where I discuss the limitations of business schools in addressing such important yet broad problems. Only now, 2014 onward, are microgrid industry associations beginning to take birth. In Appendix One, I describe efforts that might be undertaken toward policy advocacy in favor of microgrids. One may say that *power* has been in recent decades a relatively ignored part of the broader electrical engineering discipline, compared to, say, software or computer science. In addition, when fuel cells, wind turbines, and diesel and gas generators are part of the generation mix, to what academic discipline does renewable energy belong?

The multinational companies in this space have, given the hundred-year-old stability of the business, little reason to be dynamic or creative. They are a quasi-monopoly in different regions or markets. Yet AT&T of old was monolithic and a monopoly too, and nevertheless transformed dramatically.

CLUSTER OF MICROGRIDS AS TELECOM INTERNETWORKING

In September 2015 in New Jersey, I inquired at Bell Labs about the internetworking problem among a cluster of microgrids and whether there would be parallels with internetworking among telecom networks? Apparently, such internetworking is a well-understood and well-addressed problem, and it could therefore be extended to intermicrogrid collaboration. Naturally, there would be differences since a microgrid both generates electricity and manages loads, unlike a telecom network.

Still, had we access to Bell Labs today, we could put this problem on its agenda. Are there equivalent labs in energy, and what are they doing in the microgrid space? Except for early work on the CERTS microgrid at Berkeley, the U.S.-based national research labs (NREL, PNNL, Sandia, etc.) and EEI (Edison Electric Institute) appear to do little to address this intermicrogrid coordination issue. Moreover, we need several prototypes deployed, for different use-case scenarios. Do any microgrid clusters, working with each other, optimally and automatically, exist anywhere? Has anyone tried, say, ABB, Schneider Electric, GE, or startups?

Figure 2.4 shows microgrids of various sizes, interworking with each other, sharing information and resources, and yet working as an integrated, comprehensive electricity solution. Each microgrid can work independently when required, and work as a "federation of microgrids" otherwise. The microgrid cluster may or may not be hooked to the surrounding macrogrid. As best I can tell, no one has designed and deployed such a microgrid cluster.

Figure 2.4   A Federation of Microgrids

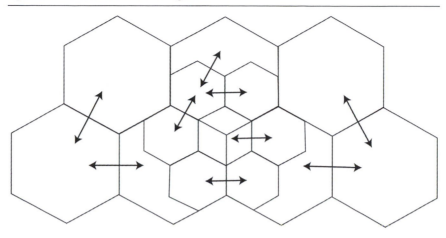

Figure 2.4   A Federation of Microgrids

FINANCIAL ANALYSIS INTEGRATED WITH
TECHNICAL MODELING

With advances in solar panel technologies, the launch of relatively inexpensive batteries, and the availability of small gas- or diesel-based generators and fuel cells, it is possible to design a stand-alone electricity delivery system that is both convenient and economical. How economical? In states such as Hawaii, where electricity rates are over $0.40/kWh, it certainly beats grid electricity pricing. In California, where the average electricity rate per household can surpass $0.25/kWh, it is economical too. In rural parts of the unelectrified world, where kerosene burning is the source of light, it also makes economic sense; costs for light effectively surpass $0.40/kWh.

The question arises: If we were to design an electricity system from the ground up, from first principles, in a greenfield market, and we had access to today's technologies—solar, battery, and more—how would we design the electricity system? How would we deploy it:

- With economic justification, in places where we already have the electricity grid, which is in most of the world?
- In the unelectrified and intermittently or poorly served parts of the world?

The first question is the tougher question. To deploy a new electricity system in the electrified parts of the world, we would need to uproot what exists, repurpose some elements of what exists, and substitute some parts of it altogether. For most people, the grid works. Why bother tweaking it? What exists has economic value;

should we not recover that investment first, through the elaborate regulatory system we have developed over a hundred years? Why not let sleeping dogs lie? Why fix what is not broken?

And for regions where supply is intermittent and unreliable, why not improve what exists, at incremental costs, rather than replace it with the stand-alone new microgrid? For countries like India, and many parts of sub-Saharan Africa, why not add a few more conventional power plants, even new nuclear ones, and augment supply to meet existing demand and then extend the grid to remote areas, even if uneconomically, by a system of cross-subsidies—the urban and more populous parts of the system, in effect, subsidizing the rural and uneconomical one? This is exactly what was done in the United States, for instance, when nationwide electrification or telephone service began, through a Universal Service Fund equivalent.

To be environmentally sensitive from a climate change perspective, we can deploy large solar or wind farms and feed the generated power to the existing grid, and thereby augment supply to meet demand, extending the grid to unserved populations where possible.

Yet the trend is clear. Whether we like it or not, sooner rather than later, by design or by a million cuts, the grid's glory days are over. Microgrids upset the current dispensation and therefore the power centers vested in today's solution. On the benefits side, the new infrastructure will be greener, cleaner, and cheaper and allow for local control. Expanded entrepreneurial and new business participation will create jobs and give birth to creative and innovative new solutions, inside premises and outside.

When microgrids proliferate, franchise boundaries disappear. An Electricity 2.0 company may offer services anywhere in the world, and yet, thanks to the Internet, manage its operations from a central location, also located anywhere in the world. When the cost structure is lowered through the repurposing of today's assets in microgrid architectures, value locked up in today's hierarchical grid will be released.

When we expand the boundaries of the industry to include broadband access, new value is created, as explained in Chapter 8. In sum, both the reduced cost base and the new revenue opportunity help the public. The broadband ISPs have ill-served the public; their speeds have been slow and the flow of their bits has been asymmetric—download oriented, not upload oriented—to favor centralized services. Electric utilities entering broadband space may create a new tier of services favoring "edge" businesses, where businesses and consumers host their own content and applications, to complement what is offered through the giant data center–based services of today. This expands the economic pie dramatically, empowers businesses and households, and thereby further contributes to the public good.

ECONOMIES OF NUMBERS, NOT SCALE

The central premise underlying the arguments here is this: the economies of scale achieved through large size—giant generation and giant transmission to reduce unit costs—may be surpassed through economies of large numbers of microgrids, organized in clusters, resulting in an overall lowered cost structure. The reorganized electricity infrastructure creates possibilities for new value creation not possible with today's network topology. It is therefore in the public interest to make the transition to a new industry structure for Electricity 2.0.

IS THE NEW APPROACH WORTH IT?

This is a valid question to ask as, clearly, value is destroyed when something that works, today's grid, is consciously replaced by something else, a cluster of microgrids. For instance, when microgrids proliferate, we need less of the transmission grid, less of central station generation. Their value is impaired and economic lives curtailed when microgrids are deployed.

Further, we need different or less regulations, and thus an entire organization has to be repurposed, with likely loss of employment. While jobs within the existing utilities may be lost, new ones will be created with microgrids, and the net result may be more jobs, not fewer. New initiatives emerge from the network edge, by small- and medium-sized businesses, rather than from the center.

Many of us believe—intuitively and instinctively—microgrids are important, but we do not know if they are economical. Finding little in the literature on the topic of microgrid economics, I decided to study the topic with the help of graduate students. All of Chapter 3 is devoted to my efforts to answer this question.

THREE

Toward Off-Grid Campuses: The Design Challenge

The illiterate expression "given data" constantly recurs. . . . It appears to have an irresistible attraction to mathematical economists because it doubly assures them that they know what they do not know. It seems to bewitch them into making assertions about the real world for which they have no empirical justification whatever.

—F. A. Hayek

A STORY OF MICROGRID ECONOMICS[1]

Until 8:30 P.M. on November 27, the last day of the Fall 2014 term at IIM Kozhikode (IIMK), no one anywhere in the world was in a position to tell me the cost/unit of electricity when solar panels, batteries, and diesel generators are combined to produce electricity for a system of approximately 1 MW, with a plant lasting about 20 years and with batteries requiring replacement every five years.

No one had apparently modeled such an integrated system, as best my research revealed, until we did it that day. Since 3 P.M., a team of graduate students with engineering and finance training from IIM, and four students with engineering and technology backgrounds interested in microgrids from TU Delft, the Netherlands, had been working in my office. Several months of prior effort had led up to this all-hands meeting of the microgrid team. Our question: For the IIMK campus, with its office buildings and classrooms, what would the economics—dollars per kilowatt-hour of electricity—of a stand-alone microgrid be?

I thought this exercise was important because it would send an important market signal. Are stand-alone microgrids economical, compared to electricity from the traditional grid? If not, how far away are we from grid parity? Our system offered a consolidated look at the state of the industry, with multiple technologies working in conjunction with each other and also incorporating the geographical and weather-related features of the service area, such as available rooftop surface and solar irradiation. In contrast, grid electricity prices are uniform across large territories and mask the cost variations across geographies.

MICROGRIDS: CONSEQUENCES OF COMPETITIVE COSTS

If the cost/unit was above $0.30/kWh, it would imply that microgrid technologies were not ready for prime time, in many markets, as stand-alone systems in competition with the existing electricity grid. We would have to wait for further advances in solar panels, or batteries, for the economics to be "right." If the cost was closer to $0.20/kWh, it would indicate that microgrids could compete with grid electricity as stand-alone systems, in many markets. In the United States, most analyses of microgrids study grid-tied systems. This misrepresents the underlying economics of microgrids, since battery costs can be reduced or eliminated in grid-tied systems.

The important larger questions, beyond the dollars per kilowatt-hour of microgrid electricity, we sought answers to were: What happens to the electricity business model when microgrids can deliver greener and more reliable electricity at lower prices than the grid? What happens to the regulatory infrastructure if barriers to entry are eliminated, and the shibboleth of *natural monopoly* no longer holds? What happens when customers have choices among several electricity service providers in every market?

Photographs of the campus are given in Figures 3.1 and 3.2, and the load we tried to design for the campus is given in Table 3.1.

Figure 3.1   Overview: Academic Hill of IIMK Campus, a ~1-MW System

Figure 3.2   11-kV Lines Entering the Academic Hill of IIMK Campus

Currently in San Diego, my electricity bill to San Diego Gas & Electric (SDG&E) averages approximately $0.24/kWh, even though, with only my son and wife in the house most of the time, I avoid hitting the top-pricing tier. My neighbors pay a much higher average price for their electricity.

Table 3.1a IIMK Electricity Bill

Arrears as on October 7, 2014				Date of Previous Reading	August 31, 2014		Supply Voltage	11 kV	HT
Disputed	Undisputed			Date of Present Reading	September 30, 2014		Billing Type	DPS	
Contract Demand(kVA)	75% of CD (kVA)	CD (kVA)	130% of Connected Load (kW)	Average MD (kVA)	Consumption (kWh)	PF	Section	Kunnamangalam	
750.0	562.5	975.0	1,783.01	797.21	182,620	0.96	Circle	Kozhikode	

Reading Details (kVA, kWh, kVAh & kVArh) for September 2014

1. Energy Consumption(kWh)

Zone	FR	IR	MF	Units
1	132,2067	130,8862	12.00	158,460
2	348,260	344,777	12.00	41,796
3	477,957	472,524	12.00	65,196
Total				265,452

2. Energy Consumption(kVAh)

Zone	FR	IR	MF	Units
1	225,6885	223,3701	12.00	278,208
2	0	0	12.00	0
3	0	0	12.00	0
Total				278,208

3. Energy Consumption(kVArh)

Zone	FR	IR	MF	Units
1	0	0		0
2	0	0		0
3	0	0		0
Total				0

4. Demand (kVA)

	Readings	MF	Units
1	76.131	12.00	913.57
2	50.252	12.00	603.02
3	38.851	12.00	466.21
5. Factory Lighting			0.0
6. Colony Lighting			0.0
7. Generator			4,352.0

Average PF = kWh/kVAh 0.95

Table 3.1b IIMK Electricity Bill

Invoice

	Unit	Rate (Rs.)	Amount (Rs.)		Amount
1. Total Demand Charge				9. Other Charges	
a. Demand Charge—Normal	914.0	350.000	319,900.00		
b. Demand Charge—Peak	0.0	350.000	0.00		
c. Demand Charge—Off Peak	0.0	350.000	0.00		
d. Excess Demand Charge—Normal	164.0	175.000	28,700.00		
e. Excess Demand Charge—Peak	0.0	175.000	0.00		
f. Excess Demand Charge—Off Peak	0.0	175.000	0.00		
Subtotal (a + b + c + d + e + f)			**348,600.00**		
2. Total Energy Charges					
a. Energy Charges—Normal	158,460.0	5.100	808,146.00		
b. Energy Charges—Peak	41,796.0	7.650	319,739.40		
c. Energy Charges—Off Peak	65,196.0	3.825	249,374.70		
Subtotal (a + b + c)			**1,377,260.10**		
3. PF Incentives/Penalty			−17,215.75		
Total Energy Charge			**1,360,044.35**		
4. Energy Charges on Lighting load					
a. Factory Lighting	0	0.0	0.00	10. Total (add 1 to 9)	1,851,337.31
b. Colony Lighting	0	0.0	0.00	Plus/Minus (Round Off)	−0.31
Subtotal (a + b)			**0.00**		
5. Electricity Duty	1,360,044	0.100	136,004.44	Less 1. Advance at Credit	
6. Electricity Surcharge	265,452	0.025	6,636.30	2. CD Interest	0.00
7. Duty on Self-Generated Energy	4,352	0.012	52.22	3. CD Refund	0.00
8. Penalty for Nonsegn. of Light Load				**Net Payable**	**1,851,337.00**

(Rupees Eighteen Lakh Fifty-One Thousand Three Hundred Thirty-Seven Only)

THE MODELING EXERCISE

About 10 days earlier, Subhashree,[2] an MBA student and a chartered account-ant, had developed a *pro forma* financial template for a stand-alone microgrid business, with cash flow, income, and balance sheet statements. To test the model, I gave her my top-of-mind estimates of capital and operating costs to see where we ended up with electricity costs. We were not surprised by our early estimates; the cost of microgrid electricity could be as high as $0.35/kWh, and, for my guess-timates, breakeven was not in sight, and the net present value (NPV) was negative.

Now we were working with real information—prices of specific batteries and panels from online sources; operating information about diesel consumption and its costs; and the load profile data at 20-minute intervals for the academic hill of IIMK from the institute's electrical engineering department.[3]

Three teams had been working feverishly in my office since 2 P.M., huddled around my desktop and two laptops. Technical and engineering inputs, along with financial assumptions, were proposed, discussed, and then fed into the spread-sheets. Are balance-of-system (BOS) costs, at 30 percent of the costs of panels, reasonable? Should solar panel and inverter prices be toward the high, medium, or low end of what is indicated on the web? Should depreciation be straight line or *sum of the years' digits*? What proportion of the financing should be equity, what fraction should be debt, and how would that affect the cost/unit? What should be the cost of money? Should the cost/unit be calculated for the designed capacity, or for usage? We ignored all subsidies and government incentives.

One version of the spreadsheet was on Soumya's laptop, another on Jan's lap-top, and the third was on my desktop, worked on by Subhashree. By 8:30 P.M., we had our preliminary answer: $0.32/kWh and a small positive NPV, assuming only debt financing and a relatively short project life. We then tweaked the duration of the project, added an equity component to the financing, refined operating costs assumptions, lowered the cost of money, replaced the five-year-life batteries with longer-life batteries, and finally arrived at approximately $0.20/kWh, with assumptions we could all agree upon. Breakeven was well past year 15, and the NPV was positive, but not a large number.

TWO CASES OF DEMAND: BUSINESS OFFICE AND RESIDENTIAL NEIGHBORHOOD

IIMK's academic hill represents a microgrid with a daytime peak load due to air-conditioning for classrooms and offices. For operating costs, only fuel costs and maintenance were included; the staffing is largely in place, and we assumed only modest new staffing.

How would the design and economics for a microgrid of about the same 1-MW capacity be different for a residential neighborhood, with evening peak load? We modeled a 120-home homeowners' association (HOA) in San Diego. The broad layout of homes is indicated in Figure 3.3. For modeling purposes, we assumed

Figure 3.3   The Layout of a Homeowners' Association, San Diego

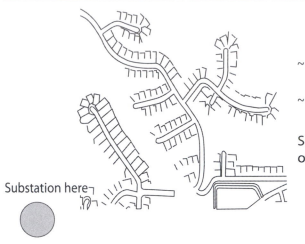

~ 120 homes

~ 1 MW average load

Sufficient rooftop and open space

Substation here⌐

the HOA would be one among many under common management. Beyond maintenance, supplies, and cleaning costs we assumed only the costs of a fractional employee per MW. We also considered the case of a microgrid owned by a utility that would not incur any new staffing expenses at all. We assumed our solar panels, batteries, inverters, and related infrastructure would be located at the substation of the current utility in the neighborhood. On December 12, we had our HOA answer: $0.25/kWh. Once again, NPV was small and breakeven was years out—not an easy investment decision. And just like the case of IIMK campus, this number could vary depending on our assumptions.

With stand-alone microgrid electricity costs between $0.20 and $0.25/kWh in 2015, based on our best-effort analysis, I feel comfortable in predicting that unit prices will fall to around $0.15/kWh by 2018. Grid-tied solar electricity in India in late 2015 is already at $0.13/kWh and lower. In other words, microgrid pricing, with distributed generation, can be in a competitive range in a short time.

No one today knows the consequences when a less than $4 million investment can create an infrastructure providing electricity to about 120 homes *cheaper* than grid electricity. If we assume volume discounts for capital deployed for panels, batteries, inverters, and BOSs; optimize the deployment of generation sources; and include some *demand-side* management and wait for the technologies to mature for another two years, I have little doubt that microgrids of approximately 1-MW capacity can comfortably compete with grid electricity. My conclusion: We are potentially on the cusp of a transformative change in the topology and business model of the electricity industry.

It is true that the prices we have arrived at are higher than typical grid prices—in parts of the Midwest United States, for instance, the prices of electricity are half those in California and comparable to the price of electricity generated using diesel alone. However, coal-based power leads to carbon emissions, typically not yet factored in today's prices. The real costs of traditional electricity are in fact much higher. Moreover, while the prices of fossil fuel–based electricity will inevitably rise, those of renewable generation–based electricity can be expected to continually fall in the foreseeable future. The renewable energy technologies are a new S curve representing disruptive innovation; today's performance can be expected to improve with time. In addition, governments often subsidize electricity, making it unclear what real electricity costs are. Finally, grid economics deteriorates rapidly as we move away from population centers; rural areas may not have sufficient populations to cover the costs of grid extension. Grid extension strategies invariably involve cross-subsidies from urban to rural users. Microgrids can be deployed in urban areas practically as easily as in rural areas.

Even where grid electricity is currently cheap, it is often unreliable and sporadic; microgrid electricity will be predictable and green, reliable and resilient. Reliability has a value that is unmeasured today but borne through the use of "captive" diesel-based generation. Today's grid is also wasteful. In India, approximately 20 percent of electricity is lost during transmission and distribution; about 10 percent or less is lost in developed markets.

EXPLORING SOLAR PROJECTS ON CAMPUS

Before starting the microgrid analysis, we had experimented with several small solar electricity projects on campus. For instance, we implemented the solar pathway lighting project described in Box 3.1, and I first wrote about this in *The Hindu Business Line*.[4] We also studied implementing solar-powered e-bikes for the campus, in partnership with an electric carmaker in Bangalore. For instance, we proposed solar charging stations at the bottom of the hill on which the campus is located, near the campus main gate, and also on the top of the hill near the academic buildings. Could we maintain a fleet of, say, a dozen e-bikes, charging users a nominal fee for each commute? Today, about half the students have motorcycles and use fossil fuel for their transport. Around 2013, there were no credible e-bike makers in India, and unlike in China, where e-bikes are everywhere, there are few to none in India. The off-grid microgrid modeling project was thus an extension of the efforts already under way.

Box 3.1 Toward Off-Grid Campuses

Indian Institute of Management Kozhikode's (IIMK's) academic buildings are located on the top of a steep hill. Even geared bicycles can climb up the slopes only with difficulty. As a result, scooters and motorcycles, but no bicycles, abound on campus.

Walking up the hill by the winding road can be a strenuous aerobic exercise. It also takes time. The destination—the offices buildings—is in sight, though reached only by huffing and puffing. The humid Kerala climate means the pedestrian is sweaty and uncomfortable during the climb.

SPIRALING LIGHTED PATHWAY

The winding road may be bypassed by a nearly spiral stairway with handrails that reaches up approximately 150 feet, with minor straight stretches for a pause. This *appears* to be a faster way to go up or down. In fact, it passes through heavy foliage and tempts climbers to pause to admire the sights and catch their breaths. At night this stairway has not been usable; it is dangerous. Snakes and scorpions are sighted nearby.

Since November 2013, solar-powered LED lights—22 lampposts that are about 12 feet height and evenly spaced along the path—have lighted this stairway. A 0.75-kW panel installed at the side of the road charges the batteries that light up the lamps. The lamps turn on at sundown and shut off with daylight automatically. At night, they lend a new beauty to the hill—dark all around, yet containing a lighted path upward into the sky and down toward the Milma Store, Kerala's milk cooperative dairy outlet.

At any given spot on the path, about three or four lights are visible due to the foliage and the turns. The pedestrian has to keep faith—every few steps reveal a new lamppost, and the next stretch of the path. This lighting solution is stand-alone, self-sufficient, and untethered to the state electricity grid, the campus's first yet admittedly small off-grid project.

MICROELECTRIC UTILITIES FOR CAMPUSES

The next steps are obvious: lighting additional pathways spread across the campus and installing solar panels on rooftops. Rooftop solar panels could charge UPS (uninterrupted power supply) batteries supporting computer networks and power fans and lighting for offices and classrooms. They can heat hot water for hostel bathrooms and for cooking in the kitchens.

Does the economics work? It increasingly does, as the costs of solar photovoltaics have fallen dramatically in the past three years, while grid electricity prices will rise due to coal shortages, pricing of emissions, and growing demand. India's electricity demand will inevitably grow; per capita consumption in the country (90 W/person) is about 1/4 that of China (395 W/person) and about 1/15 that of the United States (1,402 W/person).

Emerging economies like India and many African nations have little legacy infrastructure—they are ideal sites for new experiments.

Campuses, in fact, will be the preferred first locations for next-generation electricity services through microgrids. They have concentrated populations on private land and thus face few regulatory barriers. A worthy goal for them would be to go off grid—to be independent of the electricity grid, using it only as backup. All educational and corporate campuses (IIT, NIT, IIM, engineering colleges, etc.) can substitute for traditional power in stages for the next several years, measuring progress by the percentage of the power supply supplanted by renewable energy each year and the corresponding electricity bill savings.

Further, could solar canopies at campus parking lots charge e-bicycle batteries? E-bicycles can climb IIMK slopes—fuel-lessly, noiselessly, and cleanly. Students have estimated the capacity and costs of the solar panels and batteries required to make this happen. They have designed e-bikes as part of class assignments.

MICROELECTRIC UTILITIES AS LABORATORIES

Solar energy solutions on campus serve as a laboratory for entrepreneurial experimentation; for studying technical aspects of panels, batteries, inverters, networking, and demand management; and for understanding industry-restructuring issues—business plans including strategy, product development, positioning, and marketing.

As regulated monopolies, today's utilities offer commodity electricity, to all customers in assigned geographies. A microelectric utility may not be so constrained; it will compete with today's utilities along many new dimensions. What will today's utilities do to counter this competition?

In 15 years, we may expect tens of thousands of microgrids-based small utilities because the economics of power generation no longer depends on scale; small plants can be as cost effective as large ones. And it takes less money to begin producing electricity; the barriers to enter the service have fallen.

Will the new companies focus on particular segments across a large geography, say, street lighting or residential solar deployments, across a state or nation? Or will they concentrate on many solutions in a particular, smaller geography, that is, a one-stop shop for everything solar in a town—from residential power to street lighting and water pumps for irrigation to powering cellular towers?

How electric utilities evolve remains among the most gripping, unfinished, and suspenseful stories in the industrial history of our time. As a result of contending regulatory, technological, and business issues, the new electricity will be clean, economical, reliable, and universally available, in rural markets and urban markets alike, and come from a number of suppliers, including the incumbent utility. Campuses as optimal battlegrounds will lead the way.

COST/UNIT FROM A MICROGRID SYSTEM: WHAT DOES IT MEAN?

Consider the multiple use cases for microgrids. In the microgrid MBA class I taught for HeatSpring, David in Nigeria proposed a microgrid for a hospital and an airport. Gillian wanted a microgrid for a town center on the U.S. East Coast. Santiago wanted a microgrid for a small village in an equatorial jungle. Rudy wished to design a microgrid for a military base. Some use cases have daytime peak load, others in the evening. What is the load profile for a hospital or airport?

Some use cases expect grid connectivity, and some are off grid by design. While generalizations can be made, each system is unique and needs custom design. And the basic design is not too difficult. A smart and experienced engineering team of approximately three people can design each solution. Then we create a capital budget and include the operating cost, and a savvy finance person finds out the NPV and breakeven.

Let us assume David's hospital, Santiago's village in the jungle, and Rudy's military base are off grid. What is the cost/unit? Let us assume the town center microgrid is grid-tied with four hours of battery backup. Suppose the cost/unit is $0.25 for an off-grid system with a 15-year breakeven and $0.20 for a grid-tied system and a 10-year breakeven. Is that attractive, given both costs are higher than what we pay for grid electricity today? What are the drivers of aggregate economics: the relative contribution of capital costs, operating costs, cost of money, or the sensitivities, in the overall economics?

Let us further assume that, while the price/unit of grid electricity will continue to rise at approximately 5 percent per year, the price of the microgrid system will fall at 5 percent per year. In that case, when do the two curves—the price of grid electricity over time and the cost of a microgrid system over time—intersect and cross over? Let us say in five years.

Should we wait for five years before investing in the microgrid system? Not necessarily. Because in a competitive deployment arena, there is an *opportunity cost* to deploying late—someone else may lease access to the physical assets where the solar panels, batteries, and other microgrid equipment need to be deployed. This could be the substation for a serving area where the transformers and control room are. It could be the cellular tower where the fiber-optic cable hub is. It could be the open space in a neighborhood or a parking lot. So the deployment decision has to be made between today and five years out when we expect the microgrid economics to surpass the grid economics. There is business risk, and cost, to deploying too early and a business cost of being shut out of the opportunity by deploying late.

What should the microgrid developer charge customers? Should electricity be offered at low cost to gain market share, with the expectation of recovering the losses incurred once the cost shift occurs in favor of microgrids, over five years hence?

From the customer perspective, how large should the discount to grid pricing be to make the switch to microgrid power? How to factor in the inconvenience of construction, for example, related to microgrid deployment relative to the price advantage? Will his or her rooftop be a part of the generating mix, or will the microgrid infrastructure be located at a central location, albeit one that will probably be much closer than the nearest power plant supplying grid electricity, so that the switch is invisible and seamless?

After considering all this, a project finance person looking at both the financial analysis and the operational difficulties may well say: forget it. Stick to grid-tied multi-MW renewable projects. Sign a PPA (power purchase agreement) with the utility, and our money supply is assured.

MICROGRIDS AS SUBSTITUTES AND COMPLEMENTS

My hypothesis: Microgrids will become mainstream and not simply be limited to remote, inaccessible places and their population pockets. They will compete with, and substitute for, the macrogrid, *and* be a complement to it. The question is how? What has to happen for my street with 12 homes, or the neighboring strip mall, or any housing society, or any airport or any hospital to have microgrids?

Among the missing pieces until now has been microgrid economics. We did not know whether microgrids, save for remote locations and special instances, were viable. Are we still in the *research* mode, or are we ready for *investment*? Now we know the breakeven is approximately 19 years, and the NPV is approximately $500,000 for a capital investment of $3 plus million, and the economics will improve only with volume discounts and technical advance.

Nevertheless, this economic outcome appears disheartening. Why would anyone having an existing grid for electricity access invest in microgrids? Who will invest in such projects, except when one has to? Is it the desire for independence, for autonomy, or for greater use of renewable energy sources, despite economics?

CAPITAL PLANNING AND THE IMPORTANCE OF OPERATING COSTS

Besides economics, among the additional missing pieces includes *capital planning* in design for a given load. For instance, how much solar, how much battery, or how much diesel/gas generator should be deployed, such that the overall capital costs are the lowest? This nonlinear, integer-programming problem appears to be unsolved by the engineering profession or by operations research experts. Perhaps Homer software has a solution of this kind undergirding it.

This absence is not a showstopper, however, as we can use a *rule of thumb*–based solution, not elegant, but workable; we did such estimates while modeling the IIMK system. Once the capital is deployed, how to run the microgrid optimally? That has been addressed in several good papers.

Interestingly, the *capital efficiency* gained by optimization likely does not affect the overall economics significantly, say, no more than 10 percent. Our sensitivity analysis reveals that the NPV and breakeven are most affected by operating costs, and less capital costs. While capital costs are large and upfront and hold us back with sticker shock, even small operations costs—cleaning panels, fuel costs, maintenance, salaries, and office expenses—are major drivers of aggregate economics.

To improve aggregate economics, that is, reduce operating and capital costs, and enhance reliability, could we automate, standardize, and deploy microgrids in large numbers, in clusters, as a federation of microgrids?

HOMEOWNERS' ASSOCIATION AS UNIT OF ANALYSIS

Assuming our analysis of the San Diego HOA is right, it appears that the infrastructure used by SDG&E (San Diego Gas & Electric) for providing electricity is *less economical* than the corresponding microgrids, even today. Is this incentive enough for the HOA to become its own electricity provider, in other words, defect? Is the hassle of creating the substitute solution worth the effort? Should an entrepreneur or a new entrant in the electricity business approach the management of the association and offer to implement a microgrid for them, with suitable incentives, does that push the homeowners' association into electricity autonomy?

Can the HOA buy out its fraction of the macrogrid from the incumbent investor-owned utility? Or lease some equipment and the distribution cabling from SDG&E on terms the utility charges itself? What is the cost of the electricity loop that enters the neighborhood and terminates at the meter?

Should the HOA form a cooperative, it may lease space at the serving substation for placing equipment—solar panels and batteries. Or, the open spaces around each home and on rooftops may be sufficient for solar generation—no need to lease space from the utility. The HOA may split the service territory into street-sized microgrids and combine them as needed. Thus, the HOA may be one microgrid or be constituted of several microgrids working cooperatively with each other.

A new service provider may seek access to the incumbent electric utility's infrastructure to provide competitive electricity services. The incumbent utility may make available its current distribution infrastructure—cabling to individual customer homes and businesses—to the new provider on the same terms as it makes available for itself.

UNBUNDLING THE LOCAL ELECTRICITY LOOP

This type of resource sharing, with access to the utility's infrastructure as a matter of legal right, was exactly what was done in the case of *unbundling* of the telephone local loop. The competitor had the right to service a customer by paying for the local loop. The new provider also had the right to place its equipment and technology at the telephone company hub—*collocation*. The substation of an electric utility can be the collocation point for electricity service providers.

If the telephone local loop can be unbundled and made available to competitors, so can the electricity loop. Thus, local electricity loop unbundling, with the substation as the focal point, will give rise to competitive DG-based electricity competitors. A competitor may locate its generation assets—solar panels, batteries, control gear, more—at the substation itself, or on rooftops, or in any suitable open space. The cellular towers in a neighborhood might equally be focal points for providing next-generation electricity. The fiber-optic cable feeding the cellular tower may be an optimal asset for the management of the electricity distribution assets of the future.

ELECTRIFICATION? ABSOLUTELY. GRID EXPANSION? NO

With continuously falling prices of solar panels, advances in inverter technologies, next-generation batteries, and the use of diesel- or gas-based generation where absolutely necessary, a new electricity paradigm has emerged. To call it *distributed generation* (DG) understates the development. To call it distributed generation (DG) understates the development. However, it is technically accurate to describe it as such. With microgrids, what has emerged is in fact the next-generation, broad-based electricity solution itself, characterized by local generation, local consumption, and operating autonomy. We may question, with no exaggeration, whether the electricity business is intrinsically a wide-area networking business—the grid—at all, except for major industrial applications. Economical microgrids suggest electricity to be a *local* solution.

With microgrid advances, rural electrification is a solved problem; only execution—that is speedy and effective implementation—remains. A determined government, in India or in Africa, can achieve 100 percent electrification in less than 10 years. How many microgrids does India need, perhaps a few hundred thousand? Will the electrification with renewables lead to an entrepreneurial boom with attendant innovation?

To determine the microgrid economics for a roughly 1-MW system, Box 3.2 summarizes the design challenge we presented to the team of IIMK and TU Delft students. For the TU Delft students, this was an internship project with a grade. For IIMK students, we had the project included as a part of an advanced financial modeling course, and thus also graded.

Box 3.2 The Campus Microgrid Design Challenge

Goal. To make the IIMK campus a prototype for a scalable, replicable, and stand-alone microgrid for deployment across the country, in both rural and urban areas. The design must accommodate local generation by multiple means and demand-side management.

Microgrid design challenge. Use solar panels, batteries, and gas or diesel generators, such that the Academic Hill can work as a stand-alone, off-grid system. The specific design questions to address include the following:

- How much should be the capacity of the solar panels? Of the batteries? What should be the capacity of the diesel generators?

- Given the load profile, what generation source should primarily supply electricity for the various hours of the day? What should be the source during peak hours? How should the batteries be charged? Using solar? Using gas and diesel generators?

- Use the microgrid to charge the UPS system used for office LANs in all three faculty blocks and the administration buildings.

- Assume the economic life of each of the solar panels and gas generators is 15 years and of batteries is 5 years. Assume reasonable cost of money and a suitable depreciation method. Make suitable assumptions for operating costs, staffing (incremental), office space (incremental), and other administrative expenses. Use discounted cash flow for assessing overall project feasibility and determine the NPV.

- Assume electricity bill each year rises by 5 percent due to fossil fuel price increases. The total cost for each year must be less than the corresponding year's electricity bill. Estimate the cumulative costs and cumulative *revenue* for the system, and calculate the breakeven in months from launch.

The IIMK campus, spread over 100 acres, is comprised of two hills—academic and residential—with a road connecting them. The campus is located in Kunnamangalam village, with a population of ~ 50,000, and is located about 25 km from Kozhikode city, with a population of 432,097, according to the 2011 census. For microgrid design purposes, each of the academic and residential hill may be treated as distinct systems. *The focus of this study is only the academic hill.* The electricity consumption and charges for the academic hill are given in Tables 3.1 and 3.2.

The student population, approximately 800, consists of master's and doctoral students. The academic hill houses three faculty blocks of three stories each, each with 30 offices, with several classrooms nearby. Two classrooms seat approximately 70 students each, and two others of somewhat smaller capacity seat about 55 students each. There are also smaller conference rooms, two for each faculty block, for doctoral seminars and meetings that seat about 15 persons. All classrooms are air-conditioned and have advanced audiovisual equipment.

The academic hill also has the administration building, computer center, distance education studio, videoconferencing room, and library. There is an auditorium for seating approximately 300. There is a separate Management Development Program (MDP) building for executive education that has hotel-style accommodation for about 100 people, a restaurant, and a larger auditorium for seating over 500. The MDP building has four classrooms for seating about 60 students, smaller conference rooms, and administration offices. The faculty strength is approximately 65. At any given time, there is at least one executive education program with participant strength of about 40. The residential hill has housing for faculty and staff, as well as two guesthouses. The residential hill population is approximately 500.

Electrical load. Each of the academic and residential hill is served by two 11-kV HT lines from Kerala State Electricity Board (KSEB). At the entry point for the academic hill, there are also two diesel generators of 1,250 kVA each and one 500-kVA generator. The maximum demand for the academic hill, not including the MDP complex, is approximately 900 kVA with a 0.9 power factor. The connected load at the academic hill is 4 MW.

KSEB charges IIMK a special *educational institution* tariff at Rs. 5.10/kWh. Peak rate, from 6 P.M. to 10 P.M., is 1.5 times the base rate. Off-peak rate, from 10 P.M. to 6 A.M., is 75 percent of the base rate. From 6 A.M. to 6 P.M. is the normal rate. For comparison purposes, note that the commercial tariff is Rs. 10/kWh. For approximately 1 hour each day, the power goes "out" and the diesel generator fires up. Diesel costs Rs. 60/liter. The average cost of diesel-generated power is Rs. 18/kWh.

FOUR

Microgrids: Common Intersection between Developed and Emerging Economies

To the naive mind that can conceive of order only as the product of deliberate arrangement, it may seem absurd that in complex conditions order, and adaptation to the unknown, can be achieved more effectively by decentralizing decisions and that a division of authority will actually extend the possibility of overall order.

— F. A. Hayek

Much attention has been devoted to clean-burning biomass cookstoves. Traditional firewood burning for cooking is among the major sources of ill health related to smoke inhalation. Yet little research has focused on solar-powered induction cooking. Can it be done? If microgrids are used—shared, local infrastructure of a certain size—it is possible. Why induction cooking? Because anyone who has used the compact and portable cookstoves will recognize the clean and nearly kitchen-independent cooking now possible. I have seen homemakers make *dosas*—sour dough crepes—in the living room while watching TV and participating in social conversation with visitors. But almost no work exists on this topic. Concentrated solar to steam to cooking—this path has been implemented in several Indian temples where cooking is done daily on a large scale.

Similarly, LEVA—Light Electric Vehicle Association[1]—represents the growing battery-powered electric bike industry, yet solar-powered electric bikes constitute only a small portion of their sales. Solar umbrellas charging electric bikes ought to be everywhere in hot, sunny India, but they are not.

COOKING AND GAS GRID INDEPENDENCE

Like many homes in the United States, my mother's home in Mumbai has piped natural gas for cooking. My mother also maintains a LPG cylinder "just in case," though she has not used it for months. With the LPG cylinder, she is *gas grid* independent. In fact, the gas grid is a relatively new introduction. Our family was gas grid independent all through my growing years. We relied on kerosene as a supplement to LPG for a while. I remember pumping the kerosene stove, an impressive brass contraption, and cleaning its tiny pinhole by pushing a fine wire attached to a metal handle. Through this pinhole rose the pressurized fuel that reached the burner. It typically gave off a blue flame with some hiss. Occasionally, the flame turned yellow or flickered due to impurities in the fuel.

On occasion, my mother also cooked with charcoal, especially while making rice, believing that the slow cooking brought out the flavors better. The lighting of the charcoal stove was a semi-elaborate process. We had to light a tiny kerosene-drenched piece of rag as starter flame. The smoke as the charcoal lit up was expected to go out of the kitchen window since the stove was kept near it. But some smoke ended up staining the ceiling and walls. It is perhaps two decades since either the kerosene or the charcoal stove has been used. The store that sold charcoal does not exist anymore either. Of course, we did not know that our cooking methods were contributing to global warming.

Over two decades later in early 2011, at IIM as a visiting professor, I heard of induction cookstoves that everyone around me was using. I was puzzled at first, never having heard of them or seen them in the United States. I knew microwave cooking, but this was different. It was also different from resistive coil-based cooking, an altogether new means of boiling water, heating milk, and roasting *chapattis*. The only condition was that the cooking vessel needed to be flat-bottomed, with a certain amount of iron content for the induction heating to occur. The cookstove makers fortunately bundled a set of cooking vessels with the purchase.

I bought an induction cooker, not wanting to go through the process of getting an LPG cylinder. The boiling efficiency, ease of maintenance, and the fast cooking possible through my little machine are extraordinary. With it, I am gas grid independent, and potentially fossil fuel independent, too, if I can get the electricity from sources other than coal burning.

Back in the United States, I checked with Sears; they do sell induction cookers, portable units like the one I have, but only from the catalog, not in stores. IKEA now sells cooking ranges with induction-cooking surfaces and promotes their efficiency in boiling water in its sales video. Unlike a flame or a resistive coil, there is literally no waste in heating—all energy goes directly to the food being cooked.

ELECTRICITY'S ABSENCE: FRUSTRATING, INITIATIVE SAPPING

Electricity in India, as in the United States, whether in urban, rural, or semiurban areas, is "piped" in over long distances. The IIM campus has a diesel generator that takes over when the grid "dies," which happens for about two hours every night. It takes a minute or so for the diesel generator to take over from the macrogrid; there is darkness for those moments. Everyone is used to it.

Elsewhere in India, grid outages last for hours—8, 12, 14 hours or more a day in certain places. And those are electrified places. As I mentioned before in the Preface, about 300 million Indians have no electricity whatsoever—no cables, no power sources. They live by flickering kerosene lights and cook using biomass. Until 2010, I was innocent about the state of the country's electricity affairs, believing that electricity was more or less universally available, though intermittent. I believed India was 100 percent electrified, at least as far as cabling was concerned, though outages—load shedding—have been a daily experience of life in India ever since I can remember.

I vividly recall the moment one afternoon in early 2011 when I read a commencement speech by Jairam Ramesh, the then minister of Environment and Forests, on my office computer. He mentioned the absence of electricity for over 300 million Indians. I thought there was a mistake in the text, that he meant 30, surely not 300 million! My discovery of the absence of electricity for so many people altered my view of economic development. I started thinking about electricity first, before phones and broadband Internet.

ECONOMIC DEVELOPMENT AND ELECTRICITY

Growing up in electrified Mumbai with reliable supply, I thought the principal barrier to India's economic development was the absence of the telephone, and later the Internet. My assumption was: give people broadband connectivity and a telephone, and entrepreneurial economic growth would occur across the country, bottom up, almost spontaneously.

My interest in the telephone was also based on a poignant personal experience. I had graduated as a chemical engineer and was to be interviewed for a job posting in Germany and Singapore. The company representatives arrived at Mumbai and stayed at the five-star Taj Mahal Hotel. I lived in Mumbai too, but our family in the 1980s had no telephone. So the visitors sent a telegram from across town, about 15 miles away, to our home inviting me for an interview. I was temporarily about 50 miles away and living at a guesthouse at the factory location in Taloja, where I worked in my first job as an engineer trainee. That factory location too was inaccessible via telephone. At the factory, a petrochemical plant for manufacturing fertilizers, there were lots of intercom phones, one on each desk, but only two *outside* lines; naturally, each was always busy.

So my father visited my company's headquarters in the heart of Mumbai and informed them that I was needed for a meeting in Mumbai. The Mumbai office made a "trunk" call to have me return to Mumbai to attend this meeting. The process took two days. The experience was unbelievably frustrating. Telephones, clearly, were not the luxury the government of India believed they were; they were a basic necessity for transactions. What kind of economic planning was the nation doing, I wondered, if it did not supply adequate numbers of telephones?

At graduate school at Syracuse University a few years later in 1984, I discovered that economists did not understand the importance of telephones in economic development; there were practically no research papers or articles on the subject. My experience of telephony's absence led me to think less of the economics profession. Why haven't economists recognized the importance of telephones? How is it that they have missed out on their importance in economic development, in human welfare? Why did India's policy elite treat the telephone as a luxury?

Dissatisfied with the state of affairs, I shifted my focus away from chemical engineering and toward the telephone as an instrument for reducing transaction costs, facilitating commerce, bridging distances to alleviate anxiety, and thereby enhancing welfare and potentially economic growth. Later, my focus shifted to broadband Internet.

Those without electricity, however, are denied both phones and the Internet, along with light, fans, refrigerators, and livelihood beyond sunlight hours. Large numbers of people are denied the option to participate in society fully, simply because of the accident of birth in rural, unelectrified, untelevision-ed, untelephoned, and un-Internet-ed India. I can only imagine the liberation and empowerment provided by electricity, though I would like to claim some inkling of it, thanks to my frustrating experiences with the telephone's absence and the daily lessons learnt from load shedding in India.

To be without electricity in our age is a condemnation beyond imagination. Yet a billion and a half people across the world are relegated to this primitive existence in electricity's absence. It is a moral imperative of our time to make electricity, and thereby the bounty of the Internet, including education and entertainment, available to everyone. No child need any longer live an unempowered life, prevented from being the most he or she can be.

WIRES AND ELECTRICITY: NECESSARILY LINKED TOGETHER?

TV signals are delivered to a home wirelessly. Telephones also work wirelessly. Yet for electricity, cables have historically been necessary. Wireless TVs and wireless phones need wired electricity. Thus, electricity cables are a perquisite for other kinds of networks. The farther away from population centers one moves, the less economical electricity cabling becomes. Thus, electricity for a remote village dweller remains inaccessible and, with it, the benefits of light beyond sunlight; TV for entertainment; telephones for anxiety reduction, transactions, and communications; and refrigeration for food storage.

But electricity cables, at least across long distances, are no longer necessary to obtain the basic benefits of electricity anymore. Thanks to technical advance in the past few years, superior economics of solar, stand-alone SHS (solar home systems), and better yet microgrids, electricity can reach even the most remote

Figure 4.1   Microgrids: Distinct Purposes, Reliability vs. Access

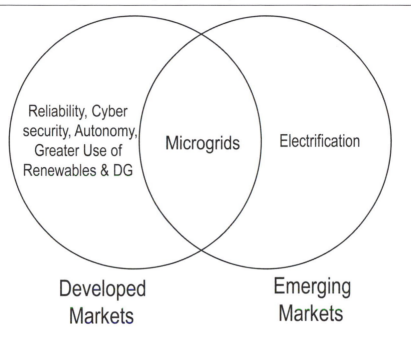

villages. No grid is necessary—for light, phone charging, TV, Internet access, and so forth—with generation and consumption becoming increasingly local.

At one end, with SHSs, we have grid independence via solar on rooftops supported by batteries, or micro gas turbines, or fuel cells, that is, electricity as local as a home. With microgrids "the local" can be larger, say, a population of 2,000. Can a street with sixteen homes be a microgrid? I do not think we know how *small* a microgrid can get. Clearly, the microgrid makes sense for emerging economies and unelectrified regions. Microgrids equally make sense in the developed markets. In Figure 4.1, I show how microgrids may be deployed for distinct purposes in emerging and developed markets, for access and reliability. Yet the technology can be the same. However, the kind of industrial-grade microgrids we need do not exist, as I wrote in *Renewable Energy World* in July 2014.[2] The absence of microgrids R&D, let alone their deployment, is among the astonishing missing pieces in today's electricity industry.

Let me describe the state of the art for the illustrative unelectrified village of Dharnai, Bihar, already mentioned in Chapter 2, and then examine microgrids' applicability yet absence in San Diego. In Figure 4.6, I illustrate what might happen if correctly designed microgrids—fully functional, with all services that a traditional electric utility provides—were to be overlaid on a city like San Diego. The Dharnai project should have led to the creation of such a cluster of microgrids.

GREENPEACE INDIA'S DHARNAI PROJECT IN BIHAR STATE

Here is a summary of the pioneering Dharnai microgrid project completed by Greenpeace, the details of which are available on its website.[3] About 89 percent of the population of Bihar state lives in rural areas, nearly all dependent on kerosene for lighting. About half the villages in the state are electrified, but electricity availability is limited; the average per capita consumption is about 125 units a year, about a seventh of India's national average, and one hundredth of that in the United States.

Dharnai has a population of about 2,400 people and about 450 households. The microgrid installed has an overall capacity of 100 kW, 70 kW for 60 solar street lamps and 30 kW for 10 solar-powered water pumps of 3 kW each. Two hundred eighty solar panels are installed on the rooftops of government buildings, private buildings, and homes; there are inverters and a battery bank.

Greenpeace addressed administrative and organizational issues as it deployed its system. It has a subscription model, with BASIX[4] Urja as the operator for maintenance and collection. CEED, Centre for Environment and Energy Development, an NGO for grassroots-level awareness building, is also involved.[5] A VEC, Village Electrification Committee, oversees the villager interest, determines affordability, and contributes to setting prices. There are several product and service tiers, for residences and businesses, comprising numbers of light, phone charging, fan, and TV use. The 400 families each consume electricity for about eight hours per day.

The microgrid capital investment is Rs. 2.75 crore, or about $500,000, that is, $5/watt installed, rather high but necessary for an early demo project, and likely to drop with volume deployment. The annual maintenance and operations cost is Rs. 13 lakh each year, or $22,000, that is, about $2,000 per month.

The remarkable part of the project is that the developers addressed several *product-markets* in one project and managed them as a single operator. They created four product packages—two for residences, one for retailers, and one for water pumps. This, of course, happens with any utility today—it is a provider of all services to all people. Customers pay for their service using a prepaid model via mobile phones; see for instance, Simpa Networks, a phone-based payment solution.[6]

Dharnai project is a fascinating case study at many levels. Instead of the project becoming a prototype for future microgrids, it in effect, shut down.[7] Why? Because the existing distribution utility of Bihar state decided to power up the village by using the grid. The prices were lower than microgrid prices, and naturally, the macrogrid supported all applications, many of which the microgrid could not.

Among the lessons learned: One, for microgrids to be successful, they must be fully functional, and support all macrogrid applications. Two, expect the grid operator to challenge the microgrid operator. Three, the prices of microgrid services must be lower than grid prices. Four, the question arises: Could the microgrid services work better if offered as distinct *product-markets*, rather than offer all services to all people, as a traditional grid does? Five, assuming a cellular tower nearby, could the tower have served as an anchor tenant for the microgrid, and thereby allowed the economical deployment of a more robust, fully-featured service set?

Figure 4.2   Product—Market Matrix

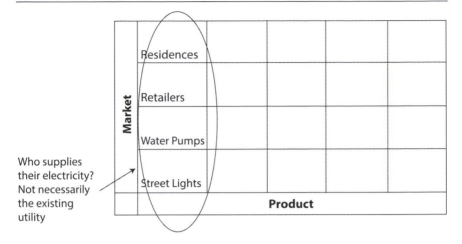

My view is that the several product packages can be distinct businesses, as illustrated in Figure 4.2. On the Y-axis, we have distinct verticals or markets - residences, retailers, water pumps for agriculture, and street lights. On the X axis, we can identify the precise product specifications that meet the needs of each of the markets. Why should each *product-market* not be a distinct business? What is more, each can be an entrepreneurial start-up[8]—each business generating its own electricity, buying equipment in volumes, and deploying beyond local markets, even nationally. Further, some of the businesses can be managed as franchises. I have described this in greater detail in Chapter 7.

The village already has mobile phones. While the report does not note this explicitly, there must be a local cellular tower, likely powered by diesel, in the neighborhood. There might be a fiber-optic link for backhauling the cellular traffic to some mobile switching center from the cellular tower.

Could the economics of the overall electricity system be enhanced if the cellular tower were treated as an *anchor tenant*—a customer of the system, a model discussed on the World Bank's forum on microgrids?[9] Further, if the solar panels are monitored for their performance by an Ethernet connection, could we not use the same infrastructure for providing Internet access? Whereas the solar-based electricity generation infrastructure is strictly local—generation and consumption—its management can be a part of the Internet and thus over extensive geography. The electricity service provider could expand the monitoring infrastructure to offer Internet service. Or conversely, an ISP can offer electricity services.

THE GAP: THE INTERNET AS BINDING GLUE

Between the SHS and the macrogrid is a gap, and that gap is filled by microgrids. When a number of SHSs are tied together as an electricity system, we have a microgrid. The individual SHSs may be centrally managed via the Internet,

Figure 4.3 Microgrids of Different Sizes

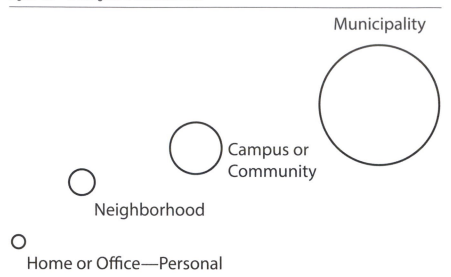

and each home system is treated as a *dumb terminal*. Thousands of such home systems can be centrally managed from anywhere in the world. It is conceivable to have *monitoring* centers, like call centers, manage this automatically, and should any home system stop functioning, a notification can be sent to the local management to troubleshoot and fix. While each home in the electricity system is self-sufficient with rooftop solar and batteries, maintenance can be centrally managed. I described such a centrally monitored yet individual SHS in *Renewable Energy World, The Innovation Imperative: ICT Companies as Electric Utilities of the Future*, November 30, 2011.

In contrast, several hundred homes in a neighborhood or village may be linked together via electricity cabling, and electricity is generated centrally in the neighborhood, and delivered to all homes. When the loads are relatively high, this system makes sense. SHSs put the customer in the electricity business, the latter is a service managed by a microelectric utility—or microgrids.

What the foregoing analysis suggests is that microgrids may range from SHSs to clusters of SHSs, or consist of centrally managed, neighborhood centric systems. Further, they can be campus- or community-sized, or even larger, say the size of a municipality, as shown in Figure 4.3. Whatever the size, the contrast has to be drawn with today's gigantic distribution network, and local autonomy—for generation, consumption, control, and management—needs to be emphasized.

THE EVOLUTION OF THE GRID

How might today's grid evolve to a future state comprising SHSs, microgrids, and the macrogrid? The end state would naturally be cleaner and greener, since microgrids will include solar panels, batteries, and in general all kinds of renewable

Figure 4.4a   Grid Coexists with SHS—No Overlap, No Microgrids

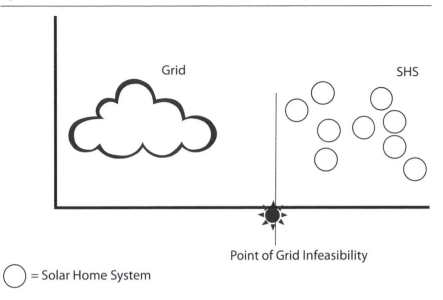

Grid

SHS

Point of Grid Infeasibility

◯ = Solar Home System

Figure 4.4b   Microgrids Complement the Macrogrid and SHS with Overlap

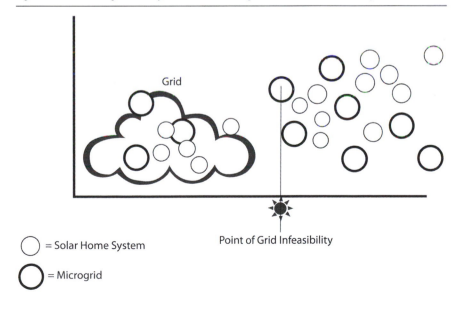

Grid

Point of Grid Infeasibility

◯ = Solar Home System

⬤ = Microgrid

Figure 4.4c   Macrogrid, SHS, and Microgrids Coexist—No Urban and Rural Divide

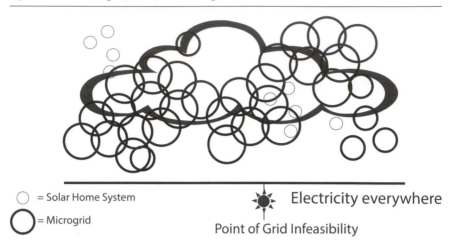

○ = Solar Home System

⬤ = Microgrid

☀ **Electricity everywhere**

Point of Grid Infeasibility

generation. The role of centralized, ultramega power generation using coal would diminish. Even nuclear generation and large-scale hydro generation might diminish. Transmission infrastructure would also lose its criticality. I foresee a timeframe of twenty plus years for this evolution to occur. In Figures 4.4a through 4.4c, I show how this might happen. In Figure 4.4a, the grid and SHSs are in distinct domains, urban and suburban vs. rural and unelectrified. The former has the grid, but the latter only SHSs. Over time, microgrids appear in both the urban and suburban areas as well as in rural areas. In the former, campuses, hospitals, shopping malls, and so forth become autonomous and self-sufficient generators of the bulk of their electricity needs, though they will remain tethered to the macrogrid for backup. Similarly, even in rural areas, several streets, community centers, schools, and so forth would have microgrids rather than SHSs. Thus, microgrids will coexist with the grid and SHSs, in urban and rural areas, as shown in Figure 4.4b. The light-lined circles are SHS, darkened circles are microgrids, and the large cloud represents the macrogrid.

Figure 4.4c shows the proliferation of microgrids in urban, suburban, and rural geographies, which coexist with the grid and the SHSs. The electricity infrastructure here is a network of overlapping networks, each generating and consuming electricity, and each much smaller than what obtains today. The point of grid infeasibility, separating the urban, suburban, and rural areas, loses meaning—the world has 100 percent electrification.

COMPLEMENTARITIES AMONG THE PHONE, ELECTRICITY, AND CLEAN COOKING

The presence of mobile phones creates demand for electricity for charging them—this is well recognized. But the telephone and electricity complementarity is greater, deeper, and more nuanced than this. To focus on phone charging is to emphasize the transactional value of electricity's complementarity with the benefits of the telephone.

The telephone is intrinsically and importantly at the application layer, not the physical layer. The emphasis on the physical device—this phone or that, this OS or that, this feature set or that—misses its strategic value. The phone's use for transactions, anxiety reduction, uncertainty elimination, knowledge gain, and so forth, especially with smartphones, surpasses qualitative benefits from any similar-sized portable appliance. After all, we can have substitutes for electric cooking's absence, say, kerosene burning. When a phone is uncharged, there is almost no substitute for the loss in utility or loss of personal empowerment.

When a phone is not charged, a phone user, a parent, for instance, does not know whether his child has reached school safely; whether there will be delays in arrival or departure due to weather; whether a decision has been made or not made; whether a taxi will reach a home or airport on time; and so on. No two phone calls are alike—a seemingly similar one-minute call across nations, or among friends reaching out to each other in the same parking lot, may be charged the same by a phone company, but one call may seal a multimillion dollar deal or a marriage proposal, and the other may simply settle a meeting time for dinner. Add to this the messaging and contact lists available with the least of today's mobile phones, and the utility of the telephone as a personal and social instrument is incomparable indeed.

As complements go, a phone and electricity are as tight complements as steel and railroads, or cars and roads, or food and drink. With smartphones the complementarity has only strengthened. A charged phone with coverage is a metaphor of personal power.

A new and comparable complementarity between electricity and clean cooking is on the horizon, but before it can happen, we need sufficient solar power and storage for each household, even poor households, for operating induction cookers and microwave ovens. When this happens, we will have fuel-less electricity for cooking. With the elimination of fuel, particularly firewood or equivalent, the pollution that it generates, with health and global warming implications, goes away. Natural gas or LPG cylinders are an intermediate, widespread solution. Yet those who have used induction cooking will attest to the miracle it represents. Thus, we have potentially a huge inflection point at hand—fireless cooking. The invention of fire—how can we understate its importance? Yet how can we overstate the value of fuel-less cooking?

For a long time, I worked on expanding the availability of the Internet to remote villages and areas inaccessible due to the lack of fiber-optic cables in remote geographies. In the United States, I worked on applications for Hughes DIRECWAY—a Ku band gigabit Ethernet platform in geostationary orbit. I visited many RV parks and saw that the best they had by way of Internet access, in the mid-2000s, was still dial-up Internet. But leave the United States, and the situation is much worse. About 1.3 billion people have no electricity access; an equally huge number have no keyboard literacy, nor English language literacy. Broadband Internet, however empowering through the knowledge it makes accessible, appeared a distant possibility. But I did not know in mid-2010 that there were no electricity cables in major parts of India and Africa, let alone any juice flowing over them.

For human welfare, the synergistic complementarities among electricity access, clean cooking, and refrigeration cannot be overstated. Yet this remains unrealized because of the absence of sufficient renewable power in rural, remote households. When coordinated with each other, the synergies create multiplicative benefits.

COMPARING ELECTRICITY, WATER, GAS, AND TELECOM IN THE LOCAL LOOP

Rooftop solar is like DirecTV or EchoStar's DISH, a satellite-based service; the sun beams down *signals* that are converted into electricity. In contrast, an electric utility delivers electricity like cable TV, water, or gas—a whole network of terrestrial pipelines and cables supports it.

A reasonable-sized home, and certainly a neighborhood, can be self-sufficient in electricity with rooftop solar, complemented by microwind, some battery storage, and a small diesel or gas generator—no network needed. We can also make our own cooking or heating gas—methane—by putting our waste food and organic trash in anaerobic digesters, though few households produce enough waste to become entirely self-sufficient in gas. Likewise we can, if we live in areas with a wet climate, harvest enough rainwater to be self-sufficient in water. Wells also allow water self-sufficiency.

In contrast, it is meaningless to speak of telecommunications' self-sufficiency. The value of a telecom network consists precisely in its ability to reach out and touch the world, and the greater the number of points it can touch, the more valuable the network. In this sense, telecommunications is genuinely a networking service—like roads—and unlike services such as electricity, water, and gas in which we can try to be self-sufficient. We cannot bottle telecom like we can bottle LPG (liquefied petroleum gas) and bottle electricity as batteries. The phone is a burner, not a battery.

Moreover, in telecommunications, the same physical wires—the pipes—can be electronically divided up into distinct streams, and each stream can support a distinct service. Cisco's technologies, for instance, allow the same cable to carry voice, video, Internet, and more from a common *multiservice* platform. Such multiservices are possible on copper cables and even more so on fiber-optic cables.

UNBUNDLING LOCAL ELECTRICITY LOOP

Nevertheless, there are many *commonalities* that apply to the telecom and electricity platforms. When deregulation happened in telecommunications, the Central Office, the building that housed the *switches*, was made available to competitors on the same terms—costs, among others—as the phone companies, the so-called Baby Bells, obtained it for themselves. To determine the costs of the different elements of the telephone infrastructure, the network was *unbundled,* and particularly valuable was the unbundling of the *local loop* that touched customers.

Why was the phone infrastructure made available to competitors? This was allowed because the phone companies are regulated businesses, providing a public good, and their cables are a part of the *natural* monopoly infrastructure. Others, besides the phone company, have the right to use it to offer service. And similarly, people ought to have the right to services from other similar monopoly network service providers besides the phone company, such as electric utilities.

The electric utilities' local loop—the wires that enter our homes and offices—is a similarly regulated infrastructure, and should anyone wish to offer services using those wires, they should be able to do so. But the electricity local loop infrastructure is not unbundled in the same way. We do not know the cost of the local loop that links the substation in a neighborhood to individual homes and buildings.

The electricity entering a home can originate from power plants located hundreds of miles away, as typically happens, or it can originate locally from solar panels, or from a combination of solar panels, wind turbines, batteries, and gas- or diesel-based generators, in other words, a microgrid. Microgrids can be self-sufficient, increasingly inexpensive, reliable, and robust—more so than the macrogrid, regarded as the largest machine in the world.

Why then do we have or need the giant grid? The answer is: we do not strictly need it anymore, except for specific industrial applications—run trains, extract metal from ores, and operate really large machines. Cargo ships and airplanes are powerful, compact microgrids. Technological advance has resulted in inexpensive electricity available from local generation methods. We have "the largest machine in the world" just because it is there, mostly for historical reasons of *lock-in,* or *path dependence,* or incumbency. If the microgrid technologies of today were available during the early part of the twentieth century, we would have hundreds of microgrids, clustered and linked to each other, supplying electricity. They would be as numerous as supermarkets, serving roughly the same number of people each.

THE BREAKDOWN OF *NATURAL MONOPOLY*

Until recently it was believed that the electric utilities are natural monopolies, that is, the barriers to enter the service were high due to capital intensity of generation and transmission, and no more than one firm could be in that business in a geography. Further, the larger the generation plant, the cheaper the per unit price of electricity—inexpensive power depended on economies of scale. Therefore, one large regulated operator was thought to be necessary for low prices. This is no longer the case.

As microgrid economics improves, campuses—college, corporate, or other—will make economic choices based on the offers made by microgrid-based utilities or the larger public utilities. Over time, we may reasonably expect campuses to break their historical links with the utility grid and go with microgrids. They will retain the utility grid as insurance and backup.

NEIGHBORHOODS AS VIRTUAL CAMPUSES

What about single-family homes on a street or in a neighborhood consisting of strip malls and homes? They are likely served by a substation, with cables running from the substation to individual homes and businesses. Can we view such neighborhoods as *virtual* campuses? Yes, we can. While the cables running from the substation to individual homes are managed by the electric utility, they really are, like the telecom infrastructure, a kind of public property. Should a provider wish to use that infrastructure to provide "greener" electricity, there ought to be no barriers—the local electricity can be from a microgrid; no transmission lines are necessary.

COLOCATION AT THE SUBSTATION: CLECs AND CLEPs

Another concept in telecommunications that ought to be applied to electricity, but has not been, is *colocation*. The substation in a neighborhood may be likened to a central office in telecommunications. Now just as the local loop is a public good, so too is the central office. If a telecom service provider—competitor—wishes to place its equipment there, it has the right. Competitors locate their equipment in distinct cages, literally, and offer services to customers. This gave rise to competitive local exchange carriers—CLECs.

We could similarly have competitive local electricity providers—CLEPs. The CLEPs can use locally generated electricity from microgrids and inject it at the level of the substation for their customers. They need not depend on the transmission infrastructure to bring it to neighborhoods from large power plants. They can save costs as a result.

In the unbundling of the local loop in electricity, there is one issue that distinguishes the electricity infrastructure from the telecommunications infrastructure. The electricity infrastructure cannot be shared between two electricity providers; the local loop has to be a monopoly for one electricity provider. This has been the existing distribution utility offering service over expansive geography. There is no reason that this cannot be another company, at the level of the substation, similar to collocation in telecom. Who decides who has the right to be a competitive electricity provider at the substation level? The answer: the community, the customers themselves. Some people think that the natural service territory for electricity service ought to be the municipality—therefore, *municipalization* of electric utilities is occurring in Europe, especially Germany, and to an extent in the United States. Equally, Community Choice Aggregation is occurring in several states in the United States too. In both instances, the service territory is much smaller than the typical franchise area of an investor owned utility.

But the municipality is still likely too large a geographical area; economical electricity with microgrids can be provided at even smaller geographies. The question is:

How many microutilities does a market need?[10] My view is: the smaller units could be campuses, neighborhoods, communities, enterprise zones, hospitals, and the like. It is still not known how small a microgrid can be while remaining competitive with the larger utility. Intuitively, it appears that microgrids can be quite small—covering a village or a block—and yet be cost effective.

EQUAL ACCESS IN ELECTRICITY

A community may decide: "For the next ten years, my electricity provider will be a new electricity company. Their electricity is cheaper and it is cleaner because they use solar, gas from waste, fuel cells, and wind turbines in their generation mix. They offer tools for efficient energy management in the home which the incumbent utility does not." And if the new microelectric utility does not deliver as promised, the community may switch to another competitive service provider, or back to the incumbent utility, which in the interim may have deployed its own cleaner, cheaper, and more efficient electricity.

This condition, where a customer chooses among service providers, is called *equal access* in telecommunications; we chose long-distance carriers in this way. The local loop telecom company, the Baby Bells of the past, offered us the choice of our own long-distance provider. As customers, we may choose among several electricity providers, each of whom leverages our local electricity loop for service. Unbundling, collocation, and equal access were mandated and implemented as a result of telecommunications deregulation. This ushered in competition in traditional wired telecommunications. When wireless personal communications services were introduced, the telecom revolution reached a new level.

One crucial difference between the telecommunications infrastructure and the electric utility's distribution infrastructure is this: whereas the wires in the telecom infrastructure can be electronically parsed into distinct service streams, the electricity infrastructure cannot be *multiservice*, at least for the most part, today. It is true that Internet *can* be provided over power cabling, but that has not become mainstream yet. Perhaps with the development of microgrids, it might. For instance, Cisco has a multiservice platform for cable operators, but not for electric utilities. Moreover, as indicated on the previous page, the cabling toward the customer side of a substation has to be serviced by a single provider—sharing of that infrastructure for electricity provision is technically not possible today. Thus, there is the need to assign or license a service territory to someone for service provision, a monopoly situation. But this can be for relatively small geographies, and this will allow entry to thousands of new microelectric utilities. The question is how to determine the geographical *size* of each market? And *how* to distribute them among contending service providers? The telecom industry divided the United States into over 500 BTAs—basic trading areas—and auctioned them.

ONE SOLUTION: AUCTIONS

Do auctions also apply to electric utilities? They could. A state (or federal)–level authority, say, a Public Utilities Commission, may auction off geographic service areas to service providers. This book proposes that infrastructure be auctioned off to the service provider who offers the best service to a community, say, a desired percentage of renewable energy in its generation mix, better price, greater reliability, value-added services, or whatever.

I propose the geography—the market, however defined, and however small— be divided up, at the substation and downstream levels, into zones for microgrids. And those zones may be auctioned off to service providers, say, for 10-year terms. The local governing body of the campus, or the virtual campus, or the neighborhood, can negotiate terms with the microgrid supplier for its electricity. The FCC conducted spectrum auctions mapped to geographical markets in the mid-1990s—BTAs. The BTA map of the United States is given in Figure 4.5. The BTAs may be too big for electricity, and each BTA may accommodate many microgrids. In Chapter 6, I address in greater detail how this might happen.

In Figure 4.6, I have shown the San Diego area overlaid with circles representing microgrids, each self-sufficient and autonomous in its functioning, perhaps owned by distinct organizations, and yet working collaboratively with each other.

In the United States and in many parts of the world, the telecom regulatory authorities know how to conduct spectrum auctions. That institutional knowledge may be extended to Electricity 2.0.

Figure 4.5   United States Basic Trading Areas (BTAs)

Figure 4.6   San Diego: Illustrative Microgrids

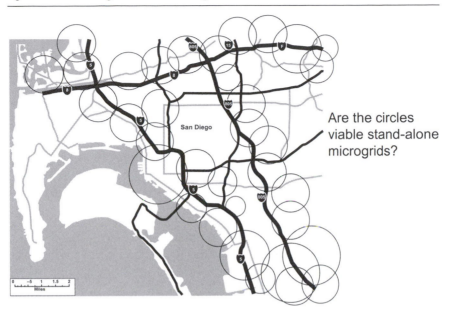

Are the circles
viable stand-alone
microgrids?

PRODUCTIVITY COSTS OF ELECTRICITY'S ABSENCE

In the advanced economies, the uses of electricity are available, more or less, on demand. Blackouts are rare, though extreme weather events sometimes cause outages of long duration. The conditions are otherwise in emerging economies. For millions in India and around the world, livelihood prospects set with the sun. Homework cannot be done effectively with kerosene lamps. Even when electricity is available, it is perennially on the verge of going out, sometimes for long periods, and this creates stress. Elevators may not work; refrigerated food may get spoilt. Internet access may not exist just when you need it for work or homework. The economic productivity of a population gets curtailed.

New entrepreneurial ventures have to take into account the presence or absence of reliable electricity. Investments have to be made with *captive* generation plants, and a factory may not rely on grid electricity. The costs of diesel electricity are several times more than grid electricity when it exists, and yet the cost of such captive power has to be borne by anyone making investments. The economic losses from unreliable electricity are huge indeed. The United Nations and its secretary general have done well to focus on Sustainable Energy for All (SE4All).

At the household level, SHSs are a boon. Households become self-sufficient in at least light, fan, and phone charging. Nancy Wimmer's book describes the organizational, technical, and operational challenges of deploying such systems, in village after village, in Bangladesh. This is the SHS-as-appliance model, with a service team ready to help, and available locally should anything go wrong and need attention.

The mobile phone complements such a system—it can be used to make payments and to seek customer support. In the future, the phone network can also be used to remotely monitor the health of the SHSs, and such monitoring for preventive maintenance can scale to large numbers. In other words, the ICT infrastructure complements the electricity infrastructure.

BRAND WITHOUT A NETWORK

During the mid- to late 1990s, the telephone companies hired a lot of managers from consumer goods industries, from P & G and Unilever, Sara Lee, and Bausch & Lomb. This was an attempt to bring a consumer focus, competitive ways, and the approach and metrics of brand managers (e.g., unaided recall of a brand name) to telecom employees with traditionally network-centric, utility, and monopolistic ways. Suddenly, the company had two distinct cultures—visibly and audibly so.

One group had MBAs, who were better dressed, talked sharply, and were skilled at PowerPoint with graphs. Suddenly, focus groups sprung up in city after city for deciding prices, for choosing images, and for deciding the text that accompanies advertisements. This group had little knowledge of the network and its intricacies and therefore received subtle and sometimes unsubtle scorn from the network people. Nevertheless, the numerical strength and power of the MBA group rose, due to increased marketing budgets. More women joined telecom than ever before.

Astonishing, even breathtaking, new thoughts entered the telecom world and were debated in conference rooms and corridors, as a result of this influx. One of the ideas bandied about for a while was: since the brand, customer acquisition, and customer service are paramount metrics of the company's performance, can we outsource the networking aspects—from equipment purchases to maintenance, control rooms to cellular towers—to a specialist networking company and focus on brand management and customer relationships? Is not networking management with the elements that constitute it—switches, towers, cables, control rooms, billing systems, and so forth—a commodity? Specify the performance parameters, and hold the network management company accountable; the rest is brand?

This was heresy to the traditional telecom employees, who were already resentful of the frequent press releases, advertisements, unprecedented budgets, and media centricity ushered in by the new employees. The old-timers asked: If not the network and its reliable operations, what is a telecom company?

Consider the market cap of a telecom company: What component may be attributed to the network and its performance, and what component to the brand and new products, customer acquisition, customer satisfaction, and retention initiatives under its banner? In terms of the Open System Interconnection (OSI) layers that traditionally define the telecom network, physical layer to application

Table 4.1 Comparing Telecom And Electricity Infrastructure

Attribute	ICT (Information and Communications Technologies)	Traditional Energy
Industry Evolution	20+ years ahead of electricity deregulation	"Carterphone" stage; concerned with the impact of DER on grid reliability
Climate Impact	Relatively minor, unless data centers are included in the architecture of ICT	One of two major *contributors* to global warming
Competition	Historically regarded as a natural monopoly. Competition from overlay networks	Historically, regarded as a natural monopoly. Competition from rooftop installations, homes and commercial
Network Topology	Point-to-point or person-to-person; occasionally point-to-multipoint, streaming or broadcast; "metering" or measurement as central location or server	Point-to-multipoint, quasibroadcast or streaming; meter as point of demarcation between premises and the wide area network
"Natural" Network	Truly a network service in that stand-alone telecom network is meaningless	Network service because we tap into concentrated sources of energy such as fossil fuels. Not truly a networking service. We can have stand-alone network service, say, for a home, campus, or factory
Appliances and Applications	Landline and mobile phones; Internet via laptops, tablets, TVs, and smartphones; voice, data, and content services	Lightbulbs, fans, refrigerators, air-conditioners, microwave ovens, induction cookers, TVs, radios, irons, vacuum cleaners, and so on
Industry Evolution	20+ years ahead of electricity deregulation	"Carterphone" stage; concerned with the impact of DER on grid reliability
Climate Impact	Relatively minor, unless data centers are included in the architecture of ICT	One of two major contributors to global warming

layer, we now had a marketing communications and brand layer on top of the application layer. The company, in effect, was sought to be split horizontally—the cake and its icing. I foresee a similar influx of the professional brand manager, and the rise of the marketing function, in the electric utility industry. How is electricity different from telecommunications? What are the parallels, and what are the contrasts between the two? What the electric utilities are likely to face—This script has played out before.

NOTHING LIKE THE MOBILE PHONE IN ELECTRICITY

When wireless technologies began to transform the wireline telecom business, the pace of change was rapid, and the scope of change was also large; we were then in frame-breaking mode. The changes were breathtaking. From brick-sized cell phones, to clunky cell phones, to flat and thin phones, to flip phones, and now smartphones—the pace of change has been relentless.

There is nothing quite the equivalent of the portable cordless home phone, let alone the mobile smartphone, in electricity. There is no new physical product as proxy, or as representative of electricity 2.0, in the customer's hands. The electricity revolution appears to parallel the competitive transformation in the wireline business, where the CLECs began to accompany regulatory changes such as *unbundling of the local loop* and *colocation*.

FIVE

Divest and Fractionate for Value

Nothing except for nature can transform the world as swiftly as can business—for better or for worse.

—Amy Larkin

Electricity has historically been a relatively homogenous product in homes and offices, typically AC. Now with *distributed generation,* that is, electricity produced as a function of location—say, rooftops—as well as technology—say, photovoltaics—electricity can be produced economically at a smaller scale. It can be generated as DC power and used as such for home electronics or LED lighting. Such technological possibilities allow new business formations and novel business models. This chapter describes how such *fractionation* can be understood using traditional and certain new dimensions, or variables.

The fractionation creates opportunities for entrepreneurs to create stand-alone businesses based on DC electricity. I describe that in Chapter 8. In this chapter, I wish to focus on what incumbent utilities might do.

Normally, electricity, however produced, is transformed into the common denominator of 110 V AC or 220 V AC. Now with renewables, say, solar photovoltaics combined with batteries, DC electricity generated may be used as such. Such DC power is what electronic appliances need. A whole lot of electricity demand can thus be met by new technologies, with no overlap with traditional AC electricity. Thus DC and AC electricity can be mapped to different uses and constitute distinct *product-markets* from a business development viewpoint. Such DC-based applications can be an overlay on today's applications based on grid electricity, with practically no intersection with the existing infrastructure. This is but one instance of a distinct *product-market*. Many such electricity applications can be splintered off from the traditional application set, each a distinct new business.

The electricity network may break up—*fractionate*—into specialized networks (as shown in Figure 5.2), for example, for street lighting, traffic signals, water pumps, or highly fine-tuned networks with tight performance requirements for research. The scale of operations for such distinct *product-markets* can be small or large and unbounded by geographical restrictions.

One thing is clear, however: the classical way of analyzing opportunities, by considering the *product-market* or the Ansoff matrix, does not entirely hold. The *product*—electricity—and the *market*—demand for it—are known entities. Normally, in typical opportunity analysis, and for determining a business direction to pursue, it is sufficient to specify the *product-market* and propose strategies for pursuit—to expand into a new market or develop new products, or both. But in assessing opportunities in renewable energy, in addition to *product-market*, we need an additional dimension of *location* to fully develop business options. In Electricity 2.0, the importance of location is novel, as explained in the following text.

Whereas typically *product* is a function of technology, in renewable energy, the *product* is equally and also a function of *location*. Further, location as latitude–longitude combination is insufficient. We also need to consider the *spatial* aspects of the solar (or wind) collection surfaces. Is it east or west facing or located on a roof?

In the raw materials to product conversion in traditional electricity production, the raw materials are in a relatively confined form—in drums, inside pipelines, in storage tanks, in ores—and are typically concentrated. With wind and solar power, the raw materials—wind and sunlight—are dispersed and our access to them is a function of location.

Location—including geographical and physical attributes—are now more important determinants of electricity production than before. The *input-to-output* transformation function for electricity can no longer be easily "boxed," that is, confined to a production plant or a reactor or a dam.

MONETIZING SPACE

Space projected on to two dimensions is surface, and, therefore, space includes surface. Built-up space, such as buildings, may be differentiated among east-, west-, and skyward-facing surfaces for purposes of solar radiation collection and in turn may be distinguished from natural space—the attributes of a hill or mountain and water bodies such as lakes, rivers, or canals. Locations differ in their suitability and capacity for renewable energy production because we need to consider how the electricity generation surfaces, in a particular location, are configured or laid out.

Therefore, for electricity generation,

Space > geography > surface—built-up or natural > location

We may *leverage space* by concentrating the sunlight incident on it by using Fresnel lens or suitably designed glass spheres or reflectors with parabolic surfaces. Thus,

Product$_{electricity}$ = f (technologies and location, including the geography and physical attributes of real estate)

Technologies$_{electricity}$ = f (photovoltaics, wind, geothermal, and spatial attributes)

Feedstock = f (location, say, availability of sunlight, wind in a place)

Market = f (customer segments, their number, attributes, and needs)

The feedstock—sunlight or wind—is geographically dispersed, and its utility is a function of latitude, climate, and topography.

Normally, product can be a proxy for technologies, especially when one kind of technology delivers a certain kind of product, and there is one-to-one mapping of technology and product. So we may have a *technology–market* matrix too. For instance, since the technologies for thermal, nuclear, and hydroelectric all generate the *same* kind of electricity, we can distinguish among these *production means*—the technologies—as characterizing electricity, for instance, hydroelectric power or nuclear power.

The point is, with solar generation, two distinct kinds of technology are implied when we consider the *technology–market* matrix: one, the technologies for converting sunlight into electricity, and, two, the technologies relating to spatial attributes of where the photovoltaics (or other technologies) are deployed. And even within photovoltaics, we may distinguish between thin film and crystalline, and so on.

Students of retail marketing are familiar with the importance of location through the injunction to focus on, *location, location, location*. Similarly, we always located factories close to rivers or seaports, with proximity to transport hubs and population centers. Location has always been recognized as important from a retail perspective; it now matters from the electricity supply or product generation perspective. Normally, *location, location, location* refers to the effects of retail location on demand or factory location on transport costs; now *location* also matters for electricity production costs. As it relates to solar renewable energy generation, we may also use the phrases *surface, surface, surface* or *space, space, space*. We can thus also have *location-market* matrix. I discuss this more fully in Chapter Seven and while describing Figure 7.2. Some locations may be good for electricity generation, others more attractive because of customer concentration, and therefore revenue potential. How might the locations be then prioritized? A utility may need to study their service territory from either a product generation perspective or a revenue generation perspective, or both.

We always located factories close to rivers or seaports, with proximity to transport hubs and population centers, when we sited factories. Now, location matters even more than before because it is directly related to the production of electricity. Remoteness has typically been a negative in businesses—it increased costs. Now, remoteness often represents *lowered* costs of electricity production. Whereas products, including centrally generated electricity, once flowed from centers to the periphery, now Electricity 2.0 flows from the periphery to the center, or from anywhere to anywhere, or from the centers found everywhere, and to anywhere there is demand, however small.

FRACTIONATION DRIVERS

The foregoing discussion points to the differentiation possibilities of what has traditionally been a relatively uniform product. Each of the customer segments, products, technologies, locations, or spatial attributes may be combined in distinct ways to create new businesses. The question is: Who will undertake such *fractionation* of the existing business? The answer is surely entrepreneurs and new business initiatives of a variety of companies, say, real estate companies or IT companies, and equally the existing utilities. I address the entrepreneurial opportunities in Chapter 7. Here let me explain why existing utilities should take advantage of the new business opportunities presented by the metamorphosing electricity industry.

"When you are falling," said Joseph Campbell, "dive." Applied to the electricity industry, this strategy for incumbent distribution utilities suggests: "Don't dilly-dally, don't prevaricate—plunge headlong into restructuring." Absent such repurposing, with both *investment* and *divestment,* the present assets of distribution utilities will become less valuable over time, lending credence to the utility "death spiral" speculations that, while plausible, are not inevitable. Admittedly strong medicine, but the alternative is certain decline.

The Electricity 2.0 industry will comprise of thousands of new competitive and innovative players. The infrastructure will be greener. The electricity supply will be reliable, resilient, and, in the longer run, more valuable and even less expensive than today's. With new entrants, customers will have a choice among service providers. Should homeowners and businesses become partially their own personal electric *utilities*—prosumers—there will be thousands of microutilities coexisting with microgrids and the macrogrid.

How might this *divestment* and *restructuring* be done? The experiences of the telecommunications industry offer parallels. The concerns expressed when telecom was restructured are being voiced now by IOU (investor-owned utilities) executives. For instance: "Will the integrity of the 'grid' be compromised by third party, distributed generation (DG) equipment?" In telecom, the concern was: third-party telephone instruments may cause harm to the telecommunications network unless the equipment was manufactured by AT&T and the Bell System. These fears proved unwarranted in telecom.

This book suggests electric utilities might be among the growth stories of the next two decades provided they address the following opportunities:

- Pursuing *select-product* markets for themselves
- Restructuring the network and making strategic investments in telecom technologies as explained briefly later in this chapter and in Chapter 8

- Splitting the service territory into smaller units—microgrids—to release the full potential of existing assets, enabling investors to realize the best gains and benefit from advancing technologies
- Selling off the split-up smaller units to qualified investors and next-generation operators, and even buying select service territories, that is, rationalizing service territories based on product and revenue potential.

These strategic initiatives are discussed briefly in the following text and in the remaining chapters of the book.

ELECTRICITY 2.0: THE CENTER DOES NOT HOLD

The Electricity 2.0 metamorphosis breaches traditional industry boundaries; it is increasingly difficult to isolate where electricity ends and information and telecommunications technologies begin, and vice versa. Why? Because fiber-optic cables are already a part of electricity long-haul cables; the smart grid is essentially an ICT overlay on the electricity network; solar panels may be regarded as analogous to remotely managed terminals of the Ethernet; cellular towers are anchors for rural electrification and complementary to the substation in urban and suburban areas; the proliferation of data management on either side of the meter—inside homes and in network operations—results in a qualitatively distinct infrastructure more aligned with computer networking; and fuel-based and rotating generation systems are replaced by passive network elements such as batteries and photovoltaic panels with nonmoving generation options.

When these technological forces combine with the macro forces illustrated in Figure 5.1, the situation calls for corporate leaders to confront and address fundamental business choices. Figure 5.1 shows the electricity industry at an inflection point at the center of converging forces—business as usual will surely take the industry along the path of decline. Positive strategic action may hold the trajectory, and should new initiatives work, the reformulated industry may even find itself on a growth path.

Besides select *product-markets* to focus on for the future, and in addition to deploying microgrids—the macrogrid writ small—with substations as hubs, for instance, the inflection point in Figure 5.1 suggests the need for corporate new business development efforts. Given the potential trajectories, what might the incumbent utility do to embark on the growth path rather than slide down the path of decline? How to position the company as the utility of the future? What new assets need to be acquired, or grown internally, and what sold off—divested—to other service providers? Perhaps some markets and assets may complement other players better, and certain other assets may be more aligned with the incumbents' strategic goals.

What new S curve, a new trajectory or two may be launched? In other words, the utility has to ask the classic strategy question: "What business are we in?" and depending on the answer, therefore, "What then do we do?" Some of these issues are addressed in Chapter 8.

Figure 5.1   Electricity Industry Trajectory

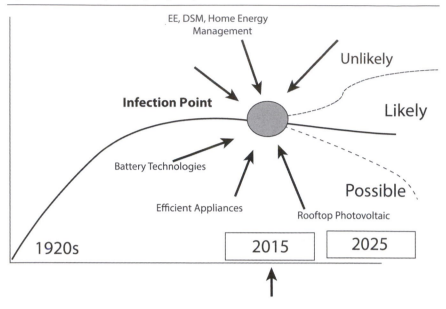

Briefly, the proposition of this book is that the incumbent distribution utilities must answer all four questions—selectively address new *product-markets*; reconstitute the current infrastructure into a *cluster of microgrids* interfacing with the macrogrid and with other microgrids; and leverage today's right of ways and assets to enter *the next-generation broadband ISP business*, which also includes the entertainment business, for example, and thereby compete with today's telecom companies.

Why is telecom an opportunity? By no means have the recent developments in telecom in the United States been either uniformly laudable or exemplary. Consider that the United States has one of the most expensive mobile phone services and poorest Internet infrastructures in the advanced economies.

DIVEST TO REALIZE VALUE

When AT&T was split into the Baby Bells, it was transformative. When spectrum was auctioned in the mid-1990s by breaking up the nation's geography into major trading areas (~ 50) and basic trading areas (> 500) for the 2-GHz auctions, this was revolutionary too. The reconstitution of the electricity industry may appear radical, but the United States and the rest of the world has experience doing something similar.

When the Internet first made its appearance, the phone companies thought: now we get to sell the consumer another telephone line, dedicated to the Internet, in addition to the existing POTS line—plain old telephone service. The POTS business, in fact, is in terminal decline, thanks to wireless telecom. The *second line* has become the principal entertainment and high-speed Internet line—AT&T's U-Verse, for instance—fed by fiber-optic cable to the neighborhood. VoIP technologies are taking over POTS, a topological revolution, among other things. These transformations in telecommunications are mind-boggling and occurred in roughly 20 years, a relatively short time.

Comparable changes loom on the electricity horizon. Until now, the electricity infrastructure, except for local differences in generation technologies, has been uniform across the globe. In the future, this need not be.

The topology of the future electricity network may be a cluster of microgrids—see Figure 5.2—occasionally stand-alone and sometimes interacting with each other, and the microgrids may coexist with other topologies, including the present top-down one-way infrastructure.

Just as *long-distance* (or inter-LATA and interstate) traffic and *local-exchange* traffic were once separate and managed by AT&T, MCI, and Sprint and the Baby Bells, respectively, so too the transmission network may be viewed as analogous to the interexchange network, and the local distribution providers may be compared to the Baby Bells; they can work synergistically. The point is: while lessons from analogies must be drawn cautiously, the telecom industry's restructuring offers guidelines and hope for the emerging electricity industry, as regards divestiture and auctions, and regulatory tools such as local loop unbundling, collocation, and equal access.

"If it ain't broke, don't fix it" does not apply to the electricity industry. The system is environmentally, topologically, and economically broken and obsolete. But it works—so did pagers when cellular phones arrived and horse-drawn carriages when the automobile appeared.

Despite technological advance, and the possibilities of personal power through rooftop solar and batteries, the industry ownership structure, and the regulatory framework, remains eerily the same. Yet the animating force around which the industry is built—the natural monopoly assumption—no longer holds, even in distribution, as individual homes seek progressive grid independence, a kilowatt-hour solar at a time. Competition in electricity distribution does not need overbuilding; the electricity loop may be unbundled as happened in the telephone industry to usher competition.

Users will continue to press switches in their habitual ways, but they need less electricity, delivered in different ways by new players.

"Nothing except for nature can transform the world as swiftly as can business—for better and worse," says Amy Larkin, yet the drumbeat of climate change talk presents few meaningful business options. And business initiatives within the industry, while good, are in fact incremental, within known industry boundaries, and amount to tinkering. For instance, New York State's Reforming the Energy Vision (REV), smartening the grid through fancy meters, introducing microgrids to assure power availability during the next storm by East Coast states, the

RPS (renewable portfolio standard) mandates, environmental laws restricting emissions, postemissions capture and storage technologies, energy efficiency, and demand-side management, while fine, do not fundamentally measure up to what is needed for Electricity 2.0.

The times call for dismantling and restructuring of the electricity infrastructure. We confront a (re-)make or upgrade decision, the latter seemingly easier. The right thing to do is to reconstitute the system, to dive.

FRACTIONATE

Figure 5.2 makes the point that the macrogrid can splinter into microgrids, organized as clusters, interacting and resource sharing among each other, to give rise to both clean and less expensive electricity that what obtains today.

But there is an additional point that needs to be made, namely, that we may not assume that the breakup of the electricity infrastructure of today only leads to a smaller, yet functionally similar grid as today. In fact, as barriers to entry into the electricity business have fallen, it is not necessary that new startups will create merely microgrids. They may in fact splinter the market into *product-markets*, and focus on select ones, independent of geographical boundaries. This is partially shown in Figure 5.3, where each rectangle represents business opportunity for entrepreneurs or new entrants into electricity. The reason I say partially is because on this diagram there is no way to suggest that each rectangle may be vast in scope, even national or global. For each *product-market* segment, franchise boundaries are meaningless. Consider the transformation under way: Besides individual homes, water pumps for irrigation, streetlights on a campus or in a city,

Figure 5.2 Topology of the Future Electricity Distribution Network

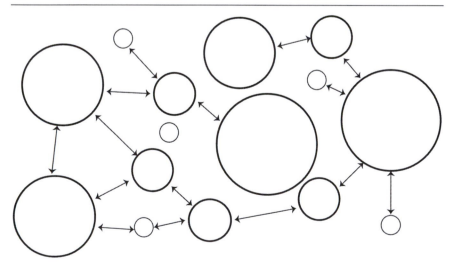

Figure 5.3   *Fractionation* into *Product-Market* Segments for Greater Value

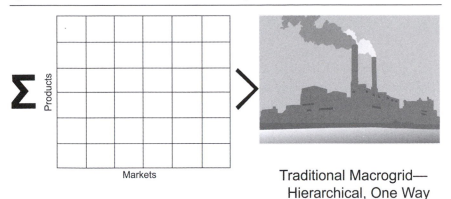

Markets

Traditional Macrogrid—
Hierarchical, One Way

sprinkler systems for lawns, and traffic signals can be grid independent with comparable or superior economics. Each rectangle represents a distinct *product-market*, a service potentially independent of electric utilities. Besides entrepreneurs and new entrants in each *product-market* rectangle, even the facilities management departments of businesses and campuses can manage today's utilities' functions—generation, local networking with comparable performance metrics as utilities—in effect, no utilities necessary.

Further, what Figure 5.3 proposes—and this is only an assumption—is that when the business is splintered in this way, the aggregate value of the components surpasses the value embedded in today's macrogrid. It is plausible to say so because the new service providers might benefit from economies of scale and geographical scope when they are focused on select *product-markets*, they may find opportunities for revenue growth through new services on the customer side of the meter, and so forth.

The question arises: by what path may we reach Electricity 2.0? Sound economics must undergird such fundamental transformation as proposed here. The economics of *product-markets* is straightforward and require standard business plan development as described. Choose a rectangle of interest in Figure 5.3, and calculate the costs and revenue potential for it, say, for solar-powered water pumps. If necessary, the geographical scope can be expanded to leverage the same fixed assets.

ECONOMICS OF MICROGRIDS: SUBSTITUTION

Microgrids are new, and their economic modeling is complex. This is why we focused on them in Chapters 2 to 4. To the question "Are they economical?," our answer is that they soon will be, even as stand-alone systems, let alone when grid tied or tied to other neighboring microgrids to form a cluster. Thus, even the prospects for individual microgrids or microgrids in a cluster look good.

We need to compare the economics of microgrids with the economics of the existing macrogrid and show that the former is superior to the latter, even without considering environmental and climate change externalities. Then a case may be made for *substitution*, provided the benefits are compelling enough.

Let us assume the microgrid is a stand-alone business with a certain market value. If the economic value of the microgrid surpasses the economic value of the macrogrid *for the same serving area*, then we have an argument in favor of micro-grids and strategic action. But how can we compare the value of the electricity network of today, which is an aggregate, with the value of small parcels of the grid, comprised of hypothetical microgrids? Today, electricity prices are standardized over a huge customer base; costs are also in the aggregate. Microgrid economics, in contrast, require local and specific assessment of the generation potential, geographical attributes, and revenue potential of a local market. One method to compare the two might be to *levelize* the valuation problem to the common denominator of $/kWh.

In the case of IIMK's microgrid and also for the homeowners' association (HOA) of 120 homes of approximately 3,500 sq. ft. each in a neighborhood in San Diego, in Southern California, as described in Chapter 3, this has been our goal—to compare apples and oranges—from an economics of production view, even when the end product is the same electricity.

Knowing the load profile, we designed a microgrid comprised of solar panels, batteries, and gas-/diesel-based generators for the HOA. We assumed the hardware would be installed at the serving substation. We used web-based prices for solar panels, inverters, and batteries. We assumed typical setup and operating costs, inter-est rates, and project life. Given today's costs, what is the price in $/kWh, at which we could offer electricity using microgrids? Our answer is less than $0.20/kWh.

Now $0.20/kWh is lower than the average price paid by the residents of the HOA in that particular neighborhood; the highest pricing tier is over $0.35/kWh, which nearly all homes reach each month. We concluded that this HOA could peel away from the grid and save money. Other select HOAs in California, neigh-borhood by neighborhood, substation by substation, can similarly bypass the grid.

The economics may be improved by sharing resources among a federation of microgrids in the neighborhood—battery banks, common solar deployment loca-tions, centralized network management. Some microgrids could be, say, business parks with daytime peaks, and others primarily residential microgrids. Economics may also be improved by new *behind-the-meter* services, by network optimization, by demand management, and by seeking volume discounts on equipment.

Finally, when we have a cluster of microgrids, working synergistically with each other, we need less of the transmission infrastructure and little of the centralized generation assets for service. Those costs are largely eliminated. Of course, some new costs are added. Clearly, more work is needed in microgrid modeling than what our little exercise at IIM has accomplished. Nevertheless, we have enough

Figure 5.4   Value from Clustering Microgrids Surpasses the Value of the Corresponding Macrogrid

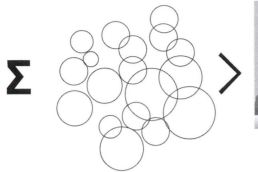
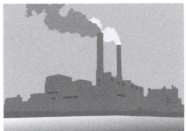

Traditional Macrogrid—
Hierarchical, One Way

evidence to conclude: a cluster of microgrids represents greater economic value than the value of the aggregate, consolidated grid. This is shown in Figure 5.4. For the *market* value of such a cluster of microgrids, we may use industry-standard EBITDA or revenue multiples.

While fractionation and substitution of the macrogrid by microgrids are valid strategies, it is likely that the greatest benefit from reconstituting the present grid will come from porous and flexible industry boundaries. We now turn to that topic.

WHAT DEATH SPIRAL? AMONG THE MOST ATTRACTIVE INVESTMENTS

By far the greatest impact on electricity economics, however, will arise from slackening industry boundaries and letting telecom services become a part of the electric utilities portfolio of services. We now turn to that proposition. Already, the World Bank tries to leverage the presence of cellular towers in rural areas to piggyback electricity access. But that is simply the start of a bigger story.

With competition for microgrid services and competition also for *product-market* segments, will the utility business shrink? Not necessarily, provided the IOUs think of opportunities more broadly. Literally, the electric utilities need to think outside the box, ignoring their historically clear-cut but increasingly fungible industry boundaries.

Consider what EPB, a nonprofit municipal electric utility in Chattanooga, Tennessee, has done. It has built the United States' fastest ISP infrastructure offering 1 gigabit per second bidirectional broadband for $70/month. More of EPB's ISP business is described in Chapter Eight as part of industry structure transformation. Other utilities can also become broadband ISPs, one microgrid at a time, as suggested by Figure 5.5.

Figure 5.5   Augmenting Revenue via Broadband

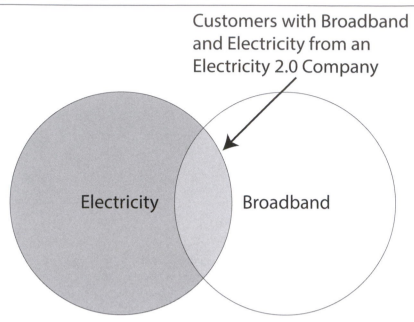

The United States has long had a subpar broadband infrastructure—both in terms of raw speed, gigabit per seconds, and as regards upstream speeds—not even megabits per second for the most part—a fraction of download speeds. The de facto duopoly of the cable companies and the telephone companies has ill served the U.S. consumer with their paltry speeds, at high price, and indeed, this has likely affected entrepreneurial opportunities for economic growth.

The customer has been shoehorned into becoming a *consumer* of content, and less a generator of content, especially rich content. Should a consumer generate rich content, the options for sharing it have been constricted by this capillary-sized upstream speed.

EPB changed all that. EPB therefore is the preferred ISP for Chattanooga, Tennessee, not the telecom or cable companies. Why cannot all electric utilities replicate the EPB success? They can. Even if a fraction of the customers of an electricity utility get broadband from them, and this represents as small a revenue stream as, say, $30 incremental per month, the economics of the overall electricity system improves dramatically, and the electric utilities of today become among the most powerful network service providers of tomorrow. Yes, there would need to be a network upgrade of the present electricity infrastructure, and while expensive, it is likely incremental to what the electricity companies already have. Perhaps, the top-down and largely one-way electricity network topologies today are unwieldy and obsolete platforms for a host of future services, including broadband. They may need to split up into microgrids to become next-generation, symmetric-broadband ISPs.

In deploying symmetric gigabit broadband, several times the speed of today's Internet, the electric utilities will attract the best residential and business customers from today's broadband ISPs—the cable and telephone companies.

In starting with a brand-new yet incremental cost infrastructure, the electric utilities overcome the limitations of today's telephone and cable companies—speed deterioration due to distance from central office (CO) locations with DSL technologies of phone companies, and the fact that the coaxial cable bandwidth is a shared resource among entertainment channels and broadband. Starting an ISP business with green field infrastructure, anchored in microgrid or substation-sized service areas, likely has compelling advantages. While the network topology and configuration of electric utility–driven broadband may be novel, the competencies necessary to deploy them are well established.

Will the regulatory environment permit wholesale electricity industry participation in broadband services? The public interest clearly lies in encouraging such competition. The good news might be that local regulatory bodies can initiate action—cities and municipalities, in addition to state-level leadership—and the federal role may be limited. The existence of many nuclei for such action promises to deliver the needed transformation more rapidly.

Whereas the cable and telephone companies bundle entertainment, telephone services, and broadband today, the electric utilities may bundle electricity, security, home energy consumption monitoring, and similar services as well. Internet-based streaming content delivery already threatens the satellite-based hub and coaxial cable–based distribution of cable companies. Electric utilities can accelerate this trend.

More interesting to consider are the economic consequences—for towns and cities, and the nation as a whole—of the entrepreneurial energies unshackled when high-speed upstream broadband makes a host of new services possible. The duopoly of telephone and cable companies has effectively strangled such upstream-bandwidth-based products and services.

With respect to *product-markets* into which the electricity business will splinter, it remains an open question whether today's electric utilities retain any competitive advantage. Surely, they have the hard-and-soft assets to be significant players, yet the barriers to entry are low, and nontraditional energy service providers have compelling advantages too. All considered, electricity distribution companies, therefore, with the right strategies, might be among the most attractive investment prospects today, should they focus on microgrids and ISP services.

LOCATIONAL BENEFITS AND COORDINATION COSTS

While every substation and its related customer base can be a unit for analysis as a microgrid, the valuation of microgrids needs to take account of not only the revenue potential of the customer base—as is traditionally done—but also the electricity generation potential of the same service territory, and the revenue prospects from ISP services.

With microgrids, and unlike what obtains with the macrogrid today, the costs and pricing, and therefore valuations, are explicitly local. Thus the economic potential will vary across geography; we can have locational benefits, in suburbs and rural areas with lots of open spaces, or disadvantages in dense urban areas, where the generation potential may be limited. Yet the revenue potential in urban areas will be high and offset the disadvantages of generation prospects. Naturally, with locational variations, we might have *locational pricing*.

ECONOMICS OF *PRODUCT-MARKET* SEGMENTS

In addition to microgrids, with electricity and ISP services, the industry may splinter into *product-market* segments. What might be the market value of such segments? Consider a university or college campus with streetlights. Each lamp-post with a LED lamp may be powered from a solar panel and battery located at the pole itself, or the cabling of the entire set of street lights may be consolidated at a central location. A battery bank and solar panels may be sized to meet the load of the lamps. This will be a stand-alone, special-purpose solution, scalable to other campuses, to municipalities, and so forth.

Similarly, we may have solar- and battery-powered water pumps for irrigation, grid independent or a part of a telecom network, yet independent as regards electricity generation and use. How big or small can such businesses be? It is conceivable to have a street lighting business for a campus alone, that is small, and is run by the facilities management or the maintenance department of a campus. On the other hand, street lighting service may be a multinational business run by, say, a Philips or GE with campuses, municipalities, and cities worldwide as customers. The financial analysis would be straightforward enough for such projects.

CONCLUSION: FALLING, THEREFORE DIVE

Assuming merit in the foregoing arguments, what electric utilities should do suggests itself: for new neighborhoods, and for select residential or business locations, get into the microgrid business and install microgrids with infrastructure upgrade to also offer broadband ISP services. Further, get into select *product-market* segments too, and do not limit services to historically regulated service territories. This is both defensive and offensive, as new entrants, likely from outside the traditional electricity industry, will also enter the microgrid and *product-market* segment business. Finally, conduct a zero-based assessment of assets and divest those not critically required for Electricity 2.0. This may be certain service areas not complementary to core future operations or located in remote areas.

As microgrids proliferate, the role for regulators remains an open question. How do they encourage the emergence of microgrids, that is, market entry, and therefore customer choice, in both electricity distribution and broadband? Who will facilitate coordination among microgrids? Who will develop the standards for it? Inter-microgrid trading and collaboration, and microgrid–macrogrid interactions, will be fascinating developments to watch. Will inter-microgrid collaboration occur due to market mechanisms, aided by light-touch regulations, or would we need direct policy intervention, subsidies, and support?

What about the existing infrastructure rendered fallow should microgrids extend to multiple neighborhoods? It has historical value because of sunken costs. Should the assets be written down or written off? Recovering stranded costs through the rate base and today's regulatory mechanisms appears retrograde when the regulations-driven business model itself is obsolete.

The electricity infrastructure, fractionated into microgrids with broadband Internet in the service mix, or as comprised of distinct *product-market* segments, is more valuable than they are in the aggregate today. The sum-of-parts valuations likely surpass the aggregate valuations of IOUs. Therefore, the strategy suggests itself:

- Electric utilities may be reconstituted into microgrids—under their own ownerships or be split up and sold off to qualified buyers—to realize the full value of current assets and future prospects.
- Substations with their corresponding customers and generation prospects, collocated with cellular towers, might be suitable hubs to begin this process.
- Electric utilities may become broadband ISPs to augment the electricity revenue stream.
- Electricity distribution business may be disaggregated into select *product-markets*, with national or even global scope.

Should electricity distribution companies not embrace this change—reconstitute their networks—their market valuations will face an accelerating decline. They will be dragged into Electricity 2.0 business willy-nilly, absorbed into the roll-up strategy of a vigorous new enterprise, and at discounted valuations.

SIX

Define and Auction Market Blocks

Gregory: *Is there any other point to which you would wish to draw my attention?*

Holmes: *To the curious incident of the dog in the night-time.*

Gregory: *The dog did nothing in the night-time.*

Holmes: *That was the curious incident.*

—Sir Arthur Conan Doyle, in "Silver Blaze,"
a Sherlock Holmes story

. . . though we cannot make our sun
Stand still, yet we will make him run.

—Andrew Marvell

ELECTRICITY 2.0: THE DOG DOES NOT BARK

The next-generation electricity dog, to borrow from Sherlock Holmes, "does not bark" at least as energetically as it should; it smells, at best whimpers.

Rory Christian, Environmental Defense Fund (EDF) director and New York Clean Energy, said: "New York gave birth to the electric power industry 130 years ago and is now boldly innovating its way toward the clean energy economy we need in the 21st century."

"As advances in telecommunications and information systems create new opportunities for energy services we could not imagine just a few years ago, the outmoded utility business model that rewards monopoly utilities for selling an increasing amount of electricity from a centralized, fossil-fueled power plant to customers is out of sync with what we need now."[1]

Very good. Christian recommends, "1) transitioning from traditional rate of return regulation to performance-based regulation; 2) fully valuing all costs and benefits associated with distributed energy resources; 3) removing barriers to non-utility entities participating in energy service markets."

While valid, the first recommendation is "within the fold"—of the nature of management consultant recommendations to corporate heads, essentially tinkering with the existing system, "reforming" it. The second is an operational recommendation: "Let us find the costs and benefits of generating today's electricity from distributed generation sources." Christian does not say what we do next once we complete this analysis. These two recommendations qualitatively differ from the third most important one, namely, "barrier reduction" for "non-utility entities" to "participate" in energy "service" markets.

What "non-utility entities," say IT companies, real estate companies, hospitals, and others, are expected to "participate"—Christian does not say "compete"—in the new electricity world? Does a "service" market include "generation" and "value-added, premise or location specific, products and services"? Above all, the recommendation begs the question: How? How do we foster market entry in Electricity 2.0?

FALTERING NEW MARKET ENTRY: POLICY PUSH MISSING

What is needed is full-blown competition in the electricity business, especially in distribution. Competing new entrants—full-solution providers in large numbers—are in the public interest. Solar installers are a beginning. They are a point solution. We need a system-wide, competitive, comprehensive, scalable, and national solution. Else, we would muddle through a solar panel at a time, in kilowatts not megawatts. And this can be done as described in the following text.

Solar installers collectively have little political heft, and grid-tied renewables merely co-opt potential competition. Microgrid talk in the northeastern United States narrowly defines the public interest as the desire for *resilience*, a complement to *reliability*. No one has initiated and led a full-throated discussion about what constitutes broad-based public interest, from first principles, in the new electricity regime. What New York State is attempting to do is, for all the revolutionary language, incrementalism. It surprises me how people tiptoe around the electric utilities business and how few challenge the status quo vigorously. Sure, David Crane, the former CEO of NRG Energy, speaks his mind, but he is an exception.

In the unraveling of the old AT&T, regulatory and entrepreneurial energies (pun fortuitous) both led to the transformation of the traditional wireline business, before wireless technologies upturned the industry altogether, and tore apart traditional industry boundaries. Curiously enough, in the epicenter of entrepreneurial activism, the United States, the entrepreneurial response to changing industry structure in the electricity business appears weak. Where is the MCI of electricity? Who's McGowan? Clearly, there are parallels between telecom and the electricity businesses. What telecom lessons might be applicable to electricity? Who will drive the inevitable transformation in the emerging electricity industry?

I had the following argument with Milind Padalkar, a doctoral student, and we reached the conclusion that a synergistic mix of public policy and entrepreneurial initiatives, by new entrants and by existing companies, perhaps from outside the electricity industry, might accelerate the industry transformation.

To my question, "Why does the next-generation electricity dog not bark?," he offered:

The more I think about it, the more I am convinced that it will not bark.

"Why?" I asked.

From the perspective of strategy, telecom and energy might arguably be comparable industries. Both have similar industry ecosystems and structures, both involve massive investments, both are basically B2C businesses, and both have traditionally merited regulatory superstructures. Both are not really 'free market' entities. But the comparison fails on a couple of key points. First, after establishing endpoint connectivity, the marginal cost of servicing an extra telecom consumer is roughly zero, whereas for energy it is not.

If you have solar installation, the marginal cost of generation is also roughly zero, admittedly only during daylight hours. Only fuel costs make today's electricity different from telecom, or from the electricity of the future. Batteries can make electricity fuel cost independent. Why is the marginal cost of an additional electricity customer also not close to zero?

The second and perhaps a fatal reason why metaphors from one cannot translate to the other is that telecom is an "inventory" business whereas energy is a "flow" business.

Busy-hour erlangs[2] may be viewed as *inventory,* I suppose. Essentially, we establish and allocate connections, and while they are generally plentiful, during busy hours they become scarce. But, with IP networks, and routing instead of switching, there is abundant fiber optic capacity and distributed processing so that Skype becomes practically "free." Only wireless networks have scarcity because of shortages at the cell level at peak hours.

We need to distinguish between local flow and wide area flow. We have structured electricity to be a local and *wide area* flow business, thanks to the concentrated energy in fossil fuels or dams. But with rooftop solar power, or other forms of distributed generation, we only have and need local flow, including local battery flow. Generate locally, charge locally, and use locally. Wide area flow in the future will likely be only necessary for megacities, furnaces for smelting, for railways, and large factories. For residences, campuses, and buildings (offices, hospitals, etc.), we need only local flow.

The human mind generally grasps static phenomena quite well but is particularly uncomfortable with dynamics where flows, rates of change, and second- or higher-order phenomena are involved. While entrepreneurs flourish by sensing and exploiting discontinuities and/or information asymmetry (either structural or temporal), they are not exempt from these human limitations.

"While this is generally true, how does this apply here?" I countered.

The same can be said about the enabling environment and socioeconomic structures. At present, I believe these are configured for entrepreneurship in inventory-type, not flow-type, business models.

Not so. Why should it matter for entrepreneurship whether a business is a flow or an inventory business? Local flows are eminently amenable to widespread entrepreneurship—service businesses. Walt Patterson calls electricity *infrastructural* and less *flow*. Flow primarily occurs because of burning fuels and transporting electricity over long distances and also because there is no storage, that is, inventory. But don't batteries change that?

Therefore, I believe that the right form of energy entrepreneurship and the enabling environments are likely to be quite different.

Yes, the parallels with telecom are just that—tools to compare and contrast and to draw out the differences. The policy environment has to match and foster entrepreneurial initiatives in electricity and in energy, more generally.

How should they change? I think that is a fit question for research. That may be the explanation for why the dog does not do more than just sniffing and whimpering. It will not bark.

My thesis is, for the electricity dog to bark, at the level of society, we need to focus on *local* and *infrastructural*. It is like a well in the yards in Kerala homes—local water generation, local consumption, and infrastructural. Sure, we can have some piping and therefore flow, but that is local. Similarly, if we *render electricity markets local,* we can have plenty of electricity entrepreneurship. The key is to define local markets and offer rights to new companies to provide services to them. Can this be done? Yes.

We do divide geography by substations today. The service territory division could be done by homeowners' associations, by streets and neighborhoods, by basic trading areas (BTAs) and metropolitan trading areas (MTAs), as was done for wireless auctions in the United States, or by *circles* as was done for telecom in India. We ought to determine a credible way to *divide geography,* and there are several ways to do that.

DIVIDING GEOGRAPHY: KEY TO CLEAN, ECONOMICAL FUTURE ELECTRICITY

If we divide geography in some coherent way and auction the right to provide electricity services in a given territory—say, in India, a district or *panchayat*—we can have a lot of electricity entrepreneurship. This is among the principal theses of this book.

One key difference between telecom and electricity is this: the greater the *reach* of the telecom network, the greater the direct public good; every telecom user benefits. Thus, *telecom is inherently a networking business with positive externalities.* With local electricity, the benefits of electrification remain typically local. It does not matter to a resident of New York whether an African village gets electrified, at least in a direct way. But with an African village connected to the Internet and with phones, each person's reach and accessibility increases and therefore collective welfare.

Electric cables everywhere are the equivalent of coverage. In electricity, we have near-universal coverage, except for the 1.2 billion people in the world who do not have, and of whom roughly 300 million are in India. Historically, electricity coverage has radiated out from the center, just like in telecom, but with distributed generation, it can originate at the network edge and remain at the network edge. Extension and linkage with the rest of the grid is optional.

Given the local character of Electricity 2.0, strictly speaking, the grid is not essential. Its existence is a historical accident. Consider: Were we to have today's technologies, would we have the grid as we have it today? Likely not. Probably, we would build microgrids consisting of solar, batteries, gas, or diesel generators, possibly including wind turbines, and be self-sufficient in our home, street, or neighborhood.

Perhaps we would have a grid for applications such as mining, or for ore smelting, say, in the manufacture of steel or aluminum, or perhaps for megacities with high-rise buildings—but for most other applications, for residential communities or buildings, we would not need the grid.

For purposes of reliability and resiliency, for reducing overall capital costs, and for leveraging the relatively different asset endowments of different neighborhoods, we would connect the microgrids to each other. Thus, with the benefit of today's technologies, were we to start on a fresh slate, we would build a cluster of microgrids and not the centralized generation, transmission, and distribution infrastructure that we have today. Of course, electricity would flow in both directions, and each microgrid may share several links with adjacent microgrids, for give-and-take of electricity as needed.

I hesitate to call this topology a *transactive network*; sure, there would be transactions, but calling this arrangement *transactive* is akin to a physical-level description of an application-level phenomenon. This happens in telecommunications too. A call is not a call; "I'm home!" from someone abroad for long or returning after a semester of school, or "Will you marry me?," or "You've won!" can also be described in transactive terms, as the opening and closing of circuits, and be tracked by time and minutes of use. And just as a call is not a call—some are transactive and some are strategic—so too calling the electricity flow among microgrids *transactive* deflates the value of the new topology, which is a federation of microgrids. Microgrid clusters are likely to be resilient—more secure from cyber threats and during natural disasters like snowstorms. For end users, the electricity supply will allow local control, be cheaper and greener, and be more reliable.

While the grid is not strictly necessary, we do have a grid that largely works rather well. How then do we accommodate the new electricity possibilities? Does the existing infrastructure preclude better future possibilities?

Four things to consider:

1. Barriers to enter in the electricity business are falling—economies of scale are no longer needed for low-cost electricity.

2. Energy efficiency gains have affected demand due to superior appliances—flat panel TVs, LED bulbs, for instance

3. Demand substitution has already begun—solar on rooftops and parking lots, for instance.

4. Electricity from the new solutions will likely be cheaper than today's electricity—solar plus battery solutions are already cheaper in California and Hawaii. But even more, for regions that have no electrification, the price-per-unit equivalent is over 40 cents/kWh. Organized right, with SHS and microgrids, this is an easy price to beat; electricity access, and even plenty for the entire world, is within reach.

We recognize that with the new technologies, the cost for Electricity 2.0 drops substantially from what obtains today. The drop in cost will be even greater if carbon taxes or other mechanisms that incorporate the environmental costs of carbon emissions are implemented.

DEFINING ELECTRICITY MARKETS: CONSIDER INDIA

India's scandal-ridden coal block allocations—to mine, transport, and burn coal to produce electricity—appear quaint in the age of solar photovoltaics. India could instead define, then auction, solar blocks. Rather than focusing on coal available in select and ecologically sensitive regions of the nation, and therefore controversial to mine, India could focus on "mining" sunlight available everywhere.

Besides solar strategy—tens of gigawatts of solar hype in the news—India and the world need a "geography" or "coverage" strategy for renewable energy. A BTA type split of a nation into markets mentioned before is one way that serves as an illustration of how it might be done. The default in India appears to be grid-tied solar, which topologically parallels today's centralized generation. Such deployments augment supply, cleanly. Clean and plentiful are good, yet not enough. We need to address access, a dire need in India and many parts of the world.

HOW TO DEFINE MARKET BLOCKS

What might solar blocks, or more broadly, optimal market units, look like? They could be variously defined as parking lots, school grounds, campuses, office buildings, railway stations, streets, neighborhoods, housing colonies, malls, census tracts, substations and their corresponding customers, railway rights of way, or a combination of several of these. Each state, municipality, or administrative jurisdiction may define solar or market blocks in its own way and auction them. The auction winner would install solar panels, batteries, inverters, and related electricity generation infrastructure on its solar blocks and its real estate, including rooftops and parking lots, for instance, and service the customers in its territories.

One question is: How small should the blocks be? The smaller the block size, the greater would be the number of new entrants bidding for developing them, for each may be less expensive and permit greater participation. And the greater the participation by new entrants, and by existing players, including today's electricity distribution companies, the greater the public interest, and also lower costs and better service.

Instead of a few state-owned or regulated giant distribution companies, we may have a mix of hundreds of thousands of private, public, and quasi-public service providers. We would obtain the best economic outcomes—in terms of quality, choice, affordable prices, reliability, resilience, new services, and more—from competition among a large number of players in the electricity markets.

Further, broad-based participation in developing solar blocks would foster market-based solutions and reduce reliance on regulations. The regulators need to only establish performance standards, establish multiyear, yet time-bound, contract durations, and ensure safety; the management of electricity services can be with private players, including cooperatives and *panchayats*.

THE SUBSTATION AND ITS SERVICE TERRITORY AS MARKET BLOCK

One easy way to define a block may merit particular attention—the substation. It may be an ideal location for hosting solar panels, batteries, inverters, and other equipment for distributed generation. The downstream distribution cabling may be used as it is used today. There is no point in overbuilding; therefore, this asset may be made available to new competitive suppliers as shared infrastructure, as *unbundled local loop*. More than one service provider may be colocated at the substation and deliver their product to customers. With minimal disruption, and without customers even knowing it, the substation can become a renewable energy hub, managed by the auction winner.

Also worth exploring is whether cellular towers in proximity to a substation might be better or equivalent or complementary locations for deploying renewable energy hardware. The cellular towers' power requirements might make towers "anchor tenants" of locally generated electricity, especially in rural areas, and complement residential demand. In the future, both broadband Internet and electricity services may be bundled as a service, for which an early partnership with a cellular provider may make sense.

PRECEDENT FROM TELECOM

This proposed restructuring of the electricity infrastructure may appear radical at first glance, or even unnecessary, as, after all, the grid, sort of, works: why fix something that is not broken?

First of all, whether we like it or not, distributed generation will continue to grow, driven by economics. The unit cost of the solar and battery system has almost reached grid parity in many parts of the world. While renewables-based electricity costs are likely to fall, costs of grid-based power, typically generated using coal, will continue to rise.

Second, the incumbent electricity suppliers worldwide face a stark choice; they either join the distributed generation trend or are left behind, progressively losing demand first and then customers.

Third, the new electricity is cleaner and more environmental friendly.

Fourth, what is being proposed here was already done in telecommunications— the local loop was made available to competing providers from the central office.

WHO LEADS?

Who will lead this revolution, fragmenting the electricity infrastructure to make it future oriented? India can afford to be bold and has little to lose, except its disenfranchised, unelectrified population of several hundred million. A chief minister of a progressive state may initiate a move. Or, in the United States, some CEO of an investor-owned utility will see the writing on the wall and begin to parcel out the service territory and offer it to bidders.

The important thing to recognize is that the value of the sum of the parts—the parcels of service being auctioned off—exceeds the valuation of today's grid. In Chapter 5, we also suggested that the valuation of the sum of parts when the market is split into *product-markets* also likely surpasses the value of today's grid. In breaking up the market, the leadership of a utility, or a progressive chief minister, would only release value tied up in yesterday's dying infrastructure.

As Elon Musk has said on several occasions, when fundamental transformations are under way, we may not think by using analogies, but rather should do fundamental analysis, from first principles. Thus, such policy initiatives as *feed-in tariffs* in $/kWh are interim and transitional measures at the end of the day; *kWh* as a consumption measure does not truly measure the benefit or utility of electricity.

In the economically developed nations, the demand for electricity is falling, due to a number of driving forces depicted in Figure 6.1, and with it electric utility revenues. With electric car charging, there might be new revenue to shore up what is lost to efficiency and substitution, but solar changing may meet that new demand, not necessarily the existing grid. What should electric utilities do? They have no choice but to join the new electricity transformation. How might they join the transformation?

Figure 6.1   Forces Causing Demand Loss, Therefore, Revenue Loss

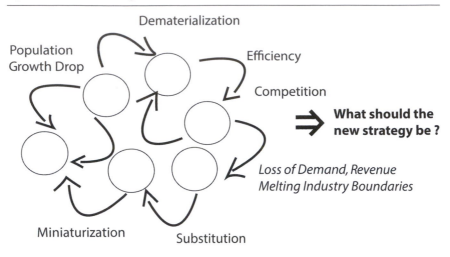

Dematerialization

Population
Growth Drop

Efficiency

Competition

⇒ **What should the
new strategy be ?**

*Loss of Demand, Revenue
Melting Industry Boundaries*

Miniaturization   Substitution

The Electricity 2.0 dog has to bark and hunt. For that to happen, positive public policy must encourage new business development and entrepreneurship. For all the talk about *solar* and distributed generation, the fact remains: the "renewables" industry is still in the latent market stage—Geoffrey Moore's "chasm," let alone the takeoff, has yet to be reached, as shown in Figure 2.1. Nevertheless, demand drop, and therefore revenue loss, for the distribution utilities has begun.

MEGAGRID OBSOLETE

It is time to acknowledge that the electricity industry as we have it is in trouble, perhaps dying, unless drastically restructured as proposed in Chapter 5. The utility death spiral report by EEI (Edison Electric Institute), and talk of decline, is everywhere. Economies of scale do not hold in electricity production any longer; instead, we have economics of large numbers. We do not need giant transmission infrastructure to haul electricity from one place to another for most applications— we may generate locally, consume locally, and trade locally with neighborhood electricity producers.

We may obtain the same reliability and resilience that the megagrid provides through a *federation of microgrids,* even when they are owned and managed by different players. We need a framework for cooperation, which might be established by relatively simple regulatory guidelines.

SEVEN

Entrepreneurial Opportunities in Electricity 2.0

Instead of submitting to the order, you create it.

—Alan Watts

MICROGRIDS AND SPECIALIZED GRIDS

If I am the mayor or governor of a town or state devastated by a natural calamity such as a hurricane or earthquake that knocked out the electricity supply of my residents and left them without electricity for two weeks, what might I do? My reaction might be the same as that of Governor Dannel P. Malloy of Connecticut, as articulated by the commissioner of the Connecticut Department of Energy and Environmental Protection, Daniel Esty:

> Our microgrid strategy aims at providing a mechanism at facilities like hospitals, sewage treatment plants and prisons where the power must stay on. The second element of the strategy centers on trying to provide core services to the public and being able to give some downtown areas the ability to stay up and be island-able during a storm. We're hoping to keep *police and fire stations, a place to charge cell phones, perhaps a school as a warming center, a grocery store, a gas station, a bank and a pharmacy in some number of communities,* in a place supported by distributed generation and that could remain up and running, providing those essential services while the grid is down. [emphasis added][1]

STREET LIGHTS, POLICE, AND FIREFIGHTER GRIDS

The organizing unit is now a function, namely, policing or firefighting. Can Governor Malloy have a *police electricity network*? Here is how it might work.

A police official decides that, no matter the severity of the next hurricane, my police station shall remain powered through solar, battery, and biogas generators. My immediate neighborhood of several thousand residents have a place to charge their phones, seek warmth, have electric lights, and boil water even when the rest of the grid is out.

Let us say about 10 such police stations in a few adjoining towns design this capability. Can the police stations be linked and managed in a coordinated way using the Internet, backed up by satellite links, in case the terrestrial Internet links are down? This would constitute a reliable and resilient police microgrid. Though not serving a contiguous territory, it would be interlinked for basic services. We could similarly have a firefighters' microgrid. Similarly, a mayor may decide that either his town's streetlights might each be stand-alone with solar panels and battery or several of them may be linked to share common storage or solar panels, and thus form a pico- or microgrid of, say, a dozen to a hundred lamps. And one street lamp among, say, 25 might be backed up with a biogas generator, so that it survives even the strongest of hurricanes.

POST OFFICE, SCHOOL, WATER PUMP GRIDS

A case may be made for having quasiprivate micro- or picogrids, managed by Internet connectivity, that are self-sufficient in the generation of their electricity, exactly as Connecticut proposes. Just as networked police stations, fire stations, and street lights can constitute private microgrids, we can similarly have a post office grid, a water-pumping grid, or a school grid. From today's all-electricity-services-to-all-people, we now move toward fragmented, special-purpose electricity solutions.

ENTREPRENEURIAL OPPORTUNITIES

Water Grid Independence: Solar Pumps–Aided Stored Water Area Network

Urban India cannot easily be water grid independent. In the four-story apartment building where I grew up, piped water from the municipal corporation is collected first at a storage tank on the ground floor and then pumped to storage tanks on the terrace on top of the buildings, and from there each home draws its water from taps. This municipal water comes from several lakes surrounding Mumbai. It is supplied only for several hours each evening. The cycle repeats itself every 24 hours. The Mumbai municipal water supply, unlike that in the United States, is not continuous.

As water supply has become scarcer, and in any case for backup and resilience, housing societies have begun to drill their own water wells—bore wells—and these supplement the water supply from the municipal corporations. If the water from the bore wells was sufficient, we would have *water grid independence* for the housing societies.

In Kerala, where I have lived off and on for the past four plus years, a casual walk off the main roads reveals a remarkable sight. Nearly every stand-alone home has an open well in its yard. A pulley with a rope and a bucket hangs over it. Each morning the residents draw water by throwing down the bucket and pulling up the rope. The homes are thus *water grid* independent. Sometimes they pump the water to terrace or roof-based water storage tanks.

Solar installers—entrepreneurs—are now commonplace even in India's tier-two cities, and solar-powered water pumps are increasingly common. Could solar installers specialize in solar water pumps? Both for the housing societies and for Kerala homes, we can have water grid independence aided by solar power.

LAMP AREA NETWORKS AND LOCAL AREA WATER NETWORK

We have sprinkler systems for single-family homes in the United States. Let me call them local area water network (LAWN). In homes, we can have an overlay network of USB plug points around a home—for TVs, entertainment systems, phone charging, and light. Both sprinkler systems plus home electronics could easily operate on solar- plus battery-based DC power and thus be grid independent, that is, not use any utility electricity at all. Office buildings too can similarly parse out lighting, computing, and entertainment loads away from the main electricity supply and have them work on DC power. I have already described in Chapter 3 the pathway lighting system on IIMK campus that is off grid. An extension IIM seeks to implement is to make all streetlights on campus also grid independent—lamp area networks (LANs). To the extent such applications take hold, the utilities face demand reduction.

Who would manage such home and office area DC grids and campus lighting, each a distinct *product-market*? It could be facilities management or the electrical engineering department of the campus. Or they could be managed by entrepreneurial start-ups.

WHO IS BEST TO CREATE SPECIALIZED GRIDS?

If a private IT company, or an entertainment company, approaches Governor Malloy and offers to build such a private police or fire station or hospital network for electricity, what might the governor do? Should it be allowed? Do laws prevent any private provider from offering such a service? Should the incumbent utility have the right of first refusal? What department or *function* within the existing distribution utilities today can deploy such microgrids for emergent needs?

Assume the newly created position for such microgrids is within the existing distribution company and reports to the CEO. What organizational form—division, department—can best pursue such opportunities? What might be the level of such a position, director, vice president, or higher? How will the accomplishments of such a function be measured? The revenues of the regulated core business will dwarf the revenues of this position.

The typical elite school MBA does not join the utilities business, historically regarded as boring; the attractions of finance, marketing, or consulting are greater. After all, the regulated utilities are regarded as a quasi-public sector job. It takes a particular personality type to accept the peculiarities of a regulated business and, day in and day out, deal with government regulatory staff and address public policy issues in state capitals and Washington, D.C.

The utility as an organization is driven primarily by operations—engineering, maintenance, and support functions, and the utilities *regulatory compact*—and less by customers and markets. The utilities do not need, and barely have, any marketing function. After all, the core undifferentiated and unbranded product has been defined and stable for decades, even a century. The Public Service Commission regulators and their staff have been the true customer of a utility. The paying customer has little say in what a utility does, except insofar as he or she votes for the politicians who appoint members of the state commissions or Federal Energy Regulatory Commission.

In the normal business world, notions such as *stranded cost* recovery, illustrative of regulatory jargon, appear quaint, even absurd. Costs are routinely incurred, and written off, when a normal business faces a competitive challenge from novel technologies–based solutions and substitutes. Where is the cost recovery from condemned paging or payphone assets? Gen X and Y barely know what a public telephone is—how can they or their parents be held responsible for the recovery of those costs incurred decades ago? There is intertemporal inequity here in the name of *regulatory compact*. Is it not true that in the emerging world of reduced barriers to entry in electricity, and given that scale economics is no longer necessary for unit cost reduction, the regulatory compact is dead?

BEGIN AT THE BEGINNING

Suppose we begin on a clean slate, and assume the technologies of today, yet place ourselves in the year 1900, what would we do to spread the benefits of electricity? My conjecture is that we would divide the nation into bite-sized markets and small population clusters, and offer them electricity using a mix of solar, battery storage, and gas-based generation.

And because we would occasionally need to trade electricity with our neighboring electricity supplier, we would figure out a way of exchanging my surplus with his, and occasionally vice versa. We would, as neighboring microgrid operators, coordinate and balance our supply and demand.

Assuming solar is equally available for my service territory as for my neighbor, whether I would have excess electricity or not at a particular time would depend on the resource endowments of my territory. If my service territory had a lot of farmland with cows, I would generate biogas on my property from dung, or from agricultural waste, say, bagasse. This biomass may be used to produce quasi-dispatchable electricity and will give me certain benefits relative to my neighbor. My neighbor's territory might be in close proximity to a perennial water stream, and he would be in a position to use a micro-hydro generator to produce electricity, round the clock, and relatively inexpensively. Naturally, my preference would be to use what I have, and his to use what he has.

Differing Attributes among Neighboring, Small Grids

Whereas my territory might have largely homes and some retail, my neighbor might have a factory, working only one shift, say from 8 A.M. to 6 P.M., and fewer homes. The electricity consumption profile would thus vary—the peak load in my service territory would be when people started cooking in the evening and started charging their EVs. The demand for electricity for my neighboring electricity generator, with factories on his premises, would drop when the factories shut down in the evening. When I have surplus electricity, I might trade it with my neighbor, and vice versa. In sum, among neighbors with such variations, we would create a market. We would all be interested in offering clean, reliable electricity to our customers, and our trading would ensure that. We would balance our needs via exchange, barter, alliances, partnerships, mergers, acquisitions, and so forth.

On a technical level, as neighborly service providers, we might develop technologies to ensure that electricity flows smoothly across our borders in either direction. For redundancy, each of us might make partnership deals with more than one neighbor, and when buying electricity, or selling it, we would seek the best price in our exchanges. Do such exchange relationships among service providers require the state as referee or umpire? No planner or regulator need feel the burden of, "My God, how can I guarantee the smooth and reliable working of 'the grid'?" Markets will work to ensure the reliability and robustness of the resulting internetwork of grids. This is not an ideological stance; rather, it is the recognition of the role and value of distributed transactions among many, as occur in market after market.

The main point to note is this: the natural monopoly in the electricity business is dead. Many new entrants will enter the market, whether the regulators or utilities like it or not. They will value the grid of the future and work to coordinate its smooth functioning. Viewing the electricity business from a lens colored by today's utilities perspective misses out on the possibilities that a business viewpoint provides.

When market mechanisms ensure the coordination of multifarious activities, with individual actors within it negotiating the best outcomes for themselves, what is the role for regulators? Would they be as policemen? Their role might be as boundary setters, defining the parameters within which the entire coordination system works. It would be light-touch regulation. Where would the public interest lie in such a market? In ensuring no one has a dominant and monopolistic role—through antitrust regulations; through ensuring reliability, resilience, and security; and in ensuring no barriers to market entry.

DIFFERENTIATION OF A BASIC SERVICE

The previous example assumes that the market is divided by geographical attributes, for instance, the natural endowments of each parcel of service. The microgrids described are images of the larger macrogrid of today, writ small. They essentially share attributes of the macrogrid today. Yet this is not the only way to organize the electricity markets for the future. Can specialization lead to a different organization?

The phenomenon of differentiation of a homogenous or amorphous market is well known in the business world, particularly in retail. Note the varieties of soaps, detergents, cosmetics, and oils, or the different flavors and packaging styles of fountain drinks and sodas. Even water is highly differentiated through flavors, aeration, packaging, distribution channels, and branding. And yet we have only one flavor, more or less, of electricity. It appears strange that the electric utility of today offers the same product to all people, to all segments—consumers, retailers, industries, and all organizations large and small, public and private. It is largely the same electricity worldwide, save for differences in voltage, frequencies, and wall plugs.

A professor colleague at TU Delft described this condition as: "Electricity is the perfect product. True, its production methods vary. And we need to optimize its generation, transmission, distribution, consumption . . . to attain least cost, reliable supply, but the product *per se* is nearly perfect." Water, by this argument, is an even more perfect product. Such thinking would be anathema to the marketing department of any regular business and is the exact opposite of what is taught in core marketing courses in business schools where *differentiation* rules.

KILOWATT-HOUR AS MEASURE

Is the measurement of electricity in kilowatt-hour the best measure? Why measure in kilowatt-hour? Should not the utilities sell *benefits or* the *uses* of electricity, such as lighting, heating, cooling, transport, pumping, compressing, and powering devices, instead of consumption? If they do, should they still be called utilities? Probably not *utilities* as understood today. *If* the value delivered can be priced, and the classical industry boundaries broken, there is everything right in the business opportunity *per se*. But this is a big *If* when it comes to decision making and execution. The important strategy question for today's electricity companies is: What business are we in? Are electric utilities in the electricity selling, as kilowatt-hour, business, or in the *uses* of electricity business, and as discussed in Chapter 8, in the ISP and entertainment delivery business?

If the utility supplied electricity and charged for it based on illumination per area served, or comfort maintained through heating and cooling, or when electricity is used for car charging, billed the customer not based on kilowatt-hour, but dollars per mile driven; and bundled flat-rate Internet access and entertainment, what then would the new combo utility look like?

We have Walt Patterson's perspective—next-generation electricity may be produced entirely without fire, no combustion necessary.[2] What we measure— kilowatt-hours—is a less and less meaningful measure, since what we really seek is lighting, heating, cooling, and motion. Lumens measure value more than kilowatt-hour of electricity consumption. Even if we assume for a moment that electricity is a perfect product, should not the utility derived from electricity be measured more than its consumption?

What we really want from electricity is the satisfaction of human needs that are age old—heating during winter, cooling during summer, light beyond the sun-light hours, heat to boil water for cooking, warm water for bathing, powering electronics to push and pull computing and communications bits, and mobil-ity beyond walking. We also want to power our electronics for entertainment— images and sound. In addition, we have industrial uses too—operating smelters for ore, pulling engines for public transport, operating data centers, and the like.

The utility purists may quibble: electricity is like dial tone in the landline tele-phone industry, an undifferentiated product. We have only one flavor of dial tone, and until the mobile phones, only one, universal flavor of ringtone. Of course, there are many central office–based features such as call waiting, caller ID, call forwarding, voice mail, and three-way calling that may alert us in sim-ple ways using rings. Yet in comparison to the plethora of services and alerts that smartphones support, host, or give access to, that is a slim application world. Even today, the landline telephone infrastructure is feature-light, just like electricity is.

EXPANDED ANSOFF MATRIX FOR OPPORTUNITY ASSESSMENT

Typically, when we consider an opportunity, we use the Ansoff matrix, the *product-market* matrix to *place* it. If the matrix is $n \times m$, an intersection, say, $n_3 \times m_5$, represents a business possibility. We then specify it in some detail— demographics, segments, pricing, volumes, penetration, and so forth—to deter-mine its economic value, develop a business plan, and pursue it. We may appoint a product manager or a brand manager to manage it in a corporate setting. Often, the product is a function of the underlying technology, and we may therefore find it useful sometimes to consider the *technology—market* matrix. In the case of solar photovoltaics with distributed generation, *location* matters for electricity gener-ation. *Time* also similarly matters—the duration when the sun shines and also when it does not. Thus location may be considered a part of the overall generation technology as well as time.

Whereas the Ansoff matrix is a proper way to characterize the market segments and their attributes and evaluate their financial prospects, we need to modify the classic axes and expand them to include *location*, and even *time*. We can have *product-markets* and we can have *location markets*, and we can have *campus mar-kets* matrices, all derivatives of *product-markets*.

LOCATION IS A CONTRIBUTOR TO DIFFERENTIATION

What is the optimal location of an electricity supply solution? Is it on individual home rooftops, or on community open spaces, perhaps colocated with the electricity substation? The California Public Utilities Commission (CPUC)[3] report recognizes the importance of location and proposes that the local distribution be studied—by the utility—to identify those locations that would be ideal candidates for microgrid locations. To quote, "In order to determine the *optimum locations* for microgrid development, [emphasis added] the Commission should undertake an effort to map the distribution grid in order to best identify these locations. This effort can be done in conjunction with the development of distribution grid planning efforts." They consider factors such as propensity to fail, stability, and congestion as issues to consider regarding location. This is a grid-centric view; it would equally be valid to view the attractiveness of a location from an economic or business prospects viewpoint—for instance, revenue potential, customer access, and electricity generation prospects. And entrepreneurs may undertake such locational analysis too!

IS A HOMEOWNER IN THE ELECTRICITY BUSINESS?

NRG Energy believes, rightly I think, that it is technically possible for a suburban home to have rooftop solar panels, battery storage, and a small gas-based generator and draw no net power from the electricity grid. The home *defects* from the grid for practical purposes, though it may maintain a connection with it as backup.

Let us assume that this is technically and economically feasible and delivers, on average, cheaper and greener power than the grid. Will customers embrace it? My view is: at least some customers would like to receive electricity as a service, as they obtain it today, and not as a product, not as a new hardware appliance, with its demands for repair and maintenance. The customer does not wish to be in the electricity business; electricity as a transparent service, as exists today, has merit. The service may be provided by a small, local utility that may or may not be affiliated directly with today's gigantic distribution utility; it can be an entrepreneurial business that aggregates the demand for several homes.

With microgrids, say, at a street, neighborhood, homeowners association, or campus level, we get the benefits of electricity as a service and also local control, local accountability, and clean generation, at comparable or better economics. A homeowner may contribute to the microgrid via solar on rooftop, for instance, and such a contribution may be netted out for that customer. Some may choose to not install solar on their rooftop, and they will end up paying a higher price, though lower on average than what is obtained from today's grid.

Among the most important consequences of the end of the natural monopoly in electricity is new market entry by entrepreneurial new electricity providers via microgrids. Such new market entry is in the public interest.

Figure 7.1   New Market Entry in the Electricity Business

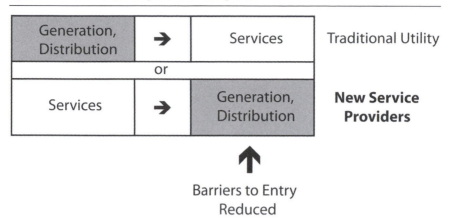

In Figure 7.1, the top row shows the traditional view of electricity services. The utility involved in generation, transmission, and distribution offers service to customers, and the service is undifferentiated—one or three phase power, at a certain voltage, with a certain current. The customer uses appliances—from light bulbs to coffee grinders to hair dryers—to derive the many uses of electricity. Yet the electricity business need not be organized in this way alone. Someone may specialize in DC power, home generated from rooftop or backyard solar, store electricity in batteries, and create an overlay network for phone charging and home electronics. Others may specialize in lighting using the same DC and LED bulbs for yet another overlay network. The point is, any service provider who has access to a customer home—from plumbers to electricians to carpet cleaners—can create a service infrastructure and reduce a customer's electricity load. For an existing home, this may for the present be uneconomical, but for new homes? This latter situation is suggested in the second row of Figure 7.1.

PHASED GRID INDEPENDENCE

Typically, for home electronics for entertainment, or phone or laptop charging, we customize electricity through wall warts that convert it into DC and the voltage we need. The power requirements for such use are low; solar panels and batteries in the backyard of a home can easily meet this energy need. If DC cabling with USB ports were spread throughout homes, we could easily be *off grid* for such applications.

Likewise, we seldom ask the question: Do street lights outside the home need the same 220(or 110)- volt 50(60)-Hz power? Can the streetlights be DC powered? Can the streets be off grid and instead be powered by microgrids? Can there be an overlay street lighting network? Grid independence for streetlights, rural water pumps, or rural households, and not *grid defection* for urban homes, appears to be a first-order need.

It is rather astonishing that a utility today provides electricity to all segments, and that *segment-specific* electricity generation is not more common. It is true that, in many settings in electricity-starved countries like India, industries have mostly diesel-generated and expensive *captive power*.

Captive power frequently means autonomous campus power—a township of an industrial town, an enterprise zone, or a college campus. But *captive* need not be confined to geography; it can be, let me call it, linearly extensive. Solar-powered water pumping can be a business unto itself, conducted on a large scale, even nationally, and independent of the grid. So also solar-powered street lighting in towns, cities, and campuses. Each application will likely generate its own power, in part, and get what additional power it needs from one or several microgrids. The fracturing of today's demand into such verticals will reduce the overall demand on today's grid.

MICROGRIDS IN A NEIGHBORHOOD: SPECIALIZATION, COOPERATION, AND TRADE PLUS LINEARLY EXTENSIVE

Consider the grayed two columns on the *Y*-axis labeled "Location" in Figure 7.2. Business school students will recognize the figure itself as an expanded and modified Ansoff matrix, where location replaces product. This makes sense since the product in photovoltaic electricity generation is a function of location and time and, of course, the technologies for converting sunlight into electricity.

A shopping mall, a college campus, an office building, and other grayed locations are each prospective microgrid sites, each with its own hub. When they do indeed become microgrid hubs, where is the need for an electric utility as we have it? Each location can have its own private electricity. The backup function of the

Figure 7.2   Location Market Matrix: Entrepreneurs in Electricity

Location			Lighting	Energy Efficiency	Cooking	Air-Conditioning & Heating	Hot Water
Generate, Use, Buy, Sell	Shopping Mall		✓✓	✓✓	✗	✓✓	✗
Generate, Use, Buy, Sell	Home, Rooftop, & Inside		✓	✓	✓	✓	✓
Generate, Use, Buy, Sell	High-Rise Office Building		✓✓	✓✓✓	✗	✓	✓
Generate, Use, Buy, Sell	School Yard & Parking Lot, Inside		✓✓	✓	✗	✓✓	✓
Generate, Use, Buy, Sell	High-Rise Residential Building		✓	✓✓✓	✓✓✓	✓	✓✓✓
Generate, Use, Buy, Sell	College Campus		✓✓	✓✓	✓	✓✓	✓✓

Market

traditional grid can be performed by adjacent microgrids. An existing distribution utility also could locate its own microgrid hub at a substation, and join the ecosystem shown here.

Each of these locations can generate and use its own electricity, and should there be any excess, or should there be any deficit, each location can both sell or buy electricity—not only from the existing macrogrid but also from each other, that is, adjacent microgrids.

If you consider all the locations listed in the columns, they reasonably can be in a neighborhood, close to each other, in a few square kilometers of geography. Thus a neighborhood can have a cluster of complementary microgrids. Such a cluster of microgrids can offer reliability, resilience, and protection from cyber- or other threats perhaps better than the macrogrid of today.

Depicted on the X-axis in Figure 7.2 are electricity uses or services. Why cannot a business be both centered at a college campus and yet focus only on air-conditioning or lighting? In other words, a microgrid need not be a full-service business; microgrids can specialize. Such specialized microgrids by use, by market, can work with other specialized microgrids across a market, however small or large. The arrows in each cell are my subjective indications of the likelihood of the corresponding services occurring; they are suggestive only.

Whether specialized or the full-service microgrid, each represents an entrepreneurial opportunity. Since the barriers to entry into the electricity business have fallen, and scale economics are no longer necessary for unit cost reduction, we may conclude that the electricity market is poised for fragmentation—it will be rendered small *and* specialized, focused, and with the potential for scope expansion to a state or even the entire nation—that is, the business can be linearly extensive.

In order for entrepreneurs to develop such solutions, they would need to know the economics of each instance in the highlighted column for a full-service microgrid.[4] And regardless of the individual variations in the economics of each, for all instances, it would be ideal if the cost/unit of electricity is less than today's corresponding average electricity bill for those locations. Technologies are driving us in that direction—it is reasonable to assume that fossil fuel–based electricity prices will rise, and distributed renewables–based electricity prices will fall over the years.

FRACTURING THE ELECTRICITY BUSINESS INTO SPECIALIZATIONS

More fundamentally, the electricity business may fracture along specializations, such as highway lighting companies, or wholesale or bulk electricity companies focused on aluminum, steel, railroad, or mining industries. Architectural firms specializing in LEED buildings may incorporate electricity-generating hardware in roofs and walls by design and use efficient appliances. They may use no fuels. This is Walt Patterson's "infrastructure" electricity from "natural ambient energy flows, including sunlight, wind and water."[5]

Figure 7.3   Metamorphic, Inexorable Transformation of the Electricity Business

		Scope	
		High	Low
Pace	High	Frame Breaking	Piecemeal
	Low	Metamorphic	Plodding

Source: Adapted from Kim, Bongjin, and Prescott, John E. 2005. Deregulatory Forms, Variations in the Speed of Governance Adaptation, and Firm Performance. *Academy of Management Review*, vol. 30, no. 2, 414–425.

Its characteristics will include two-way electricity flows and differentiation of electricity services offered by specialized businesses instead of today's *all services for all customers* model. A microgrid, at least superficially, conjures up the image of the existing large grid, writ small. When considered from the viewpoint of the modified Ansoff matrix with location markets, the business consequences are more complex. Yes, there will be microgrids that mirror the macrogrid of today, only miniaturized. Equally, the electricity business fractures and expands beyond known franchise territories or limitations of geography of today. The consequences of the end of the natural monopoly paradigm, reduced barriers to entry, and technical advance, however, are less straightforward.

In fact, so profound are the changes that in Figure 7.3, we may say a once "plodding" business, with low "scope" of change and a low "pace" of change, has moved into the "metamorphic" quadrant, with enormous "scope" for change, though at a relatively slow "pace." Yet the slow pace may not be discounted for its impact is likely to be "frame breaking" or revolutionary. Twenty years hence, we may barely recognize the transformed electricity business.

CITY-CENTRIC, INTENSIVE SERVICES BUSINESS

One version of the utility of the future may organize itself by city and, within this market, offer multiple services or applications to multiple segments. Historical network reach defines the market boundaries, and thus this approach would be closer to what utilities do today. This is the buffet restaurant strategy—a customer

Figure 7.4   Intrinsic versus Extrinsic Opportunities

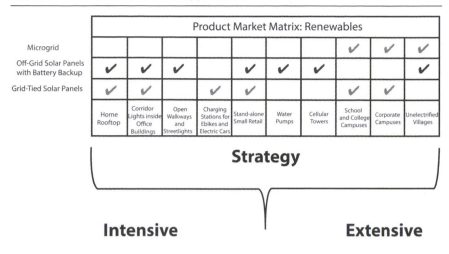

may pick and choose, and either pay a la carte, or an *all you can eat* flat price. A cable entertainment business may lead to solar installation and maintenance, energy efficiency, home security, cable entertainment, telephone, gas, water, and broadband access businesses—all utilities from one service provider.

In Figure 7.4, I show that some markets may be best served by microgrids, others are ideally off-grid, and yet others may be best served by the traditional grid, with some solar-based distributed generation baked into the solution. The urban centers ought to be treated, for purposes of utility planning, like energy-intensive industries like smelting. They represent concentrated energy demand, like subways and tramways, which ought to be satisfied by existing utilities. In suburban and rural areas, however, the largely stand-alone microgrid may be the norm, preferably linked to other microgrids, and optionally linked to the macrogrid. By check marks, I have tried to show what markets may be best served by particular solution.

But regardless, the larger point I wish to make is about two broad strategies a service provider, an entrepreneurial new firm, or an existing business entering into electricity may adopt: (1) intensive electricity services, a market or city-centric approach and (2) an extensive electricity services strategy.

SPECIALIZED, EXTENSIVE, GEOGRAPHIC SCOPE-BASED BUSINESS

A new business may specialize in street lighting and deploy its solution on city streets and campuses, on buildings and factories, in city after city, on highways, state by state, and regionally or nationally. It will benefit from economies of scale, scope, and reach. Similarly, the electric car charging business may be regional or national in scope and parallel the gas station brands like Chevron, Exxon, or Texaco, and might be branded PG&E or Sempra Stations. Yet others may specialize in hot water solutions on rooftops or solar cooking solutions for restaurants, as is already happening in India's major temples.

It is interesting to speculate what might happen with next-generation electricity services, and in what sequence. For instance, will the full-service microgrid—the macrogrid rendered small—happen first? Or will entrepreneurs define select *product-markets*, say, solar water pumps network or the traffic lights network, and parse away demand from existing utilities in chunks? Or will the facilities management departments of businesses and their maintenance staff build and manage electricity supply—*insourcing* electricity services?

NEW ENTRY: SERVICES TO GENERATION AND VICE VERSA

If a company is engaged in electric installation, say, hot water heaters, or repair, or energy-efficiency services for a campus, hospital, or a residential building, can it not also generate power for that facility, locally, using solar panels, from the facility's rooftop or neighboring open spaces? In general, the business direction would be from services to generation for the company. Equally, a generation and distribution company can enter the value-added services business for its customers, by offering services within customer premises, on the *other side of the meter*. In either case, it would be merely incremental vertical integration and readily accomplished in either direction.

A company may define its business as lighting for campuses and buildings. Today, the equipment suppliers, say, Philips or Schneider Electric, are distinct from the electricity suppliers. Yet an equipment supplier may decide to generate electricity on those very campuses using solar panels and batteries and thus become a microelectric utility for that location.

METAMORPHIC CHANGE

When natural monopoly ends and economies of scale are no longer needed for low per-unit electricity costs, what types of industry structure transformation may one expect? The pace of change is slow, yet the scope of change is potentially significant. Thus it may best be described as *metamorphic* in Figure 7.3.

While electricity is electricity and the eventual network topologies of the electricity infrastructure may be similar in today's grid-rich economies and those of the emerging world, the paths to reach that point matter. The pursuit of particular paths depends on local leadership and public policy. The fundamental barrier to the emergence of the new electricity paradigm appears to me to be the legacy, macrogrid, mind-set, and inertia of incumbency in its favor. A leadership willing to experiment in the matter of electricity provision can foster the market entry of the kinds of microgrids that constitute the optimal infrastructure of the future. Political and business leaders need to be presented with credible technical options.

These do not exist today because the microgrid of the kind we need does not exist. The technological trajectory is clear. The capabilities and resources exist, and while not trivial, are well within the realm of easy application. The implementation is missing at a time when we face a (less lofty yet more critical version of) the "man-on-the-moon" moment with profound consequences.

LIMBO OF SUBOPTIMAL EQUILIBRIUM

Even if the electricity infrastructure *should* consist of multiple, small, inter-connected microgrids, it is quite possible that the electricity infrastructure will remain in a suboptimal equilibrium, with microgrids coexisting with the macro-grid, and the cost of electricity will remain relatively high, along with continuing large amounts of carbon dioxide emissions. The decommoditization of electricity would not occur with the speed one would like or expect, and though value-added electricity services will arise, they may remain sporadic.

Such suboptimal equilibria—for example, when unemployment is relatively high and growth rates are slower than what might be—are well known to economists. The *invisible hand* of the market does not dislodge this condition. Policy intervention becomes necessary, goes the conventional wisdom. Yet *policy* is generally passive and reactive, and the *state-as-initiator* approach is a poor substitute for entrepre-neurial energies.

MCI's Bill McGowan's role dismantling the old AT&T monopoly cannot be overstated; his going to the courts and fighting was critical to transform the tele-phone industry. Nor can Craig McCaw's entrepreneurial efforts with Cellular One be ignored; McCaw prepared the ground for the PCS auctions that gave a boost to the wireless revolution. Who or what companies in electricity parallel that role of MCI in telecommunications?

It is not enough to have only entrepreneurial activity in electricity even though the barriers to entry have fallen, and technologies enable smaller-scale solutions; active public policy is essential too, on a national scale. And should public policy display insufficient dynamism, entrepreneurs may have to file lawsuits to claim their right to offer services, exactly as happened in telecom.

SEMANTIC ISSUES—GRIDS & SMARTGRIDS, HYBRID & INTEGRATED, DG & TOPOLOGICAL REVOLUTION

The discussion thus far in Chapter Four through Chapter Seven presents me with an opportunity to discuss some nagging issues about terms and definitions in Electricity 2.0. This might also be the place, at the conclusion of Chapter Seven to discuss them because Chapter Eight deals with *industry structure* issues, and Chapter Nine with renewable energy related curriculum in business schools, and thus less directly with microgrids. It might thus serve as prologue before such a change in direction.

The Grid: An Anachronism

The grid evokes images of a mesh of cables and transmission towers, linking generation plants and substations, flung over hundreds and thousands of miles, a giant spider web, almost romantic in its reach and power. When we ask a layperson what *the grid* means, the "electricity network" is the typical answer. Only secondarily does anyone say, "the Internet" or telecommunications networks, cellular or wireline or entertainment, and, only rarely, the network of pipelines that bring us natural gas or water. Yet the Internet is the true grid and the electricity grid an anachronism, even a historical aberration. By and large, electricity services only need local area networks—electricity LANs.

The hierarchical, top-down, wide-area network that is today's grid results from a historical event, the delivery of electricity generated at Niagara Falls, and carried over transmission lines into New York City. Had Edison had his way, we would have small DC grids, and whatever they might have evolved into over decades. With new distributed generation (DG) technologies, we are revisiting the existing grid topology and making it more suitable for our times. In the process, the edifice, that is, the electric utility business, stands threatened. The rhetoric of *utility death spiral* and *grid defection* fills the trade press, thanks to research reports by industry and financial research companies.

Grid Appropriated by the Electricity Industry

The grid in electricity today is more a top-down and hierarchical network and less a distributed processing and peer-to-peer network for exchange of information and electricity. Comparatively, the telecom network, thanks to edge routers and data centers spread across the telecom network, is a relatively flat, multidirectional network. The electricity infrastructure, in fact, can consist of "islands of electricity coverage," relatively isolated from each other, and only sharing links among each other for occasional emergency needs. The islands of electricity can be linked to each other for operational efficiencies and to achieve the benefits of economies of scale by using the telecom network, or the Internet. Thus, electricity is a local networking solution; the telecom infrastructure is genuinely a wide-area network. Should the word grid, then, be used for describing electricity solutions at all?

Hybrid versus Integrated

In the growing literature on electricity systems that rely on more than one generation source, say, solar panels, batteries, gas generators, and fuel cells, it is increasingly common to refer to the resulting solutions as *hybrid systems*. This is unfortunate, if true in a physical sense. Yet the value from such a system, at the *application layer*, to borrow from the open system interconnection (OSI) language, derives from its *integrated* functioning—matching loads with supply and tracking them reliably. When multiple generation sources are combined and work together, we get a hybrid system; this is merely a fact and not reflective of the value of the integrated overall system at all.

Topological Revolution

Many consider the emerging electricity revolution to be a DG revolution leading to the creation of a two-way network, distinct from what has historically been a one-way, top-down network. Others consider it a *renewables* revolution—the advent of solar panels, biofuels, fuel cells, new-generation batteries inexorably displacing the fossil fuel sources that power today's grid. Yet others characterize it as a *grid independence* revolution; the fact that it is now possible to go off grid and be self-sufficient. While each is true, I believe the revolution is equally a *topological* revolution—the rearranging of the elements that constitute today's network into a new configuration.

The hierarchical grid is being reconstituted as a cellular grid, with peer-to-peer connectivity among microgrids rather than hierarchical networking as in the past. Microgrids with smaller and more local generation, local consumption, and almost no transmission are replacing the giant generation plants and massive transmission links. We are witness to a metamorphosis, a slowly unfolding revolution; the grid of the future might be a *federation of microgrids*. The electricity remains the same as we have always known it, yet it comes from a distinctly new-generation and delivery paradigm.

Typically and ironically, when the electricity industry is represented by an image, transmission towers and cables are frequently shown, and not smoking power plants or transformers. With distributed generation, the transmission links are becoming less relevant. What image might represent the new electricity industry? Neither solar panels nor wind turbines will do.

Smart Grid and Information and Communication Technologies

Overlaying information and communication technologies (ICT) on top of the existing grid for superior operations and greater reliability; better and richer SCADA; meter as source for data collection and control—is that what the smart grid is? How is this different from normal network monitoring and control in any IT-enabled system? Or, is this not similar to automated process control in a petrochemical, fertilizer, or polymer plant, or in general in any continuous process industry? The interesting question is: Does such smartening of the grid and its elements make it easier to reconfigure the topology of the existing network, and convert it into a cluster of interacting microgrids?

EIGHT

Electricity Most Glamorous: The Enernet of Things (EoT)

Economic progress, in a capitalist society, means turmoil.

—Joseph A. Schumpeter

The Internet of things (IoT) makes news constantly, mostly as an opportunity worth tens of trillions of dollars. It includes machine-to-machine (M2M) communications, including Bluetooth headsets for phones, phones-to-car connectivity, car to home communications, and hands-free talking for safety while driving or walking. Other scenarios include connected thermostats, refrigerators, and industrial equipment controlled remotely and via smartphone applications. My interest is IoT's impact on next-generation electricity infrastructure. Here is why.

WHY ENERNET

My hypothesis is this: whereas IoT generally does not fundamentally challenge the structure of existing industries and makes the existing applications more efficient, the combination of electricity with the Internet does. A concept newly being discussed in this regard is the Enernet of things (EoT),[1] that is, the interworking of electricity infrastructure with the Internet.[2]

Enernet, a broader conceptualization, better represents the transformative, awe-inspiring changes unfolding before our eyes. It shakes up and reorganizes the topology of the grid and converts a long distance or wide area *flow* business to a local area flow plus storage business. It thereby alters the existing business model, and it encourages us to embed some electricity functions in infrastructure. Eventually, it might move us away from selling kilowatt hours to selling the uses of electricity—illumination, heating, cooling, and motion—perhaps like buckets of minutes or GB bundles in phone and data services. Enernet therefore might be a bigger deal for electricity than for other industries. Does not the *smart grid* adequately represent the impact of the Internet and information processing on the electricity grid? Not really. The smart grid largely upgrades, for efficiency purposes, what we already have. It leaves the existing infrastructure and its topology intact. It does not encompass industry structure changes as represented by what EPB has done in Chattanooga, Tennessee.

AN UNDERAPPRECIATED REVOLUTION: PIONEERING SERVICE IN CHATTANOOGA, TENNESSEE

EPB, a municipal electric utility, entered the ISP business, and through EPB fiber optics offers 1 gigabit per second symmetric Internet connectivity to their customers for approximately $70/month. That's fast and well-priced, an accomplishment worthy of recognition, emulation, and celebration.

The EPB story does not get enough press, though covered on CBS News in 2013[3] and in the *Guardian*.[4] EPB overlaid fiber-optic cable for smartening its electricity infrastructure in its service territory, but once the cable was deployed, it decided: We can build our own ISP with the fiber-optic cable. It did. And the important part is this: instead of replicating the asymmetric broadband deployments of incumbent phone or cable companies, it deployed symmetric, 1-gbps bandwidth for customers, upstream and downstream. This is revolutionary for several reasons.

One, it represents the layering of, first, electricity services, then the Internet, on the geography of a municipality. It raises the issue: What are the relationships among municipalities, electricity providers, and ISPs? Consider, for example, that Comcast, a coaxial cable-based Internet and entertainment company, partners with NRG Energy for comarketing. Why? "The core business for both NRG and Comcast has struggled in recent years. Comcast had posted straight 26 quarters of pay-TV subscriber losses until Q4 2013, accordingly to Forbes, with the loss stemmed in part by triple play bundling. NRG, on the other hand, was just downgraded by Zacks Analyst to 'underperform' in part due to the fact that about a quarter of its electricity generation business comes from coal, which is under increasing regulation." Therefore, "NRG Energy has already been working with Comcast on cross-marketing in Texas for a few years, feeding potential customers to Comcast when they call to set up new services for electricity, and Comcast was doing the same for NRG's Texas retailer Reliant."[5] Under the circumstances, cross-marketing makes sense.

Although Comcast partnered with one electric utility it had filed a lawsuit against EPB in 2009. Here is an excerpt from the interview with the EPB CEO:

Q: *What kind of response did you get from the cable industry?*
A: *We got sued. It went through the court process and eventually, we won.*

Q: *What would you do differently if you had this to do over?*

A: *It took us a fair amount of time to figure out the benefits of the network. We thought that if we had this network, that instantly big technology companies like Apple or Facebook would move to Chattanooga. That certainly didn't happen. What we found over time is how it helps our own citizens and builds entrepreneurship in our area.*[6]

A media article notes: "In April 2008, Comcast sued the Chattanooga Electric Power Board (EPB) to prevent it from building a fiber network to serve residents who were getting slow speeds from the incumbent cable provider. Comcast claimed that EPB illegally subsidized the buildout with ratepayer funds, but it quickly lost in court, and EPB built its fiber network and began offering Internet, TV, and phone service. After EPB launched in 2009, incumbents Comcast and AT&T finally started upgrading their services."[7]

Not all electric utilities have the same strategies. EPB broke the mold and decided to become an ISP—not merely an everyday ISP, but one with symmetric broadband to individual households and businesses faster than anyone else in the United States. It therefore represents a fundamental threat to the business model of traditional ISPs—AT&T, Verizon, Comcast, Time Warner Cable, and other telephone and cable companies. In contrast, the collaboration with NRG Energy is at a lower, tactical level and does not constitute an existential threat to incumbent ISPs.

Barriers to entry in infrastructural industries—cable, telephony, and, until recently, electricity delivery—are typically prohibitively high; the companies are de facto monopolies; they are protected from competition. In the distribution network, it makes no sense to overbuild. It makes sense, if required and as I have described in Chapter 4, to do what the telephone companies did—find regulatory means to share that local loop infrastructure through colocation or having a choice among long-distance carriers by presubscription or by use of dialing codes. Yet, suddenly, EPB built its quantum leap of a broadband system, challenging the incumbents.

The market signaling value of this event is enormous. The larger electric utilities may be slow, but they get the idea. They also have telecom assets that can be leveraged for retail telecom and entertainment services. Consider, for instance, the broadband infrastructure of Southern California Edison[8] in California. Even in India, Powergrid Corporation[9] has an extensive fiber-optic network as does the Indian Railways, the Railtel Corporation of India.[10]

Now cities are getting into the act. Syracuse, fed up with the slow-speed Internet offered by its incumbent ISPs, desires its own ISP business, and the mayor seeks advice from the mayor of Chattanooga about how to go about it.[11] After all, cities compete with each other to attract and retain businesses. The quality of the Internet is a critical component of a city's business climate and therefore also the push toward city sponsored Wi-Fi hotspots.

Electric utilities of all kinds—cooperative, municipal, investor-owned utilities—are ideally poised to offer bundled electricity, broadband, and entertainment services on next-generation platforms. The basic infrastructure—cables and right of ways—is there, and is being smartened via the smart grid.

This New York Times article,[12] August 7, 2016, describes how Bolt Fiber Optic Services, a subsidiary of Northeast Oklahoma Electric Cooperative,[13] has become a high speed ISP offering up to 1 Gbps Internet service plus HD entertainment and VoIP telephone service. To quote from the article, "Our electric cooperatives believe they have an obligation to economic development, so it was very natural for them to leverage the systems they have to also provide broadband," said Martha A. Duggan, a senior principal for the National Rural Electric Cooperative Association, a trade group in Washington.

ZERO-BASED BUSINESS ASSESSMENT AND REORGANIZATION

To realize the growth possibilities from combined electricity and Internet service requires breaking down traditional industry and jurisdictional boundaries; repurposing network architectures and topologies; and even restructuring the ownership structure of utilities.

Yet what choice do utilities have but to do so? The electricity business, particularly in mature markets, is at an inflection point, facing Schumpeterian *creative destruction* and decline. Utilities must make fundamental choices; business as usual is less and less of an option. Utilities probably need a separate ISP division with its own leadership focused on end-user residential and business customers, not regulators. They need a holistic view of services, uncluttered by old notions about product or service boundaries.

During times of fundamental change, when the business model itself needs revision, Clayton Christensen recommends a *zero-based* assessment of the business. "If we didn't have an existing business, how could we best build a new one?" he asks.[14] How might we answer this question for electricity?

Answer: If we start from basics, the new business might comprise of a federation of microgrids, working cooperatively with each other to offset each other's limitations, offering electricity and *broadband* access, including telephone and entertainment services, and using a variety of non-fossil-fuel-based *renewable* sources and storage in their generation mix.

Cellular towers and the electricity substations may host the solar panels, batteries, and other generation sources and equipment and be the focal point for services, as shown in Figure 8.1. For a long time, fiber-optic cores have been built into the transmission infrastructure of utilities, as stated earlier. Such fiber-optic infrastructure has been wholesaled by utilities to whoever needed it, mostly to cellular and telephone companies. While utilities obtain most of their revenues from electricity delivery, bits delivery has had a niche existence, but seldom for households and small businesses. In India, Powergrid Corporation, a transmission utility is an ISP focused on business customers; it could partner with distribution companies to offer residential broadband services.

Figure 8.1 Substation Plus Cellular Tower as Hub

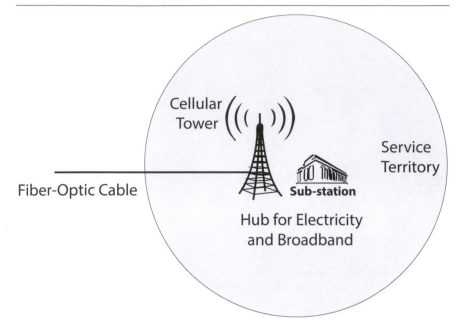

Cellular Tower

Service Territory

Fiber-Optic Cable

Sub-station

Hub for Electricity and Broadband

The intermingling of electricity with information systems—customer data management, operations control, automated metering, smart-grid-related upgrades—has been progressing apace. I have argued in the past that performance monitoring of solar panels[15] on rooftops is analogous to network management of remote computer terminals, and thus within the scope of IT companies. Equally, electricity distribution companies are ISPs too. The network topologies of electricity and telecom make them closely aligned relatives. Can the bit-delivery business become as significant as electricity delivery itself? Yes. The poor job done by incumbent ISPs—telephone and cable companies—creates such options.

SIGNIFICANCE OF EPB'S SOLUTION

Many businesses can now perform the traditional functions of an electric utility—providing affordable, reliable, and resilient power to homes and businesses. The barriers to entry in the business have fallen. For instance, a home with rooftop solar panels, batteries, and gas-based generators may choose to be grid independent. Even when homes decide to remain *grid tied,* utilities face falling demand and revenue, and the possibility of grid defection in the future. Further, competing electricity solutions can emerge quickly, and not one-home-at-a-time; microgrids can offer community-, village-, or campus-level solutions.

What then should electric utilities do? The first part of the answer is: "*Join* the solar and batteries-based electricity delivery business—*be* the change maker."

Figure 8.2   Increased Revenue and Margins with Broadband

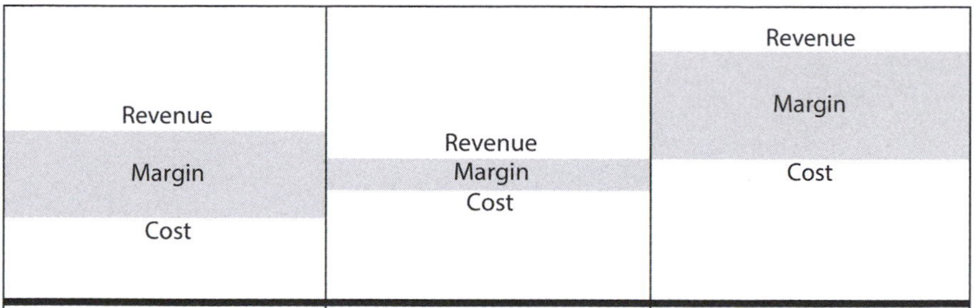

		Revenue
Revenue		Margin
Margin	Revenue	Cost
Cost	Margin	
	Cost	
Today's Regulated Business	Regulated with Renewables	Electricity plus ISP Business
Economies of scale: large scale generation for unit cost reduction. Prices expected to rise due to rising fuel costs, carbon pricing, demand drop, and grid defection	*Economies of numbers: large numbers for unit cost reduction. Somewhat expensive today, costs likely to fall, leading to improved margins*	*Economies of numbers + business expansion by leveraging current assets— rights of way, poles, cabling*
Up to 2020	2020 through 2030	2015 through 2040 and beyond

This will shore up falling revenues, but will not be enough. The second part of the answer is: augment revenues. How? The best way might be to get into the broadband ISP business. In an industry where new, nontraditional electricity service providers are expected to enter, playing defense is not enough.

EPB's service is more than 10 times faster than that typically provided by traditional ISPs for downloads and orders of magnitude faster for uploads. And EPB is not alone. Greenlight,[16] a municipal utility, offers gigabit ISP services in Wilson, North Carolina. Nevertheless, utilities in the ISP business are exceptional, and my argument is, this needs to change, for the utilities' benefit and survival.

Symmetric speeds allow new, *edge,* services of a kind we cannot yet fully imagine. For example, a personal and portable data center becomes possible; the *center* shifts to the edge of the network. What are the consequences? I think it is too early to tell, for we have never had a platform so powerful. The high-upstream speeds appeal to entrepreneurs contemplating new services.

In offering such ISP services, electric utilities likely enjoy a competitive advantage because incumbent ISPs might not easily match the built-from-scratch, yet incremental cost infrastructure. One outcome might be that the beleaguered electric distribution companies will become among the *growth* companies of the future.

The incumbent ISPs—cable and telephone companies such as Comcast, AT&T, Verizon, and perhaps Google Fiber—represent competition. By and large, they offer relatively slow, asymmetric, consumption-centric, unfriendly, and overpriced Internet access, bundled with telephone and entertainment services. With gigabit speeds, electric utilities can easily match the entertainment and telephone services of incumbents.

It is a commonplace of course that revolutions often come unannounced or are not promptly acknowledged as such. Two issues strike me as particularly salient regarding EPB's broadband: one, significance of *symmetric* broadband Internet service, and, two, the *optimum size* of operations for an electric utility combined with an ISP.

SYMMETRIC BROADBAND INTERNET SERVICE

One, symmetric broadband: the EPB broadband infrastructure, being symmetric, opens up service possibilities impossible with an asymmetric Internet, which intrinsically favors centralization of services; the symmetric version opens up uncharted opportunities for edge or customer-hosted services. The telephone and cable-based ISPs should have offered such speeds, but they have been tied to the *consumption* model of the Internet, the user as *downloader* and less as *uploader* or as *publisher*. That has favored a centralized Internet. This is against the grain of what the Internet truly is, a peer-to-peer mesh, a transactive and not a centralized, hierarchical network.

The data center as hosting site dominates over the edge computer as personal hosting site. The center of the cloud is "out there" and not in my office or bedroom. The *personal cloud* has not taken off, though we have edge storage. The step from *edge storage* to edge web hosting is not a big one. Yet ISPs and the centralized hosting paradigm have suppressed it. This is less a technical issue and more a business-model one.

Already, Internet access has been a liberating force worldwide. It can be more so with novel entrepreneurial initiatives. Today we live with the constraints of limited file sizes with email systems, and make do with Drop Box-like services when in fact we can easily have our personal and private, edge-hosted solutions on our laptops and smartphones, given Chattanooga-type access.

When I started my company, Circlelink, we needed high uplink speed because our product involved edge hosting. But in San Diego and in the Bay Area, we were lucky in mid-2005 to get a few mbps in the upstream direction. "Who can bet *against* increasing bandwidth?" said a colleague; we believed that speeds would keep increasing. When it did not happen, our venture was handicapped. We bet on symmetric broadband in people's homes in the United States by 2008, at least in some towns. In 2011, after keeping the business alive for a few years, I shut it down. Then along came EPB Fiber in Chattanooga.

If not the United States, why has some other nation not created the symmetric, bi-directional broadband Internet to enable next-generation broadband services? This is likely the case of *supply creates its own demand*, that is, if such rich broadband were available, people would begin to see the possibilities. The existence of supply allows the mind to think, imagining new services and then testing them. Otherwise we only run thought experiments. Public policy initiatives did not break this impasse; they might have, had we had visionary leadership. Then, suddenly, the launch of EPB broadband Internet has upended the *status quo*.

But do residential customers need symmetric gigabit service? Today, likely not. Some residential customers may greatly value *edge servers* in the interest of privacy, as Hillary Clinton did, and today they cannot get that—all privacy is vulnerable to the actions of data center managers, and the latter, in the interest of redundancy, replicate their data with other data centers. Further, we may not lump all residential customers under one category; some may value privacy more than others. We also need to consider business needs for privacy, and develop suitable business models.

Here are two excerpts from an interview with EPB's leadership.

Q: *Why does it matter for a residential customer to have faster service?*

A: *As a residential customer today, that don't make a huge amount of difference. You can download your Netflix movie a little bit quicker. The main difference today is for economic development purposes, you have companies that know more bandwidth is always helpful. Essentially what a gigabit service means is a bigger pipe and companies are always looking for a bigger pipe.*[17]

EPB presents the world with a test bed for next-generation technology. They have also democratized the Internet, made it more egalitarian. How did they do it?

Q: *How much did it cost and who paid for it?*

A: *We built our fiber optic network through 600 square miles, to every home and business. The fiber optic network did not just include the gig services. It also includes a "smart grid" (a home meter on steroids that sends data every 15 minutes about home energy usage.) Our total was roughly $320 million. We paid for it through one–third stimulus dollars and two–third bonding.*[18]

All electric utilities could do what EPB has done—offer symmetric broadband Internet to homes, small and large businesses, schools and colleges. As I argue throughout the book, they have no choice unless they wish to progressively lose market value, or become an acquisition target at a discount of an aggregator, a next-generation utility.

THE *OPTIMUM SIZE* OF OPERATIONS FOR AN ELECTRIC UTILITY COMBINED WITH AN ISP

Two, optimum size of operations: EPB raises the question whether a *municipality* ought to be the unit of study for future electricity or ISP services? After all, EPB serves a relatively small geography, and does not arguably have economies of scale.

Do economies of scale not matter anymore for unit price reduction? Can services under a relatively small geographical municipality be economical? In the emerging age of solar panels and batteries, demand drop, and eventual grid defection, and the rise of off-grid homes and communities, what is the *smallest* meaningful geographical unit for optimum economics?

Today's investor owned electric utilities in the United States cover vast geographies. In India, each state has its own electricity distribution company. And yet, in India close to 70 years since Independence, about 300 million people have no electricity access, and millions more have unreliable access. Clearly, the nation has failed in giving access to this most basic of empowering utility. Without electricity, we cannot have Internet access, and therefore, neither education nor participation in today's economy. The question arises: Are large geographies as service territories needed in the age of distributed generation? Should *districts* in India—over 675 as of 2014—be their own electric utilities? Should each district have several utilities? Or should even *panchayats*—over 230,000 of them—be the *unit of analysis,* that is, service territories for electricity services?[19]

In the United States during the mid-1990s, the nation was divided for wireless auctions into over 500 BTAs, and the rights to service provision distributed among bidders for that geography and corresponding spectrum. That is one way of dividing geography for service. In an article in *Renewable Energy World,* I argued that the United States could have as many electric utilities as supermarkets. Can a supermarket be a hub for solar panels, batteries, and more—just like a substation—for electricity provision? Or a cellular tower in a neighborhood?

This division and auctioning of geography, and the participation of thousands of players in the electricity and related services business is likely the way for releasing value and for the public good represented by both electricity and broadband symmetric Internet.

MUNICIPALIZATION AND COMMUNITY CHOICE AGGREGATION

With its franchise agreements with Xcel for electricity, and Centerpoint Energy for gas, expiring soon, Minneapolis, Minnesota, is reconsidering its role in service provision. Boulder, Colorado, has been trying to seize control of its electric utilities from Xcel for years. Hamburg, Germany, plans to buy back the energy grids it sold to Vattenfall over 20 years ago. But Hamburg is only one of dozens of German municipalities trying to regain control of their energy grids from private companies. We apparently have a global epidemic of municipalities seeking control of their utility and ISP operations.

A number of cities around the nation have recently formed utilities in order to create greater freedom in pursuing energy efficiency and renewable energy. Some cities have seen dramatic increase in their sourcing of renewable energy (over 50%

renewable energy in some cases) with declines in energy costs of up to 10% and dramatic investments in energy efficiency.[20]

Community choice aggregation (CCA), a parallel effort to municipalization,

> is a system adopted into law in the United States of Massachusetts, New York, Ohio, California, New Jersey, Rhode Island, and Illinois, which allows cities and counties to aggregate the buying power of individual customers within a defined jurisdiction in order to secure alternative energy supply contracts on a community-wide basis, but allowing consumers not wishing to participate to opt out. Also known as municipal aggregation, governmental aggregation, electricity aggregation, and community aggregation, CCAs now serve nearly 5% of Americans in over 1,300 municipalities as of 2014. CCA's are de facto public utilities of a new form that aggregate regional energy demand and negotiate with competitive suppliers and developers, rather than the traditional utility business model based on monopolizing energy supply.[21]

The scope of CCA as of now appears limited to electricity, and does not extend to ISP services.

THE INTERPLAY AMONG MUNICIPALITIES, ISPS, AND ELECTRICITY SERVICE PROVIDERS

Are municipalities as geographical service territories the best suited to deliver electricity and broadband Internet? Can a municipality offer either electricity or broadband, but not both? Is a municipality the *right size* for offering such services, or can the unit for deploying electricity—and broadband—be smaller, say, the size of an office building or campus or home owners' association? Even when municipalities are not fully into the ISP business, many nevertheless offer Wi-Fi hot spots in key locations. Clearly, the Internet is not simply a subscription service but also a public good, and useful for attracting businesses and encouraging economic activity.

Investor owned utilities and transmission companies also are in a position to launch their broadband services. Today, they focus on the wholesale of their fiber-optic infrastructure; little stops them eventually from extending into residential and business services, especially as ISPs and others enter into electricity space, and begin to snip away at their revenues.

The electric utilities have a longer history than ISPs. When the market cannot provide a service economically, regulations help spread the service through cost averaging, or through Universal Service Funds, as was the case with telephone services. Sometimes, the administrative jurisdictions undertake the provision of the needed service themselves. The options for municipalities, as ISPs and electric utilities, are shown in Figures 8.3 and 8.4.

Figure 8.3   Municipalities in Electricity and/or ISP Business

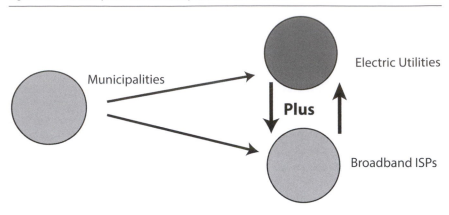

Figure 8.4   Municipalities: Neither in Electricity Nor ISP Business

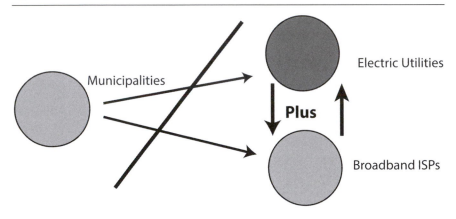

Thus, it makes sense that some municipalities have historically been electric utilities. Then, as industries evolve, and the Internet and the smart grid intersect with new generation technologies like solar and wind, new service possibilities emerge. This was the case with EPB. More commonly, the electricity and Internet services are offered by distinct, yet similarly-regulated companies as shown in Figure 8.4.

What Berlin and Boulder are trying to do is to take back electricity services from their franchisees; the municipality wishes to become an electric utility. And like EPB in Chattanooga, Tennessee, they may later choose to become ISPs.

When a municipality is neither in the ISP business nor an electric utility, but is considering entering into either domain, we have Figure 8.4. The municipality has a choice regarding what to do and in what sequence. It may (a) do nothing, which is to say, it will let the market decide who offers electricity, and who broadband services, (b) first become an electric utility, or an ISP, and (c) and then do the other.

This ongoing trend of *municipalization* is in fact a part of the larger industrial restructuring among electricity, the Internet, and ICT, or information and communications technologies. The electricity industry, thanks to distributed generation, and *local generation, local consumption,* allows for smaller and smaller, yet economical, service territories even at the level of an individual home, a street, a building, or a campus—in other words, microgrids.

But that is not all; the industry is also fragmenting into niche though large *product-markets,* that is, a *street lighting* company, a *traffic lights* company, a *solar-powered agricultural water pumps* company, and so forth, as described in Chapter 7. It appears equally feasible for a home of the future to have a *DC grid* or a *DC microgrid* powered by solar panels and batteries for electronic appliances and a regular AC grid with solar panels and inverters.

WHAT BUSINESS ARE ELECTRIC UTILITIES IN? OR, WHY CONSIDER THE ISP BUSINESS AT ALL

It is clear that electric utilities will lose demand, and thereby revenue, in mature economies, due to appliance efficiencies, some substitution due to solar deployment, and some substitution due to defection, as shown in Figure 6.1. Sure, electric charging for automobiles will offset some of this loss. Nevertheless, it is unclear as to whether the new demand will offset all the losses. It is therefore important for electric utilities to revisit the question: "What business are we in?" and include in their answer, "ISP business too."

Besides offering ISP services, and connecting their network to a cluster of microgrids, should electric utilities get into the home and building energy management business? Electric vehicle charging? Security services? Charge by value delivered—comfort, heating, cooling, motion, and not by kWh? Generally, to all these questions, the answer is "Yes"; the timing of market entry remains an issue. The other question is: *How* to enter these businesses? By organic internal growth? Or thorough acquisitions?

Service providers necessarily have to go inside premises. As the industry fractures into *product-market-location* segments, and as generation and consumption are colocated, the electricity generational attributes of a parcel of land or real estate needs to be accounted for simultaneously with its revenue potential in evaluating the electricity service infrastructure of the future.

Even in developed markets, electricity needs have not diminished; hardly that; it is simply that the demand can be more efficiently met through a host of technologies, and the traditional measure of electricity use—kilowatt-hour—is unable to capture the value of the services delivered, adequately. Raw electricity demand growth only exists in emerging markets, where per capita consumption is low, and where electricity use patterns have not differentiated sufficiently—India, China, and the developing nations of Africa.

MICROGRID ELECTRICITY: BEYOND ISPs

Should electric utilities get into microgrids? Of course, given that with solar panels and inexpensive batteries, costs of production might become lower than for coal-based or thermal power. But even if they get into these businesses, the new revenues may not be enough to avoid overall revenue decline, share erosion, and customer defection. Entry into the new businesses is necessary but not sufficient for their financial health.

Not only are barriers to entry in the electricity business falling, but also every business now is a potential electricity generator, at least a partial owner of their own *captive* power. Competition is here. With local generation and local consumption, there are no transmission losses, and less likelihood of electricity theft, as often happens in emerging markets.

From an ISP services delivery point of view, are microgrids necessary, for delivering a combined electricity and ISP solution? It is possible to create ISP services under the umbrella of an electric utility *without* microgrids, and with the present electricity network topology. To the extent a cellular tower fed by fiber-optic cable is colocated with the corresponding substation, the substation's serving area represents a microgrid for both Internet access and electricity. My expectation is that microgrids will be a reality for reasons of electricity infrastructure optimization alone. They are likely a component of a transactive, cooperative network topology of the future, as shown in Figures 2.4 and 5.2.

What might be the economics of a solution that includes both electricity supply and ISP services? In the upper middle class neighborhood of Chapter 3—a homeowners' association of about 120 homes, each home between 2,500 and 4,000 sq. ft., with 15 percent of homes having swimming pools and spas, and 10 percent homes having electric vehicles—what would happen should the electric utility offer ISP services of the EPB kind, 1 gbps symmetric, at say, $70/month? Let us assume a take rate of 30 percent in three years. The aggregate economics of both electricity services plus ISP services would make for compelling financial results as suggested by Figure 8.2.

Consider the following: let the electricity supply be based on a microgrid, with its solar panels, batteries, diesel generator, inverters, and other equipment located at the substation serving the 120 households. What then is the economics of such a combined microgrids and ISP solution? We really do not know.

At IIM, we modeled such a homeowners' association solution, and developed at least part of the solution, as described in Chapter 3. We found that by using a combination of solar panels, batteries, and diesel/gas generators, and nominal prices available on the Internet, we were able to achieve a price per unit of approximately $0.20, below the average per unit price of the grid electricity prices for that neighborhood. In essence, we have an economically viable substitute for the grid in select markets. We expect the costs to drop with volume discounts, advances in technology, and optimization of generation sources deployment.

Now if we colocate a telecom hub at the substation, in addition to the solar panels and batteries, how much would be the incremental capital cost, and what fraction of this relatively well-off neighborhood would subscribe to the 1 gig upstream and downstream service? No one has done this calculation, but it ought to be done.

WHAT BUSINESS ARE WE IN?

In "Marketing Myopia," a celebrated 1960 article in *Harvard Business Review,* Theodore Levitt wrote, "The railroads did not stop growing because the need for passenger and freight transportation declined. That grew. The railroads are in trouble today not because that need was filled by others (cars, trucks, airplanes, and even telephones) but because it was not filled by the railroads themselves. They let others take customers away from them because they assumed themselves to be in the railroad business rather than in the transportation business. The reason they defined their industry incorrectly was that they were railroad oriented instead of transportation oriented; they were product oriented."

Electric utilities may no longer define their business based on generation technologies—coal, nuclear, diesel, hydro, even wind or solar or fuel cells—as is historically done. When solar panels are *utility scale* and feed the grid, they may be regarded as just another fuel equivalent. Even large wind farms similarly belong within the existing paradigm. Rooftop solar panels, on the customer side of the meter—and which serves as a demarcation point—challenge the utilities' business model. Utilities typically have limited exposure to, and no control over, operations on customer premises for historical and regulatory reasons. And yet the competitive threat originates from the other side of the meter, from traditional customers, who in effect bypass the electricity infrastructure of today, in kW sized chunks, one home at a time. This is qualitatively the equivalent of mobile phones in the time of wireless or landline telephony.

In emerging markets where access to both electricity and the Internet is limited, electrification and Internet deployment programs have typically been distinct and placed under different ministries. A common infrastructure may now serve both needs. Opportunities exist to leapfrog old paradigms and simultaneously provide both electricity and Internet access quickly and cleanly.

To the strategy question, "What business are we in?" utilities may not only answer "electricity;" they are equally, at least, in the next-generation ISP business. Not acting on this prospect may be harmful to their business health.

WHAT DIRECTION TO PURSUE? CHOOSING AMONG BUSINESS AS USUAL, MICROGRIDS, AND ISP

For electric utilities, the choices may be mapped along three dimensions as follows—toward microgrids, toward ISP services, or business as usual (BAU). Of course, there would be overlapping areas, and IOUs are likely to do a combination of the three. My conjecture is that the pursuit of ISP services by dividing the service territory into microgrid-sized chunks might be the optimum approach. Where might the microgrids be centered? At substations, as shown in Figure 8.1. Should electric utilities get into microgrids? Yes. But the point is not *microgrids* per se as a part of the electric utility of the future; that is of course necessary. Rather, the question to answer might be: What is the best network topology for both electricity services and broadband ISP? And simultaneously, what value-added services beyond access to electricity and broadband do we provide? On our own, and in partnership?

In Figure 8.5, I have shown a traditional distribution utility facing three choices: (1) Continue as if little has changed in the industry and follow the Business as Usual route. This would include normal business strategies of consolidation and growth, in a traditional regulatory context, such as what Exelon-Pepco have done. (2) Enter into the microgrids business, as shown on the X-axis, and this would include creating their own microgrids, integrated with the grid, in select locations within their franchise territory, perhaps even outside their franchise territories. (3) Enter the ISP business, as shown on the Y-axis. It is an open question whether microgrids should precede entry into the ISP business, or the other way around. My view is: Should an investor owned utility stay on the BAU path, they will progressively lose value, through substitution, demand loss, and eventually grid defection. And much

Figure 8.5   Toward Broadband, Microgrids, or Both

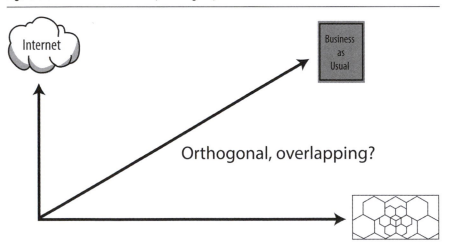

before there are meaningful losses of this kind, the utility will take a hit in the financial market. The equity analysts will see the writing on the wall (or roofs), and convert the Hold or Buy rating to Sell.

At least four forces are at work. One, *integration*—backward and forward, that is, services extending forward into customer premises, beyond the meter, and also the backward integration of renewable energy technologies on the generation side. The electric meter may no longer be regarded as the point of demarcation between utility services and the customer. Why? First, because the entire renewable generation can be on the other, *customer side* of the meter, and the electricity generated may not pass through the meter at all.

Two, *substitution,* from fossil-fuel-based generation to solar panel-based generation, batteries, wind turbines, and so forth, working collaboratively, and integrated into microgrids. One form of generation is being replaced by another; cleaner, smaller, and cheaper.

Three, *differentiation.* Instead of selling a commodity product, the utility can now *fractionate,* and offer a host of services, unbounded by geography or service territories, and represented by each cell of the product-market-location matrix.

Four, perhaps most important, the incumbent utilities face the option of *diversifying,* given that the industry is at an inflection point, and new strategic choices have to be made if the business does not want to shrink due to loss of demand. Typically, such an inflection point as shown in Figure 5.1 presents a take-off opportunity to launch a new "S" curve for a business, either through new business development, or through inorganic yet strategically complementary growth.

Offering broadband with symmetric data speeds, appears a good first step. Certainly, this appears to be a better option than consolidation, mergers and acquisitions, and related cost cutting, as is happening with Exelon–Pepco, among others. At best, consolidation buys time.

PARTNERS FOR ELECTRIC UTILITIES AS ISPs

Who might partner with an electric utility getting into the ISP business with the bidirectional bandwidth proposed here? Might it be Skype, who as a service provider needs bidirectional but not too much bandwidth? Netflix? At least in today's incarnation, it largely needs asymmetric bandwidth mostly in the downward or toward -the-customer direction. Might it be Amazon? Should municipalities be partners in the creation of such novel services? Time will tell, for the industry stands poised to expand in novel directions.

The broadband ISPs of tomorrow may not be wireline carriers alone—they may well be wireless providers, especially in emerging markets. They may not be traditional telecom providers either, nor even electricity providers. The so-called over-the-top applications providers, a Facebook or Google, may go down the seven layer OSI stack, incorporate physical assets, and become an integrated and transparent *all-layer* service provider, including an ISP. The connectivity may not be via the cellular infrastructure alone—Wi-Fi deployments create coverage pockets competing with traditional cellular voice and data services. Finally, as already discussed, municipalities are getting into the electricity and Internet space.

ICTTE: CONVERGENCE OF ICT, TRANSPORT, AND ELECTRICITY INFRASTRUCTURES

We are familiar with the UN-created acronym ICT, describing both computing and telecommunications. The emphasis on *technologies* is puzzling and unfortunate because it focuses on the physical layer, and not applications or uses. I would rather the ITU had not drawn attention to the technologies, for they change—hardware, systems, equipment, cables, and pipes—and emphasized the benefits to customers instead that remain, independent of the underlying infrastructure. It might have been better to use ICU (information and communications *uses*) or ICA (information and communications *applications*) or ICS (information and communications *services*).

After all, language matters—it conjures up images; it elevates thought or lowers it, it binds or liberates. ICT appears to be a lazily coined acronym, and its use has stuck.

In recent years, along came the smart grid, where ICT was deployed as an overlay on the electricity grid. Electricity got paired with ICT as a result. Further, with electric cars, GPS navigation, satellite radio, and services such as OnStar, Transport got blended with ICT too. A better acronym for the future might be ICTTE, where the latter T and E respectively are Transport, including Mobility and Portability, and E represents Electricity or Energy.

Or, ICTTE could be replaced by ICATE (information and communications applications) plus transport and electricity. This acronym has the benefit of being at the layer 7—applications layer—of the OSI stack. It also is more comprehensive in that mobility, portability, and transport as well as electricity are included in its scope. The smartphone combines all of the ICTTE or ICATE elements, as does a Tesla, an electric vehicle that may be regarded as an obese smartphone on wheels.

Besides traditional uses of electricity—lighting, cooling, heating, and rotating in appliances—we now have electric cars. Of course, we've always had electricity for transport, in railways and subways, but that was electricity tapped from a static infrastructure. Now we carry our electricity with us in cars, like gasoline equivalent but without any direct use of fossil fuel. And the car is a part of ICT infrastructure too through GPS and mobile 3G/4G technologies. An ICT infrastructure that tracks cars is no different from the ICT infrastructure for the smart grid. Cars with their ICT grid and the electricity infrastructure with its ICT grid are a part of the *same* intermingled infrastructure. That is, we have an *overlap* of electricity and transport, with ICT undergirding both as substrate. Or we may say this is *convergence* of ICT, electricity, and transport infrastructures.For those who manage ICT networks, both transport and electricity are *verticals* or *segments* to be managed. Thus, ICT companies can expand into both transport and electricity verticals.

One may say: this is the IoT. This is M2M communications too. But that is inadequate, and unfortunate, for that description is also at the physical layer. To capture the new intermingling, we can no longer use the acronym ICT alone; we need to include transport and electricity, and include applications, and thus ICATE is better.

In Figure 8.6, I show the interplay among traditional ICT—Information and Communications Technologies—and two new additions that contribute to a hybrid new infrastructure taking shape—T for Transport and E for next generation, distributed Electricity.

But there is more happening, both on infrastructure side, and also with electricity differentiation. For instance, the new electricity with distributed generation and renewables is no longer your father's or grandfather's electricity. In solar generation, nothing moves or rotates, and there are no magnets to generate

Figure 8.6   ICTTE, or the Enernet of Things (EoT)

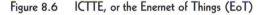

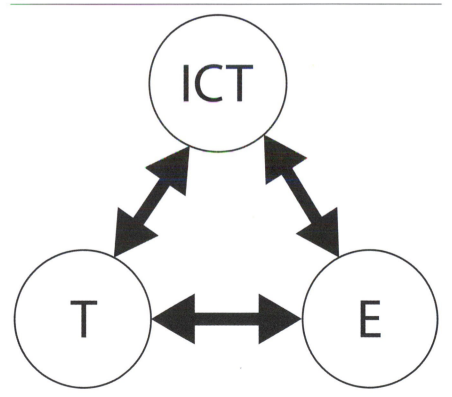

electricity. Solar panels are in fact silicon-based much like the innards of the ICT infrastructure—doped or painted sand, in fact. The new solar electricity appears to naturally complement batteries, too, that also produce electricity without any rotation or motion.

On the electricity *differentiation* front, we can parse electricity as never done before. For instance, we can create a parallel and overlay DC infrastructure for electronic appliances like music systems or computers, phones, and laptops. Such a DC network would work easily enough using solar plus battery, at low voltages. Instead of the traditional power plug, such a network would consist of USB plugs everywhere. Such USB plugs would charge phones, power home entertainment and stereo equipment and TVs, allow LED lighting, and power home sprinkler systems. Such use of a DC overlay may be regarded as a distinct *product* for a set of distinct *applications* or market. The grid electricity may continue to power refrigerators, air-conditioning, heating appliances, and continue to charge electric automobiles, another distinct *product-market.* Are there business incentives for someone to splinter the traditional electricity distribution in the home, and elsewhere? Cost savings, superior new applications, resilience, reliability, local autonomy, and control may be among reasons driving such developments.

When convergence was last discussed, it was in reference to telecommunications—convergence of networks, wireless and landline, voice and entertainment; convergence on the phone screen where many applications from different networks and servers came together. All that has in fact happened, but we do not call it convergence with any wonder or awe any more. Convergence once had the aura of offering conceptual completeness in an otherwise colliding world. But the concept lacked fundamental, intrinsic rigor, and it fell by the wayside. Regardless, the convergence was broadly within the telecommunications industry.

This new convergence of electricity, transport, and ICT is the comingling of *distinct* industries; industry *structure* change on a grand scale, resulting in awe-inspiring industrial mutation. Classic industry boundaries are becoming porous and are fusing with each other. Further, in electricity, larger is no longer cheaper—economies of scale matter less. Anyone can be in the electricity production business easily.

What about the traditional electricity business defined by generation technologies—thermal and geothermal, nuclear, hydro? Those classifications no longer hold. The paradigm of fossil fuel burning to generate steam, and then pushing that steam through turbine blades to turn a rotor within magnets, that electricity is so yesterday.

Electric utilities are in the broadband ISP business, as illustrated by EPB in Chattanooga, TN, and discussed in these pages. The converse may also be true. For industries such as ICT, residential buildings and industrial construction, and transport—roads and railways, perhaps others, it might be proper to ask the question: Are we also in the electricity business?

Do electric utilities buy telecom companies, or do Internet companies buy electric utilities? Do electric utilities collaborate or compete with telecom carriers like Comcast and today's AT&T, Google, and as yet unknown Internet or entertainment companies? Will the energy industry drive broadband or broadband drive Electricity 2.0? Will over the top and application layer companies buy physical layer companies, or the physical layer companies enter application and network layer businesses? I do not think we have a good grip on what is happening with any analytical or conceptual clarity—it is a brave new world.

NINE

Functional, Therefore Dysfunctional, Business Schools

[T]he whole thrust of academia is one that values education, in my opinion, in inverse ratio to its usefulness—and what you write in inverse relationship to its understandability.

—Gloria Steinem

A CASE FOR BUSINESS RELEVANCE: MISSING AT THE TRANSFORMATIVE EDGE

For business schools to remain relevant, in their curriculum and research, they must strive to understand the industry structure attributes and the dynamics of numerous industries. Nowhere is this need illustrated more clearly than in the emerging hybrid industry comprising electricity, ICT (information and communications technologies, or Internet), and transport. The colliding industries fuse traditional industry boundaries and permit new combinations and business models, yet this dynamism has poor representation in business schools. Nor do business schools offer tools to interpret the metamorphosis— the melting and reforming of the emerging megaindustrial system. The issues of adequately understanding and addressing emissions-related climate change and concepts like *sustainability* are further complicated when they have to be understood for their business implications; after all, electricity and transport industries are the major contributors, around 80 percent, of all global CO_2 emissions.

The shortcomings of traditional business school structures, primarily functionally organized departments, are manifest most while teaching integrative courses such as strategy and entrepreneurship, where actions at the edges—at inflection points—need to be addressed head-on as strategic business choices. This chapter proposes that industry verticals should be better represented in business schools, beyond occasional *centers* and case studies. Functionally organized and remarkably similar in their structures across nations, business schools have insulated themselves into irrelevance when it comes to addressing the critical issues of our times, particularly energy related business issues. Introducing domain knowledge of industry verticals into business schools will permit them to specialize and differentiate among themselves, to bring them in accord with the driving forces shaping our world. The situation for business schools is worse, for even industry boundaries are becoming porous and intermingling with each other, for instance, telecom and electricity, or electricity and transport, and thus including traditional industry verticals in the business school curriculum is not enough.

LIMITS OF FUNCTIONAL ORGANIZATION: CURIOUS CASE OF STRATEGY AND ENTREPRENEURSHIP

Business school faculties are organized around *business functions*—finance, accounting, operations, human resources management, marketing, and information technologies. There also exist supportive courses, including economics, sociology, and business history, for instance, broadly clubbed under *humanities*. However, two topics typically covered in the curriculum—strategy, which used to be called *business policy,* and entrepreneurship are *integrative* and not functional. Strategy and entrepreneurship presume basic knowledge of the functional disciplines.

In an MBA curriculum, they are taught in the third semester or later, once the functional fundamentals are addressed. While strategy is compulsory, entrepreneurship is generally an elective. One may argue: strategy departments exist in corporations. Is that not therefore a function? Not really because there is more art and interpretation in it than received *how-to* knowledge, unlike in, say, accounting, finance, or operations. Strategy and entrepreneurship demand a holistic view. The *unit of analysis* for strategy is the entire corporation or the business unit. Typically, the strategy of a company needs to be formulated in relationship to its industry context.

Of course, strategy *implementation* involves functional skills—planning, budgeting, and the use of tools such as the balanced scorecard. Strategy *formulation,* however, belongs to a qualitatively different realm, requiring synthesis, creativity, and interpretation of the industry structure, especially during times of change, and thereafter the definition of the goals and objectives of the company, and is often followed by investment decisions.

The emerging electricity industry is among the most dynamic right now. What tools aid in the interpretation of the environment characterized by technological advances in solar, wind, and batteries? Or consider other awe-inspiring changes in the industry in Box 9.1. No amount of functional knowledge can measure up to this task of exploring the implications of these changes, unless accompanied by specific industry knowledge, including knowledge about changes in technology, business models, and regulations. Blithe analysis, based on an industry overview, as often offered in case studies in business schools, or a cursory study will not do. Because the logic of the industry context requires both domain knowledge and its interpretation, I believe the functionally organized business schools do not, and cannot, fully deliver on their promise; in part, they fail in their educational mission.

In Figure 9.1, I show that in matters electricity, whereas policy issues, technology issues, and issues of climate change and sustainability are well addressed, there is a curious absence of business issues. The players are regulated monopolies after all, and business issues were either simple or did not merit particular attention, at least in the past. Now with reduced barriers to entry, end of natural monopoly, and economies of scale no longer needed for low unit cost of electricity, the situation has changed. Entrepreneurial startups and other new entrants in electricity are stakeholders too. New market entry, besides the traditional performance metrics of reliability, resilience, security, customer service and affordability, is in the public interest. Business issues thus come to the fore in the electricity business as never before.

Box 9.1 Issues in Next-Generation Electricity

- Consequences of two-way electricity flows
- *Cluster of microgrids,* as a honeycomb or as fractals, as the topology of the grid of the future
- Superposition of electricity and information architectures
- Reduced barriers to entry and the end of natural monopoly
- Proliferation of distributed generation
- Irrelevance of economies of scale in affordable electricity production
- Entrepreneurial opportunities resulting from grid-independent electricity
- Rise of electric cars; possible decline in internal combustion engine (ICE) cars
- Interplay among electric cars, electricity production, peak power consumption, and an infrastructure of charging stations spread about like gas stations

Figure 9.1   Electricity: Policy, Technology, and Sustainability, But No Business

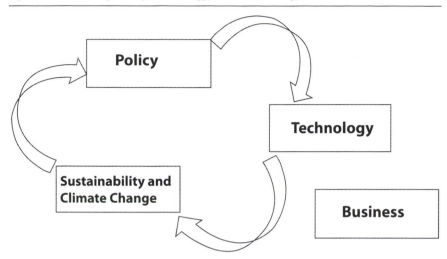

INDUSTRIES, NOT FUNCTIONS

Should business schools therefore create *electricity, transport, petrochemicals,* or *mining* departments to address industry-specific issues, distinct from engineering and sciences? The question appears rhetorical. Yet we have the *finance* and *information systems* industries represented as business departments. Within *marketing* we do have significant representation of the *consumer retail* industry, the so-called FMCG—fast-moving consumer goods. Then why do we not have *energy* or *energy and the environment* as a department too?

Rewards and accolades flow in functional silos in business schools. The journals are functional too. Traditional academic boundaries in business schools do not accommodate cross-disciplinary efforts easily. Even though critical social, policy, and leadership issues require strategic interpretation, and therefore more than functional skills like accounting, marketing, and finance, such skills earn little explicit recognition for faculty—the highly rated journals have no industry associated with them. Of course, the corollary is: Students graduating from business schools, mostly trained in functions and tools of analysis, have to undergo a whole lot of domain specific learning on the job, related to the industry they join.

Note that outlets for the *energy + environment* or *energy + transport* themes do not exist among business journals. No one quite understands the *economics of microgrids* as yet, for instance, and if we did develop this understanding, it is unclear as to whether we would publish the results in an economics journal, a business journal, or an operations research journal.

Consider the new grid topology comprising of a cluster of microgrids, as a honeycomb or as fractals, an astonishing metamorphosis of the grid as we know it, with profound business implications. Where would we publish such work on microgrids? What set of reviewers could assess the merit of such submissions? Where can we write about industry structure issues resulting from distributed generation or entrepreneurial opportunities resulting from grid-independent electricity and the many issues listed in Box 9.1?

There is a more fundamental problem. Even if there existed journals and competent reviewers, the time cycle of publications, typically surpassing a year, may make the results of that work obsolete by the time they appear in print; the industry moves too fast. To address the issues besetting any fast-moving industry, we require the time cycle of trade magazines, even newspapers, not academic journals. Academia gives little credence to the trade press. Even if new knowledge is generated—the avowed purpose of academic research—the material, as far as the industry is concerned, may be dead on arrival should we wait for academic journals.

Consider the telecommunications industry—wireless and Internet. It underwent massive restructuring with little acknowledgement of that transformation by the business school academic community. The entire paging industry disappeared without business schools making note of it. Both telecom, and more broadly the ICT, and the energy industries, including electricity, play a huge role in the economy, and their evolution has not stopped. For instance, the Internet of things (IoT) opportunity is expected to surpass $19 trillion,[1] according to Cisco. Both electricity and telecommunications would benefit from academic scrutiny, should it happen. Yet one would not know of the seismic changes in these industries by scanning any business journal.

In the emerging electricity industry, are there *policy* journals? Yes, there are. *Technology* journals? Yes. *Business, management,* or *strategy* journals? Practically none. Business school faculty members are thus unable to pursue any career objectives—publications in highly rated journals—through an emphasis on electricity, energy, environment, climate change, and, in general, sustainability issues. The net result: the world of practice and its needs go unaddressed. Year after year, presidents of the Academy of Management wring their hands and bemoan the absence of *relevance* in business research. And yet no proposal to address the absence has gained traction.

Things cannot be otherwise, given that business school *structures* are ill suited to address the practical and problem-solving requirements of business and of public policy makers in an interconnected and converging world. Industry problems, however, cannot wait—consultants offer domain-specific expertise coupled with functional capabilities. The latter being generic and relatively time independent have value as training, but not as useful, timely, and problem-solving advice. By its structure, its incentive mechanisms, and its time cycles, academia has relegated itself to irrelevance as regards the urgent and important energy-related business issues.

WORSE FOR ENTREPRENEURSHIP

If business schools face challenges in addressing *strategy formulation,* the situation worsens for teaching and research in entrepreneurship. Should business schools presume the existence of companies or firms? Entrepreneurs *create* organizations; thus we may not presume their existence. How do business schools address the nebulous, invisible force field that is the womb of new organizations? In a word: poorly.

Entrepreneurship classes typically focus on the writing of business plans that are truly *integrative*—they address functional disciplines and also require the cogent expression of the business idea. Professors and students can wrap their arms around it. However, business plan writing is among the later steps in new venture creation—a whole lot of invisible steps precede it, the stuff of nascent entrepreneurship. This phase involves the interpretation of the environment—the industry structure and technical changes in it—that helps jell the opportunity for an entrepreneur. Prospective entrepreneurs expend enormous energy, frequently for years, engaged in the interpretation and deciphering of the often intangible context of their start-up.

The metamorphic changes in next-generation electricity throw up numerous entrepreneurial opportunities. Innovations are bunching together at an accelerated pace, as written by Schumpeter, characterizing the rise, perhaps birth, of a new industry in the crucible of the present.[2] What tools do business schools offer to interpret these trends?

A special issue of *Entrepreneurship Theory and Practice* (ET&P)[3] journal, April 2016, addressed this issue in part by focusing on "the underlying mechanisms through which the *industrial sector shapes entrepreneurial phenomena* [emphasis added] and the 'bottom-up' processes through which individuals, organizations and industries interact in creating, discovering and exploiting entrepreneurial opportunities [which remain] largely under-theorized and little understood." While timely, a similar initiative ought also to be undertaken by the strategy community.

NEED TO FOCUS ON INDUSTRY STRUCTURE

The industry structure changes imminent in the converging electricity and transport industries, particularly the advent of the electric car, have little scholarly recognition in business schools. Tesla's visibility and prominence is helping to change this through cases, but the industry structure implications remain unaddressed in meaningful frameworks. Given the momentous changes, one would expect the strategy departments to focus on it. They do not; their acknowledgment of these transformations takes the form of *sustainability* or *climate change,* as topics in some classes, a dubious conceptualization at best. What does, or will, sustainability education enable the student do after graduation? What is the action verb associated with it, and what kinds of projects? A tough set of *actionable* problems does exist—see Box 9.2. However, they are cloaked under this unfortunate word and yet might remain unaddressed at the end of a course on sustainability.

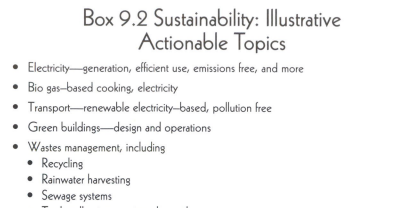

Box 9.2 Sustainability: Illustrative Actionable Topics

- Electricity—generation, efficient use, emissions free, and more
- Bio gas–based cooking, electricity
- Transport—renewable electricity–based, pollution free
- Green buildings—design and operations
- Wastes management, including
  - Recycling
  - Rainwater harvesting
  - Sewage systems
  - Trash collection, sorting, disposal

Figure 9.2   Industry-Specific Content Practically Absent in Business Schools

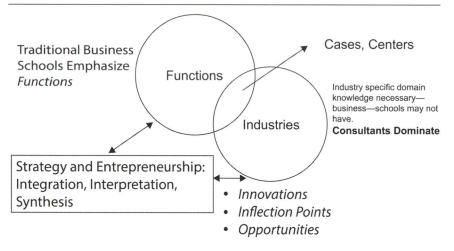

In Figure 9.2, I show how business functions, the focus of business schools, typically find little intersection with industry verticals. The intersection between "functions" and "industries" is shown to be small. Sometimes business schools have centers for the study of select industry topics, such as transportation and logistics, or information systems. More commonly, in schools where case studies are used as a tool for instruction, cases have elaborate descriptions of industries, and challenges facing the protagonists in particular companies in that industry as it evolves. Other than that, even in integrative courses such as strategy or entrepreneurship, there is little industry specific content. As a result, business schools go about their work indifferent to the pressing issues of our times in particular industries. Looking at the business school curriculum in even the most famous schools and universities, you would not know that there is global warming leading to climate change, or that COP 21 happened in Paris, December 2015. Neither the business opportunities nor threats resulting from these developments find credible expression in business schools.

Another way of looking at the situation in Figure 9.2 is to suggest that "industries" remain the focus on consulting companies, who try to solve pressing industry problems, whereas the functional problems—generic, commonplace, and requiring no particular industry domain knowledge—are apportioned for the business schools to address. Naturally, the profitability of the work of consultants is greater.

Sustainability originates from *sustainable development,* first described in the Brundtland Report as "development that meets the needs of the present without compromising the ability of future generations to meet their own needs."[4] The origins of the phrase appear reasonable when conceived, but today, instead of focusing on *development,* which is a continuing need, the adjective that qualified it, *sustainable,* has usurped all attention in the form of the abstract noun, *sustainability.* Further, it has now been paired with *climate change,* another fashionable undertaking offering politicians and climate scientists a forum for hand wringing.

Sustainability- and climate change–related decisions must translate into business initiatives for meaningful impact. Yet how can this happen without business schools and businesspersons playing their part, for instance, in defining relevant investment-grade options for existing companies, or business plans by start-ups? Thus, one of the most critical, existential issues of our times finds little place in business education; the fashionable new terms damage the causes they seek to serve.

Interestingly, even should the word survive public vetting, sustainability content, whatever it is, also crosses traditional functional boundaries of, say, finance, marketing, accounting, and operations. How then should such content be addressed in business schools and through what academic journals and trade press publications? I have chosen to write in *Renewable Energy World,* and several of my articles are listed in Appendix III. Also listed in Appendix II is the course outline of an MBA class I designed, "Strategic Management of Energy Systems," that the IIMK faculty body approved for teaching starting 2016, the first of its kind.

NEITHER CENTERS NOR CASES TO THE RESCUE

As I said before, business schools sometimes create centers for the study of special topics that do not neatly fit into traditional academic disciplines. Even that has not happened with renewable energy and electric transport—cars, motorcycles, and their charging ecosystem. Fundamental questions remain unaddressed: What is the new public interest in electricity? Is it still offering reliable, resilient, and affordable electricity, or is it in new market entry as well?

When the *case method* is used for instruction, as is frequent in business schools, the case writers often describe in detail both the industry context and the particular problem a protagonist of a business faces in his or her company. This might be about the only way business schools bring industry detail in their pedagogy. Needless to say, while helpful, it is hardly sufficient.

One expects business schools to offer guidance to students and industry, by writing articles on open-ended, timely issues; by consulting; and by including novel topics in the curriculum. But business schools are remarkably unaware about the opportunities for bold strategy making, for entrepreneurship, and for anticipating and critically examining industry structure changes that the renewable energy revolution is poised to bring about. How can business research be relevant if the faculty do not engage in addressing once-in-a-hundred-years kind of changes occurring today? The times are at least as momentous as the deployment of electricity distribution systems for the first time in the 1900s.

INVITING INDUSTRY INTO BUSINESS SCHOOLS

Among the new business schools being established worldwide, will some be organized along industry verticals, including a department for energy? For the Internet? For communications on the move? For interconnected infrastructures? For disease studies? For poverty reduction?

I am not arguing for exclusively industry-centric schools, for instance, a school for *petroleum* or *electricity* studies—they do exist in pockets—as they would tend to be more technology oriented and less business schools. But what I am proposing is bringing into traditional business schools—all eerily uniform—a far greater focus on select industry verticals, more than merely a center or two. Perhaps such centers can collaborate with incubation centers that may be housed in the same business school or a neighboring engineering school. A business house may fund such centers, perhaps in partnership with government agencies or ministries. The advisory board of such research and incubation centers may have stakeholders including investment funds, businesses, environment-related NGOs, and faculty from business and technical research. The research output of such centers must include business, technical, and financial analyses. The Tata Center for Technology and Design,[5] founded in 2012, appears a step in the right direction, though not focused on business models or energy issues alone.

In Figure 9.3, similar to Figure 9.2, shows "industries" with a greater presence in the scope of work of business schools. Depending on what industries a business school focuses on will enable it to differentiate itself from other business schools. While helpful, such progress would be necessary yet not sufficient as it related to energy. This is because the scope of "energy" transcends traditional industry boundaries, and will include "electricity," "transport," and "battery and storage" industry verticals, besides "information technologies." I have argued in *Renewable Energy World* that including "sustainability" in the curriculum does not do justice to what is needed.[6]

Figure 9.3   Functional, Therefore Dysfunctional, Business Schools

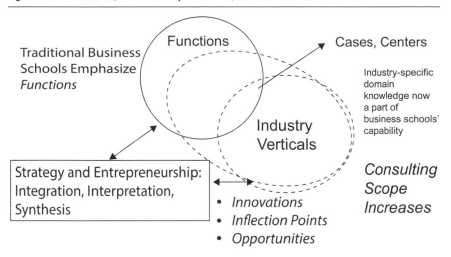

Clearly, not all schools can focus on all industry verticals; business schools will specialize. And that should be a welcome development, since it will contribute to distinctions among business schools, based on the industry verticals they emphasize, which is lacking today. The relative importance of each industry vertical would vary over time too. Specializations by industry verticals will make room for industry experts in academia, adding to research relevance. Research relevance will also increase when faculty have the opportunity to address real-life problems, with methods appropriate to the challenges at hand.

TEN

Wrapping Up: Microgrids Everywhere

If you can dream it, you can do it.

—Dhirubhai H. Ambani

Among the benefits of working at IIM, one is that executives from different industries and companies come to the campus to participate in Management Development Programs (MDPs). When I heard that senior officials of Punjab State Electricity Board were going to be on campus for a week, I offered to teach them a class on Electricity 2.0.

How would they react to the propositions of this book: that the industry would break into distinct *product-markets*? Or that small-sized service territory would be more appropriate in the future, given that economics of numbers matters more than economies of scale? Or that barriers to entry being low, neither large investments nor heavy regulations are necessary; many new entrants will participate in the electricity business.

I have wanted to run these thoughts by industry insiders. So I was excited. On a fine morning, I made my pitch and asked: "What do you think? Any questions?" A senior executive, a chief engineer of a district, offered: "Sir, you are talking all imaginary things. The industry does not work that way. This is not going to happen."

Fair enough, and not an unexpected answer. However, in response, another chief engineer, from a different district, spoke up: "Look, given today's approach, over 300 million have remained without electricity connection for 70 years. If this new approach works, I am all for trying out. It really is unacceptable that so many have no electricity."

All right, I said, "How about Punjab State Electricity Distribution Company entering the symmetric broadband ISP business? Just like EPB in Tennessee?"

That was perceived with great skepticism, too far out. I pressed further. I said, "Look, it may appear infeasible to split up the service territory into microgrid-sized chunks. But, how about the opposite? How about combining the service territories of Punjab, Haryana, Delhi, and Rajasthan into one contiguous service territory, under common management? Surely, there will be cost savings? Why should Kerala, Tamil Nadu, Karnataka not have a common management for distribution services? Could Maharashtra and Gujarat, or Maharashtra and Andhra Pradesh, be combined for operational efficiencies and cost savings?"

I continued: "If the distribution networks of different states were privatized, would not the private companies be interested in merging operations to achieve cost savings, and pass on some of the savings to customers? In the US, this is precisely what is happening. Exelon is merging with Pepco to achieve savings from combined operations, though the regulatory approvals are happening state by state."

We had reached tea break. No one surrounded me to press for further discussion, evidence I suppose that my propositions did not find favor with them.

A month earlier, at a similar MDP for the Powergrid Corporation of India, I discussed the classic strategy question: What business are you in? I presented the scenario where microgrids not only link with the macrogrid but also communicate and exchange—trade electricity, battery capacity, information, and other resources—among each other. Assuming this happens, I suggested, why do we need large, long-distance grids, except for select long-haul applications?

Electricity ought to be largely local—local generation, local consumption, and local autonomy and control. Will that diminish the role for Powergrid? We agreed it might. "What will you do about this?" I asked and suggested: Why should Powergrid not consider itself in the ISP business? In addition to the long-distance electricity transport business?

Similarly, I suggested, the Indian Railways, with its extensive network, may well regard itself as being not only in rail transport but also in the electricity and ISP business. Its extensive rights of way and its reach to remote corners of the nation make it an ideal player in telecom and renewable electricity too. Imagine solar panels all along the railway tracks, and on roofs of stations, with every station a hub for broadband services? Should the Ministry of Power, including new and renewable energy, and the Ministry of Railways be under a common leadership and a new ministry?

REACTIONARY FORCES

In December 2015, as I wrap up the book, the headline news in electricity circles is that David Crane has stepped down as CEO of NRG Energy. I have always regarded him as being among the more insightful and colorful CEOs in the U.S. electricity industry. Seeking an explanation why, I read that among comparable utility stocks, NRG's was the worst performing.

That may be, yet why has the fact not sunk in that *all* distribution utilities and independent power producers (IPPs)—the generating companies—will see falling revenues, progressive demand loss, and eventual customer defection, and therefore declining share prices? David Crane spoke candidly, perhaps to a fault, and did something about this emerging scenario, from acquisitions to restructuring. Given that the market fundamentals are stacked against traditional utilities, his company embraced distributed generation, electric car charging stations, and the microgrid business and worked on offering value-added home services. Thus, the stock market explanation, even if true, does not appear fully to explain why Crane has left. Should not his actions as CEO "cement" his position as leader, not only at NRG Energy, but also in the industry as a whole?

Normally I think what I do and express myself. Even so, in matters electricity, I wish to know: "What does David Crane think?" He has been my reference point for corroboration. I read what he writes, listen to his interviews, and seek out his speeches. When his opinions run along similar lines to mine, I feel relieved.

Utilities as investments no longer can be what they used to be. Perhaps Crane failed to explain this well to his shareholders and his board, or they buried their heads in sand. In any case, it appears that the investors are behaving more as "future takers" than 'future makers,' in the words of Jane Ambachtsheer. She writes, "All investors are "future takers" with regards to climate change in that each will be impacted by whatever climate scenario comes to pass"; however, "investors can take specific actions to make their investment portfolios more resilient. These investors can be described as 'future makers', an idea that has been endorsed up by a range of industry commentators."[1]

Despite the Crane episode at NRG, the writing on the roof is clear: investor-led and entrepreneurial-driven initiatives, plus the new business development efforts of a variety of existing companies in different industries, will transform the electricity business. The proposition of this book remains: the "sum of parts" valuations of traditional utilities—split up as microgrids or into *product-markets*—are greater than the value of the consolidated, monolithic utility as we have it. Market capitalizations, and therefore share prices, of traditional utilities, have necessarily to fall—NRG today, others in the relatively short-term future. What then do we do? Crane offered solutions that appear underappreciated; the messenger has become a victim.

The merger between Exelon and Pepco illustrates a second reactionary and therefore not a positive strategy. Since August 2015, when the DC PSC initially turned down the Exelon–Pepco merger, there has been a lot of back-and-forth about the pros and cons of the deal. In its essence, the merger appears as a strategy of *consolidation*. One can always wring out costs by combining two essentially similar entities. But the larger disruption looms—demand drop, distributed generation, and grid defection—thanks to technological advance. What strategy can counter that megatrend?

A third reactionary outcome is exemplified by what happened in Nevada, where as RMI[2] blog notes,

> Under the old rate structure, solar customers paid a fixed charge of $12.75
> a month (the same as nonsolar customers). Under the new structure, the

charge jumps to $17.90 a month in 2016, then increases by $5.15 each year until it reaches $38.51 a month in 2020. . . . Meanwhile, the rate that solar customers pay for grid-supplied power declines slightly from 10.8 cents per kWh in 2016 to 9.9 cents, while the rate they are paid for excess power delivered to the grid falls sharply from 9.2 cents to 2.6 cents, or from roughly the retail rate to the wholesale rate.

The result, write the authors, will accelerate the trend toward grid defection: "Policies that encourage grid defection may lead to a Balkanized grid in which thousands of customers simply generate and consume their own power, with increasing unit costs for any energy served by the existing grid."

But what the authors consider a negative—"Balkanized"—is in my view the nature of the grid of the future, a cluster of microgrids. In fact, this book recommends that such fragmentation ought to be encouraged by public policy and embraced by existing utilities, as widespread ownership by numerous electricity providers represents competition and is in the public interest.

A fourth illustration of reactionary forces at work comes from Dharnai, India. As already described in Chapter Four, this village had no electricity for decades, and therefore, Greenpeace India installed a small microgrid. Homes and streets got lights, and Greenpeace earned good press. Politicians visited the village. But not all residents were happy. Some said, "We want real electricity, not this fake one," as it does not support all applications, and the price is higher than grid electricity in neighboring villages. The result: the state electricity board did what it had not for decades; it extended the regular grid to Dharnai, effectively killing the renewables-based microgrid.[3]

The incumbent reactions in all these instances represent temporary "wins." It is only a matter of time before the performance parameters of the renewable solutions surpass the traditional grid. A far superior strategy would be to embrace the impending change, and for incumbent utilities to join the renewables revolution, expand into new *product-markets*, deploy microgrids, and explore the ISP option.

LET SLEEPING DOGS LIE?

"Why fix something that is not [seemingly] broken?" This thought likely holds back or delays action regarding renewables, especially in the developed economies. This partly explains their relatively slow growth, though the larger issue is likely the relative immaturity of technologies and the absence of bold public policies and institutional mechanisms driving business initiatives.

It is also true that the broken parts of today's energy infrastructure—from generation to transmission to distribution to regulations—each have such a large *time constant* that the movements of this behemoth are imperceptible; it appears stationary. But its transformative trajectory is unmistakable. It is as if a gigantic explosion has occurred, and its impact can only play out, imperceptibly at first, over 20 plus years.

Who should take the lead in mitigating the effects of the silent, invisible, and seemingly remote explosion? The initiative may or may not rest with the traditionally recognized, innovative, and powerful Western nations, with well-developed capital markets, enabling institutions, and a history of undertaking bold national policy initiatives. This is because, objectively viewed, the incentives do not exist for them to act with as great a compulsion as they do for emerging economies. Thus, the status quo may prevail for long, with reactionary resistance, a friction force.

Will leadership initiatives occur with emerging economies, aided by globally sourced and developed technologies and solutions? For emerging markets, the need for electricity is acute, sunken costs are less an issue, and, therefore, leadership actions may be easier and more affordable. Leadership in next-generation electricity may mean doing different things and differently, much like the emerging markets bypassed traditional telephony, going straight to wireless and smartphones, ignoring the historical industrial trajectory of the West. There were no stranded cost issues—simply new investments.

With distinct paths, one driven primarily by better returns on investment, the second driven primarily by need, and both driven by entrepreneurship and new business development, Electricity 2.0 will reach the same end point—a cluster of microgrids coexisting with a residual macrogrid. And the net result will be cleaner, cheaper, and universally available electricity and broadband Internet.

BEYOND CLIMATE CHANGE

Climate change *cannot* be the driver of this transformation, merely its context. Thus, unless events at COP 21,[4] and at other similar events in the future, translate into business action, we go nowhere. The greatest contributions COP 21 can make would be to define R & D priorities, leading to business initiatives: not merely research into component technologies, such as solar and batteries, but also systems-level research into intermicrogrid connectivity and communications, common resource sharing among microgrids, microgrid–macrogrid connectivity, optimization of generation resources, interworking of demand-side controls with generation, and so forth.

To date, there is little evidence of this kind of research from electricity service providers or their multinational equipment suppliers. At a time when we need Bells Labs equivalent in electricity, there is no one doing necessary pioneering research with the passion and focus of the Manhattan Project, despite the drumbeat of global climate change conferences. The physics and chemistry of global warming is clear enough—time to move beyond that. What governments might do is an open, interesting, and important question. But surely, the nation-states' role is not merely deciding among each other how much each nation is allowed to pollute and how we pay for that.

Unless policy supports large-scale entrepreneurial participation in next-generation electricity, and new entry by hitherto nonelectricity providers, we are not doing enough. We need to recognize that Electricity 2.0 is a local retail business, less a networking business, and certainly far less of a wide-area networking business than we have it today. "Local generation, local consumption, and local autonomy" has to be a policy priority. The core COP 21 issue is, how are we to achieve that, through what policy initiatives, and what incentives and institutional mechanisms?

Climate change and the accompanying term *sustainability* are pathetic and inadequate characterizations of the issues confronting the earth. *Climate change* is merely a fact that has become a fad, a distraction, and an excuse for feel-good behavior. Were I to attend COP 21 in Paris, I would feel guilty and wasteful rather than good about my trip. What we *do about climate change* is the real challenge.

Such nascent efforts as municipalization are indicative of a movement toward a new public good, but neither optimal nor sufficient. We do not know how small an economically viable microgrid can be, or why a microgrid should be the size of a municipal jurisdiction. Nations may differ in how they go about it, and the variability in policies introduced as a result is all to the good.

For instance, Meghalaya, a mountainous state in India where universal grid deployment is very difficult, may decide "all villages will be powered by microgrids; all of today's grid electricity will be used for industrial uses." Maharashtra state may decide: by a certain date, all new agricultural water pumps will be solar powered—no grid is necessary. New York State's REV initiative may come up with solutions that work well for the northeast United States, and California may come up with a solution all its own. Certain states may mandate that all university campuses of more than 1,000 students, and all hospitals of greater than 300 beds, say, become self-sufficient microgrids.

National sovereignty in many respects is increasingly obsolete, Brexit notwithstanding, as many recognize and as the image of the earth from NASA's earthrise picture has spectacularly shown. It is equally evident with climate change. In the case of the Internet, the diminishing of national sovereignty is not only palpable in its positive manifestations, as when the world's news is at anyone's fingertips but also in its negative manifestations, such as when the Internet is used for coordinating terror.

With John Donne, the seventeenth-century metaphysical poet, we have to say, "No man is an island, entire in itself." The same recognition is found in the pithy Sanskrit insight, *vasudhaivum kutumbakam,* translated, "The world entire is (my) family." The spiritual insight of oneness transcending the local and the particular, captured by the poet saint Tukaram,[5] by Edna St. Vincent Millay,[6] by Pierre Teilhard de Chardin, and long line of mystics over the centuries, and preceding the Internet or global warming recognition, needs translation into institutional terms, including know "what" and know "how." Business incentives and motivations to entrepreneurial action must flow as policy consequences of climate change meetings and the recognition of a common interconnected future.

The inadequacy of the nation-state does not mean the United Nations and its organizations are up to the task either. As David Victor[7] points out, the initiative can emerge as partnerships among the willing to launch the process, a few nations first, whose impact due to their size matters—United States, China, India, Brazil, and the European Union as a whole. Nothing quite like cooperation on this scale, for purposes other than trade or business, with planetary objectives, has happened before, unless we consider the formation of the United Nations itself.

The apocalyptic talk of climate change impacts may be viewed separately from the need to restructure the traditional electricity business on business grounds. That the traditional infrastructure needs to be broken down and reconstituted in a new industrial organization, does not need the trigger of climate change or the metrics of global warming that scientists have given us. The frustration with unreliable electricity or its absence can also be a trigger enough. Human ambitions and motivations in pursuing opportunities, technological developments, and the desires of people to be self-sufficient in their electricity needs, through solar power and batteries or anything else, would be good enough.

Energy needs to follow the Internet path, as the Enernet of things (EoT) will do. With the Internet as the binding glue, scale and scope, and therefore low cost and clean electricity, can be achieved even with discrete and dispersed microgrids.

When MCI—the original Microwave Communications Inc.—wanted to link Chicago to St. Louis via a microwave link in the early 1980s, the AT&T of that time said, "No." With "Carterphone" when an entrepreneur wanted to link its own telephone instrument to the existing telephone network of AT&T, again the company of that time said, "No." The legal actions initiated by these events have led to the telephone abundance today. Seemingly small events like these have breathtaking implications. As regards the electricity industry, and eventually transportation too, climate change may be the context, and inexpensive solar panels and battery innovations may be the triggering events.

In a memorable essay, Arvind Subramanian, now India's Chief Economic Advisor, wrote in the context of India's massive power outage: "In Lord Richard Attenborough's movie *Gandhi,* an underling of the British Empire heatedly warns his supercilious boss that Mahatma Gandhi's impending protest march to the sea poses a far greater threat than the Raj realizes: 'Salt, sir, is a symbol.' This elicits the memorable sneering put-down from the boss (played by Sir John Gielgud): 'Don't patronize me, Charles.' Is power, or rather the power sector, today's salt—emblematic of both the pessimistic outlook and promise of India?"[8]

It surely is, but the power sector is a metaphor for more, and not just for India. Its size and heft has been a blessing, and now we know it to be an albatross because it may be too large to dismantle with ease, and in the time frames set by climate change for the needed industrial mutation. Because an issue is not immediate and apparently urgent, it does not mean it is not critically important. In an interview with Idaho Public Radio, Dr. Strobe Talbott, president of the Brookings Institute, reflected upon climate change as the defining issue of our times and wondered how his young grandchildren would find the world 50 years hence? This thought about grandchildren, I believe, is a valid approach to viewing the problem, in that most of those who are alive today may reasonably have children, on a hostile, hot, and unstable plant, with coastal cities slowly sinking under ocean water melted from the Arctic regions, or other as yet indiscernible impacts.

Is the doomsday—"end of the world" or end of "life as we know it"—phenomenon inevitable? Hasn't humanity feared just such scenarios at the turn of every millennium? Guy McPherson's[9] writings on *Nature Bats Last* suggest that many believe the earth's systems are already past the tipping point and that reinforcing distinct forces—carbon dioxide emissions, plus methane from under the Arctic melting ice, plus deforestation, for example—together will accelerate the climate change effects we have begun to experience. Haven't we been on such a brink before during the Cold War? If we escaped those possibilities, why won't we now?

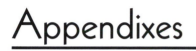

Appendixes

Appendix One

Microgrid Alliance: Policy Advocacy

INDIA AS A START

*Indian Prime Minister Narendra Modi and French President Francois Hollande launched the **International Solar Alliance** at the UN Climate Change Conference in Paris on 30 November 2015.*

"India and France have launched an International Solar Alliance to boost solar energy in developing countries. The alliance includes around 120 countries. " The goal is "to launch an international solar alliance as a common platform for cooperation among solar resource rich countries lying fully or practically between the Tropics of Cancer and Capricorn."

I have drafted a charter for a hypothetical Microgrid Alliance of India (or an International Microgrid Alliance). Microgrids necessarily incorporate "solar" and thus represent a broader solution. The Alliance can have a chapter in each of the participating countries.

GOAL

To spread microgrids in India and around the world. The Microgrid Alliance is a public policy–lobbying organization comprised of interested stakeholders.

The alliance's goal is to encourage the use of microgrids as the preferred solution for electricity access, reliability, and resilience for communities in rural, urban, and suburban areas in India and across the world. The electricity availability should be 24 × 7—"load shedding" must become a thing of the past.

CONTEXT

Given its rising demand for electricity, India is in an ideal position to leverage the emergence of microgrids. In fact, microgrids may leapfrog conventional electricity solutions in India and other emerging economies, just as wireless telecom dominates the market in many parts of the developing world. We do not need to extend today's grid, as we can have microgrids where needed.

Reliable electricity, like mobile phones, can empower previously marginalized populations. Advances in solar photovoltaics, battery technologies, and smart controls of the emerging electricity infrastructure have made universal electricity access an attainable goal.

WHAT THE ALLIANCE DOES

The alliance aims to solicit members, develop content, maintain a website, and provide forums for online discussions and periodic face-to-face meetings. The alliance website offers links to business and technical and policy resources. The web-based moderated discussion boards, and monthly "live" seminars with invited speakers, with video streaming for those who cannot attend in person, address open-ended issues of interest to alliance membership. The presentations are archived for later access.

Several open-ended challenges—some technical, some business, some regulatory—need to be addressed while deploying microgrids. The alliance offers members opportunities to solve these challenges.

Electricity access is a precursor to, and a complement of, universal broadband infrastructure. The alliance will partner with ISPs and educational institutions to facilitate access to both electricity and broadband Internet.

The alliance encourages public and private universities—IITs, IIMs, engineering colleges—to create energy research centers (ERC) focused on multiple areas essential for creating an ecosystem of microgrids.

Microgrids may be defined in various ways. Some use the term to describe small rural grids. However, microgrids with sophisticated controls, load-following ability, optimized initial costs, and efficient operations that balance the attributes of individual generating or storage components, while offering customers a full range of services, are rare.

HOW TO BEGIN

The alliance proposes deploying several prototype microgrids representing commonly encountered use cases. For instance, a typical microgrid for a school, college, university, hospital, office building, factory, enterprise zone, housing society, shopping center, malls and strip malls, and village may be built. For the load that each microgrid represents, we can define a typical configuration of generation and storage resources and determine its economics. The baseline economics for each of the previous use cases should be available to all who seek to deploy microgrids.

Early deployments may be grid-tied, where possible, and early rural deployments may be off-grid stand-alone solutions. Eventually, microgrids may interface with each other. The ownership of microgrids may be with existing distribution companies or with new private-sector players. Regulatory guidelines may be developed for ensuring the public interest through suitable ownership structures. The microgrids deployed should be spread across many parts of a country. They will necessarily take account of local variations, both on the supply side and on the demand side.

Ideally, customers—the beneficiaries—should fund the microgrids because they will see savings compared to traditional electricity or will benefit from new services. To seed the market, governments—at the center or at the state or local levels—may sponsor select prototypes and fund them initially.

WHY WOULD ANYONE JOIN THE ALLIANCE?

Many multinationals can, in principle, fulfill their microgrid goals on their own. At the present stage of the latent market, however, collaboration at the macro level and speaking with a common voice helps create the market. The alliance assures customers that the larger industry is engaged, and not just a company or two. While acting as a collective for policy and market building, individual company solutions will, of course, vary. Because customers are still unsure that microgrids can save them money, the early funding for a few installations has to be raised by someone who sees the business opportunity or by policy makers wishing to support an "infant industry." The USTDA (United States Trade Development Administration) rightly tries to do this. What might the Indian government similarly do? What can state governments do? The alliance can propose policy initiatives.

WHO PARTICIPATES IN THE ACTIVITIES OF THE MICROGRID ALLIANCE?

Corporations, public and private; operators and technology providers; regulatory entities, both at the state level and at the center; companies that today use captive power for reliable electricity access—all such entities can be members of the alliance. In general, this Microgrid Alliance, like the Microgrid Alliance—United States, allows the following to be members: grid technology companies; software and service companies; government agencies and institutions; demand response providers; academic institutions; building owners and operators; renewable energy providers; storage companies; distributed generation companies; research firms and organizations; electric utilities

Microgrids are more than macrogrids, writ small. The electricity business will fracture because the end of an industry structure is characterized by natural monopolies and economies of scale. Smaller (and eventually large) businesses focused on specialized applications may be formed, for instance, lighting companies for campuses and municipalities or homeowners' associations. Other businesses may focus on solar-powered water pumps for agriculture. Yet others may focus on automobile-charging infrastructure. Such businesses—in distinct and specialized *product-markets*—are also welcome to join the Microgrid Alliance.

ALLIANCE ADMINISTRATION AND OUTPUT

Role for the Ministry of Power, and New and Renewable Energy. Regulatory changes will be necessary to facilitate the use of microgrids. This will require bold and unprecedented leadership from the national ministries. Lessons may be derived from the transformation in telecommunications. For instance, spectrum was auctioned for wireless services; something analogous might be designed and implemented for electricity services.

The alliance has a board, advisory board, and steering committee, and charges for membership. For business entities, annual membership fees may be, for example, $1,000; for individuals, $25; for educational institutions, $150; for trade organizations, $1,000.

The alliance has an active and engaged group; the website complements its functions. It hosts rich, relevant, and timely content. The alliance transcends in scope what an energy research center at any educational institution (such as an IIT or IIM) may look like.

The alliance's scope will be national and global, on a peer level with similar alliances in the United States, for instance,[1] or its scope and functioning may parallel such professional bodies as the Academy of Management and Strategic Management Society.

Annual conference and meeting. The alliance holds a two-day annual meeting each September.

Sponsorship. Simultaneously signing up as sponsors, under academic and government stewardship, Tata, Schneider Electric, ABB, and the smaller rural players may make the alliance participatory and open, yet neutral.

Microgrid deployment news stories. The alliance actively seeks news stories on microgrid deployments worldwide, and these stories are posted on the alliance website. Dedicated and knowledgeable staff actively manage the website content.

Seminars and publications. The alliance holds monthly seminars on current topics of interest—everything from regulatory guidelines, to ownership structures, to technical issues of deployment and optimized working of microgrids.

The alliance will publish (say, two issues of) a journal each year addressing critical issues microgrid deployments face. The articles will address business, public policy, and technical issues. The journal will be accessible to industry professionals—not too technical—but cover topics in greater depth than typical trade magazines.

UNSOLVED PROBLEMS AND OPEN ISSUES

Rural application. It is now commonplace that we cannot economically extend the existing macrogrid to remote areas. Remote areas often do not have the needed (a) population density or the (b) ability to pay for the costs of electricity delivered by conventional means. Microgrids offer an alternative; they may be self-sufficient solutions, interface with the macrogrid, or interface with other microgrids to deliver needed electricity.

Urban and suburban application. Yet microgrids are not only for remote areas; microgrids may be deployed in urban and suburban areas too. For example, a housing cooperative with 32 apartments may create its own microgrid.

Optimization of generation and demand-side resources. While technological advance has made microgrids possible, we have not solved many of the technical problems necessary to make microgrids mainstream. The alliance seeks solutions to such problems. For example, in what proportions do we combine multiple generation sources—wind, solar, batteries, run-of-river hydro generators—to create the lowest capital cost infrastructure for reliable electricity for a given market demand?

Further, having deployed the capital optimally, how do we operate the microgrid economically given varying loads and changing input costs? Thus, optimization among multiple generation sources to match the varying demands of a facility—a home, office building, factory, and shopping mall—daily and across seasons is a difficult yet solvable problem, but this needs talented researchers from multiple disciplines.

Licensing microgrid service providers. How do we license a microgrid service provider? This is among the many policy and regulatory issues the alliance addresses, for we cannot assume that microgrid deployments will be done by incumbent distribution utilities alone or even by those in the electricity business.

How small. How small can microgrids be? Can they be at the level of a house? Building? Homes on a street? Homes in a neighborhood? Can all homes served today by a substation belong to one common microgrid?

Topology. How do we visualize microgrids—as a honeycomb? As fractals? How will microgrids interface with each other in a cluster? How will individual microgrids interface with the macrogrid? What models exist to enable such interconnection?

Information flows. How will information flow among microgrids? What kind of contracts will be executed *between* a microgrid and its corresponding macrogrid? What kinds of contracts will be executed *among* microgrids?

Economics. What are the economics of individual microgrids? Of a cluster of microgrids? How does the economics compare to the economics of traditional grids?

Quality standards. What quality standards—voltage, current, power factor, and beyond the traditional metrics—are suitable and required for microgrids?

Complement existing grid. As more and more microgrids are deployed, the demand on the existing grid will diminish, and the available traditional electricity may be deployed to new applications and new markets, especially industrial markets. How will this transition occur, smoothly?

Appendix Two

Course Outline: Strategic Management of Energy Systems

This is an illustrative course outline for inclusion in any business school curriculum. This can be a foundational course leading to a series of specialized courses, offered under the umbrella of the Center for New Energy Research.

Instructor:	Prof. Mahesh P. Bhave
Course Credits:	3
Session Duration:	1 term
Term and Year:	2016-plus, Term 5 or 6
Contact:	Room 307 maheshbhave@gmail.com/mahesh@iimk.ac.in +91 750 699 7189 (mobile) India

[T]he biggest change I've seen is in business. People are now looking at renewables as a business model in many more places than before.
        —Christoph Frei, Secretary General, World Energy Council

COURSE RATIONALE

The focus on the course is business—in the context of public policy, technological advance, climate change, and increasingly fluid industry boundaries.

The broad field of energy studies, especially electricity, is dominated by discussions of (a) public policy and regulations, (b) technology, and (c) climate change and sustainability. Surprisingly, businesses are underrepresented as actors in shaping the emerging energy field and therefore a livable planet.

True, today's electricity distribution companies are in the public sector, highly regulated and effective monopolies, and they are thus not businesses in a competitive market. This has begun to change, thanks to advancing technologies in solar, wind, batteries, and more.

- *Barriers to entry* in the electricity business are falling.
- *Economies of scale* are no longer necessary for low unit costs of electricity.
- *Distributed generation (DG)* enables "local generation, local consumption" and even local electricity trading.
- *Natural monopoly* arguments no longer hold the core of today's regulatory dispensation.

Renewable energy sources increasingly offer electricity cleanly at competitive prices to traditional electricity, and their economics will only improve, and eventually surpass, fossil fuel (or hydro, nuclear)–based pricing.

Despite this metamorphic change in the industry, businesses had only a token presence in Paris at the COP 21 accord in December 2015. In business schools, energy-related issues are mostly subsumed under "environment" or "sustainability," both perceived as relatively "soft" issues.

This course addresses questions such as the following:

- Do technological advances in renewable energy present new business development opportunities for existing and new businesses?
- What can businesses do, as corporate strategy, besides energy efficiency in their operations, regarding fossil fuel use, in electricity and transport, to increase revenues and profits and reduce costs?
- Could some companies (say in IT, or retail) enter the electricity business?
- What might entrepreneurs do?
- What might existing electric utilities and oil, gas, and petrochemical companies do?
- What is the role of foresightful public policy?

Course Objective: To create a cadre of business executives and policy makers aware of critical issues relating to energy trends, technologies, public policy, and the environment from a corporate strategy and public policy perspective.

Prerequisites: Students are expected to be familiar with financial tools such as discounted cash flow and benefit–cost analysis and with the Microsoft Office suite, especially Excel. Familiarity with quantifying nontangible benefits and costs is an asset.

Pedagogy: The opportunities from renewable energy in a dynamic technical, public policy, and climate change context are best addressed as a *business issue of investment.*

Cases from the trade press, illustrative current articles, and formal cases will be discussed in class.

This is a hands-on course, part traditional class and part workshop. Students will work in teams and will undertake research in detail on some of the technologies and topics discussed and present a *business initiative* or policy proposition to the rest of the class.

Each team will develop a *proposal* involving an investment (or divestment) relating to energy. Students will argue why their proposal is timely and fits with the organization's mission. They will anticipate objections and argue for overcoming them.

Students will also offer critical feedback to improve the proposals of other teams. In this process, students will learn how *new business development* projects or government policies get approved, budgeted, and launched.

Students role-play—as venture capitalist, socially responsible fund manager, bank business loan executive, CFO, CEO of an NGO, agency head, minister, ministry secretary, international climate change team negotiator—and evaluate the proposals presented critically.

To begin, student teams (a) *choose an organization,* one they are familiar with. This can be a division of a large corporation or government agency. (b) *Define a business or policy problem* as it relates to energy—electricity or transport, sustainability. (c) *Choose an applicable technology* based on the topics discussed, and (d) *define strategic fit, positioning, competitive advantage, public interest, benefits, and so on.*

Context: Energy management is at the core of sustainability. Just as management *information* systems (MIS) is taught in business schools, so too management *(of) energy* systems (MES) *or* business *energy* systems (BES) ought to be taught in business schools. This is not the case.

The world is running out of oil. The atmosphere is increasingly full of carbon dioxide and other warming emissions (greenhouse gases, GHGs), primarily from the burning of oil and coal for electricity, transport, and heating and cooling. This raises average global temperatures and leads to climate change. Anthropogenic climate change is happening at a time when the demand for fossil fuels—coal and oil—from the BRICS nations, namely, Brazil, Russia, India, China, and South Africa, is accelerating. Today's fossil fuel–driven lifestyle is not sustainable anywhere, and a worldwide search is on for credible, new renewable energy-based solutions.

SESSION OUTLINE

Week 1 From Public Policy to Business Strategy and Vice Versa: Why Strategic *Management* of Energy
- Businesses and individuals have to act, public policy has to initiate, support
- Sustainability—what does it mean?
- GHG emissions, global warming, climate change—by country, by source
- Beyond CSR (corporate social responsibility)—energy projects as new opportunities

- Oil, coal, and security—trends in usage; "peak oil"; nuclear energy post Fukushima earthquake
- "Peak water" and energy–water nexus

Week 2 Basics: Energy Literacy
- Electricity bill and metrics; gas bill and metrics
- Automobile use and its emissions impact
- Economics of power generation and distribution
- Regulatory history, natural monopoly, economies of scale
- GHG emissions calculations, for homes, buildings, and transport, by country
- Comparing energy and telecommunications—parallels and contrasts
- Historical and current review of rural electrification

Week 3 Business Consequences of Renewable and Traditional Generation
- Industry structure change in electricity and transport and oil and petro-chemicals industries
- Inflection point, metamorphic change, leadership choices—"*What, then, do we do? When?*"
- State of technologies—photovoltaics, concentrated solar, hydro, wind, and so on
- Biofuels—corn and cellulosic ethanol, algae, and so on
- Storage—batteries, fuel cells, flow batteries, and so on
- Shrinking market for traditional generation sources—coal, natural gas, nuclear

Weeks 4 and 5 Opportunities from Conservation and Efficiency
- Appliances, buildings, and vehicles and their ratings
- Demand response and peak load management
- Zero net energy buildings and campuses
- LEED, PEER, and USGBC and equivalents in different countries
- Energy conservation building codes, interfaces, standards, for example, USNAP—universal smart network access port
- Innovation possibilities—new energy-efficient products
- Renewable mandates in power mix, for example, California PUC

Week 6 Service Territories or Markets: Microgrids, District, Community, and Municipalities
- Campuses, jails, military bases, and remote villages
- Municipalization of electricity services
- Islanded generation and off-grid—NREL, LBNL work; CERTS microgrid
- Energy storage, intermittency, optimal mix of generation sources
- Federation of microgrids—honeycomb and fractals, future research

Week 7 Techno-Financial Modeling: Solar, Wind, and Microgrids
- Cost assumptions, for example, photovoltaics—crystalline, thin films; batteries
- Aggregate economics; assumptions based on geography; what-if analysis

- Financial tools—RET Screen International, SAM (solar advisory model), HOMER, and so on
- Prototypes, simulations, and market research in support of propositions

Week 8 Strategy: Porous Industry Boundaries and New Business Development
- What business are we in? Expanding scope as defense and offense
- Classical frameworks—technology–market matrix; technology–application matrix
- Driving forces; aggregate project planning; positioning and competitive advantage
- Partnerships and alliances; timing
- Strategic dissonance and disruptive innovation

Week 9 Emerging Industry Structure: Trends and Barriers
- Industry structure today and emerging competition
- Consolidation among utilities—Exelon and Pepco merger; limits to cost savings as strategy
- Utilities—Sempra Energy, SCE, PG&E, Duke, NRG, and so on, and their renewable energy strategies
- Convergence of energy, IT, and transportation; the "smart grid" and its consequences
- Electricity beyond kilowatt-hours—infrastructure electricity
- Electric and hybrid vehicles, their ecosystem; range anxiety, charging stations

Week 10 International Policy Framework: Kyoto through Paris COP 21
- WBCSD—Brundtland Commission
- UNFCCC annex I, non-annex I, observer parties; clean development mechanism (CDM); RECs, "cap and trade," carbon tax, and so on
- Low carbon strategies for inclusive growth

Week 11 Global Enabling Contexts: Comparative Initiatives
- Global survey of policy initiatives
- European leadership—Germany, Netherlands, Spain, and so on
- Energy projects in the Mediterranean and North Africa
- China—development of traditional coal-based power and solar manufacturing
- India's National Action Plan on Climate Change, Jawaharlal Nehru National Solar Mission, MNRE, and so on
- Narendra Modi's coalition of sunlight-rich countries at COP 21, International Solar Alliance
- US DoE and its laboratories; smart grid, NIST–EPRI work; automated metering infrastructure (AMI); feed-in tariffs, NEM, subsidies, and other incentives

Week 12 Synthesis: Tying Things Together
- Invited speakers roundtable
- Vision, overview of trends; career prospects in renewable energy

Week 13 Select Additional Topics
- Solar recharging of electric two-wheelers and cars
- Solar cooking, solar water pumps, solar water purification
- Rural electrification and economic development

Week 14+ Student Project Presentations

GRADES AND EVALUATION COMPONENTS

30%   Mid-term exam

30%   Final examination

30%   Final submission—presentation, text, financials, and appendix

10%   Participation

FINAL SUBMISSION

Three weeks after the last class. The final report submitted should have text (~ 15 pages, single spaced), Excel (~ 5 graphs), and slides (~ 15). Additional material may be placed in the appendix.

RESOURCES

Industry Associations, Trade Groups, Government Departments, and Ministries

International Energy Agency; International Renewable Energy Agency (IRENA); EPRI; Alliance for Energy Efficient Economy (AEEE); Rocky Mountain Institute; American Council on Renewable Energy (ACORE); California Center for Sustainable Energy (CCSE); Silicon Valley Photovoltaics Society; Galvin Electric Institute; Solar Energy Industries Association (SEIA) and Solar Electric Power Association (SEPA); World Watch Institute; World Energy Council; Prayas Energy Group; the World Bank, IMF, IFC, ADB, and the UN's SE4ALL; NITI-Aayog; Shakti Sustainable Energy Foundation; Council on Energy, Environment, and Water; Center for Science and Technology Policy; World Institute of Sustainable Energy; Energy Alternatives India; U.S. Department of Energy and its National Laboratories; Environment Protection Agency (EPA); California Public Utilities Commission (CPUC); California Energy Commission (CEC); Energy Information Administration (EIA); UNIPCC; UNFCCC; NRDC; Global Reporting Initiative; NYSERDA; and so on.

Select Latest Research Reports

References Including Select Video Clips

APPENDIX THREE

Select Microgrid-Related Articles by Mahesh P. Bhave

2015

The Mega Wonders of Microgrids, *Business Standard,* July 9, 2015.

Energy Efficiency? Quite Secondary. Generation First!. *Renewable Energy World,* May 20, 2015.

Tesla E-Motorcycles Complement SolarCity Microgrids, *Renewable Energy World,* May 20, 2015.

What Business Are Electric Utilities In? *Renewable Energy World,* March 6, 2015.

There Is Solar, and There Is Solar, *Renewable Energy World,* January 28, 2015.

Microgrids as Fact and Metaphor, *Renewable Energy World,* January 22, 2015.

2014

Microgrid Economics: It Takes a Village, a University, and a Ship, *Renewable Energy World,* September 30, 2014.

The Grid Is Coming? The Grid Is Going! *Renewable Energy World,* September 9, 2014.

A Requiem for Today's Grid, *Renewable Energy World,* August 5, 2014.

Microgrids Missing from the UN's Sustainable Energy for All Initiative, *Renewable Energy World,* July 8, 2014.

Microgrids Create Municipalization Benefits, *Renewable Energy World,* June 2, 2014.

Solar Disruption? Yes. Utility Death Spiral? Not Necessarily, *Renewable Energy World,* April 22, 2014.

Is Sustainability Talk a Distraction from What Really Matters? *Renewable Energy World,* March 19, 2014.

How Many Electric Utilities Does a Market Need? *Renewable Energy World,* January 31, 2014.

2013

More Power to Microgrids, *The Hindu Business Line,* June 5, 2013.

Microgrids by Mail Can Contribute to Rural Electrification, *Renewable Energy World*, March 15, 2013.

2012

Solar Power, Amul Style, *The Hindu Business Line,* November 2, 2012.

Solar Power on Every Rooftop, *The Hindu Business Line,* September 19, 2012.

Writing on the Roof: Competition for Electric Utilities, *Renewable Energy World,* August 17, 2012.

Smarter Grid Linking Solar Panels May Bypass Utilities, *Renewable Energy World,* June 14, 2012.

Renewable Energy in Business Schools: Apply an Investment Focus, *Renewable Energy World,* March 21, 2012.

2009–2011

For Renewable Energy Growth, Bring in the MBAs, *Renewable Energy World*, December 10, 2010.

The Innovation Imperative Part 2: ICT Companies as Electric Utilities Means Opportunity for India, *Renewable Energy World*, December 7, 2011.

The Innovation Imperative Part 1: ICT Companies as Electric Utilities of the Future, *Renewable Energy World*, November 30, 2011.

Renewables Impact on the Grid? Lessons from Telecom History, *Renewable Energy World*, September 8, 2009.

Notes

INTRODUCTION

1. Burr, Michael. May 2013. Economy of Small. http://www.fortnightly.com/fortnightly/2013/05/economy-small?authkey=239679983e0ea8e94385574aa531390f6d54ae0111fdb1ef5d698d03495b27d1.

2. Ibid.

3. Bhave, Mahesh. November 30, 2011. The Innovation Imperative Part 1: ICT Companies as Electric Utilities of the Future. http://www.renewableenergyworld.com/articles/2011/11/the-innovation-imperative-part-1-ict-companies-as-electric-utilities-of-the-future.html.

1. CENTRIFUGAL REVOLUTION: STRATEGIES FOR NEXT-GENERATION ELECTRICITY

1. The French Revolution led to the Reign of Terror and then Napoleon; France didn't become a stable democracy until the Third Republic, in the 1870s.

2. Kaggere, Niranjan. April 18, 2015. No Entry to BESCOM in 30 Flat Building, Bangalore Mirror. http://www.bangaloremirror.com/bangalore/others/No-entry-to-Bescom-in-30-flat-bldg/articleshow/46962841.cms.

3. Mahesh P. Bhave articles in Renewable Energy World at http://www.renewableenergyworld.com/authors/a-f/maheshbhave.html

4. Stewart, James B. September 24, 2015. Problems at Volkswagen Start in the Boardroom. http://www.nytimes.com/2015/09/25/business/international/problems-at-volkswagen-start-in-the-boardroom.html.

5. Solar power, Amul style—http://www.thehindubusinessline.com/opinion/solar-power-amul-style/article4058561.ece and reprinted in Renewable Energy World, http://www.renewableenergyworld.com/articles/2012/11/solar-power-amul-style-model-can-be-extended-to-solar-power-generation.html

2. MICROGRIDS FOR AUTONOMY: LOCAL GENERATION, LOCAL CONSUMPTION

1. Quoted in MIT Technology Review, India's Energy Crisis, October 2015. https://www.technologyreview.com/s/542091/indias-energy-crisis/

Dr. Anshu Bharadwaj is the Executive Director of Centre for Study of Science, Technology and Policy (CSTEP), Bengaluru. http://www.cstep.in/about/meet-the-team

2. Moore, Geoffrey. 1991. *Crossing the Chasm: Marketing and Selling High-Tech Products to Mainstream Customers*. Harper Business Essential, New York.

3. Advanced Microgrid Solutions. http://advmicrogrid.com/.

4. Bhave, Mahesh. September 9, 2014. The Grid Is Coming? The Grid Is Going!. http://www.renewableenergyworld.com/articles/2014/09/the-grid-is-coming-the-grid-is-going.html.

5. Central Electricity Regulatory Commission (CERC). http://www.cercind.gov.in/.

6. Sustainable Energy for All. http://www.se4all.org/.

7. Meghalaya Government to Start Micro Grid Systems in Select Villages. October 30, 2014. *The Economic Times*. http://articles.economictimes.indiatimes.com/2014-10-30/news/55595208_1_renewable-power-power-sector-grid.

3. TOWARD OFF-GRID CAMPUSES: THE DESIGN CHALLENGE

1. If you are interested in reviewing the latest version of the spreadsheet, contact the author.

2. The students who worked on the microgrid modeling project are Soumya Ranjan Pradhan, D. A. Subhashree, and Ankita Kumari from IIMK, and Joost van Berckel, Jan David Endtz, Huub Hillen, and Vinz van Teeseling from the Technical University, Delft.

3. We sincerely thank Mr. K. T. Bose, electrical engineering, IIMK, for helping us with the details of the campus electricity infrastructure and related information. For the template for the pro forma financial analysis, we sincerely thank Ms. Subhashree, PGP17 student, IIMK, and a chartered accountant.

4. A Beautiful Future for Small Grids. November 28, 2013. *The Hindu Business Line*.

4. MICROGRIDS: COMMON INTERSECTION BETWEEN DEVELOPED AND EMERGING ECONOMIES

1. Light Electric Vehicle Association. http://www.levassociation.com/.

2. Bhave, Mahesh. September 30, 2014. Microgrid Economics: It Takes a Village, a University, and a Ship. http://www.renewableenergyworld.com/articles/2014/09/microgrid-economics-it-takes-a-village-a-university-and-a-ship.html.

3. Dharnai Live Media Manual. http://www.greenpeace.org/india/Global/india/media%20manual_low%20res.pdf.

4. BASIX.http://www.basixindia.com/index.php?option=com_content&task=view&id=228&Itemid=231.

5. CEED. http://ceedindia.org/index.php.

6. Simpa Networks. http://simpanetworks.com/.

7. See, for instance, http://www.scientificamerican.com/article/coal-trumps-solar-in-india/

8. Lipton, Chad. May 15, 2015. Microgrids Key to Bringing a Billion Out of the Dark, National Geographic. http://voices.nationalgeographic.com/2015/05/15/microgrids-key-to-bringing-a-billion-out-of-the-dark/.

9. The World Bank Group, Collaboration for Development. https://collaboration.worldbank.org/groups/incubating-innovation-for-rural-electrification-the-telecom-energy-initiative/blog/2015/05/22/microgrids-key-to-bringing-a-billion-out-of-the-dark.

10. Bhave, Mahesh P. January 31, 2014. How Many Electric Utilities Does a Market Need?. http://www.renewableenergyworld.com/articles/2014/01/how-many-electric-utilities-does-a-market-need.html.

6. DEFINE AND AUCTION MARKET BLOCKS

1. EDF Envisions a New Electric Utility Business Model That Will Incorporate Clean Technologies, More Customer Engagement in New York. July 18, 2014. https://www.edf.org/media/edf-envisions-new-electric-utility-business-model-will-incorporate-clean-technologies-more.

2. Wikipedia: The practical measurement of traffic is typically based on continuous observations over several days or weeks, when the instantaneous traffic is recorded at regular, short intervals (such as every few seconds). These measurements are then used to calculate a single result, most commonly the *busy-hour traffic* (in erlangs). This is the average number of concurrent calls during a given one-hour period of the day, where that period is selected to give the highest result. (This result is called the time-consistent busy-hour traffic.)

7. ENTREPRENEURIAL OPPORTUNITIES IN ELECTRICITY 2.0

1. Rosenberg, Martin. September 29, 2013. Here Come Microgrids. http://www.energybiz.com/article/13/09/here-come-microgrids.

2. Patterson, Walt. 2015. *Electricity vs Fire: The Fight for Our Future*. Kindle Edition.

3. Villarreal, Christopher, and Erickson, David. April 14, 2014. *Microgrids: A Regulatory Perspective*. California Public Utilities Commission, San Francisco, CA.

4. Lahiri, Sudipta, Bystrom, Olof, Fioravanti, Richard, and Tong, Nellie (DNV GL). 2015. Microgrid Assessment and Recommendation(s) to Guide Future

Investments. California Energy Commission, Sacramento, CA. Publication number: CEC-500–2015–071.

5. Walt Patterson on Energy. http://waltpatterson.org/.

8. ELECTRICITY MOST GLAMOROUS: THE ENERNET OF THINGS (EOT)

1. A Good Dialogue with Steven Collier on the Enernet. The Emerging Enernet: Convergence of the Smart Grid with the IOT. https://www.youtube.com/watch?v=Nu9RZPTNejY.

2. While referring to Enernet, it is not necessary to add *of things*; we may assume it, or we may say *EoT*. There is no need to retain the parallel with IoT.

3. CBS News. February 28, 2013. http://www.cbsnews.com/videos/which-city-has-the-fastest-internet-in-the-nation/.

4. *The Guardian*. August 30, 2014. http://www.theguardian.com/world/2014/aug/30/chattanooga-gig-high-speed-internet-tech-boom.

5. Tweed, Katherine. February 3, 2014. Comcast Picks NRG as Electricity Partner in Pennsylvania. http://www.greentechmedia.com/articles/read/comcast-picks-nrg-as-electricity-partner-in-pennsylvania.

6. Breidenbach, Michelle. December 10, 2014. mbreidenbach@syracuse.com. As Syracuse Considers Ultra-High-Speed Internet, We Called the Mayor of "Gig City" for Answers. http://www.syracuse.com/news/index.ssf/2014/12/as_syracuse_considers_ultra-high_speed_internet_we_called_the_mayor_of_gig_city.html.

7. Brodkin, Jon. April 30, 2015. Comcast Brings Fiber to City That It Sued 7 Years Ago to Stop Fiber Rollout. http://arstechnica.com/business/2015/04/comcast-brings-fiber-to-city-that-it-sued-7-years-ago-to-stop-fiber-rollout/.

8. Southern California Edison. http://www.edisoncarriersolutions.com/.

9. Powergrid Corporation of India. http://www.powergridindia.com/_layouts/PowerGrid/User/ContentPage.aspx?PId=151&LangID=english.

10. RailTel Corporation of India. http://www.railtelindia.com/index.php?option=com_content&view=article&id=119&Itemid=172.

11. Breidenbach. As Syracuse Considers Ultra-High-Speed Internet.

12. Kang, Cecilia. August 7, 2016, How to Give Rural America Broadband? Look to the Early 1900s. http://nyti.ms/2aMZ2kY

13. Bolt Fiber Optic Services, http://neelectric.com/ffth.html

14. Berger, Warren. February 4, 2013. The 5 Questions Every Company Should Ask Itself. http://www.fastcodesign.com/1671756/the-5-questions-every-company-should-ask-itself.

15. Bhave, Mahesh. June 14, 2012. Smarter Grid Linking Solar Panels May Bypass Utilities. http://www.renewableenergyworld.com/articles/2012/06/smarter-grid-linking-solar-panels-may-bypass-utilities.html.

16. O'Boyle, Todd, and Mitchell, Christopher. December 5, 2012. Wilson's Greenlight Leads North Carolina in Fast Internet. http://www.muninetworks.org/reports/wilsons-greenlight-leads-north-carolina-fast-internet.

17. Breidenbach. As Syracuse Considers Ultra-High-Speed Internet.

18. Ibid.

19. Information about the number of panchayats is available at http://www .panchayat.gov.in/documents/401/0/USQ%201863.pdf.

20. Community Power. http://www.communitypowermn.org/about.

21. CommunityChoiceAggregation.https://en.wikipedia.org/wiki/Community_ Choice_Aggregation.

9. FUNCTIONAL, THEREFORE DYSFUNCTIONAL, BUSINESS SCHOOLS

1. Cisco CEO Pegs Internet of Things as $19 Trillion Market. http://www .bloomberg.com/news/articles/2014–01–08/cisco-ceo-pegs-internet-of-things-as-19-trillion-market.

2. Kuznets, Simon, Schumpeter's Business Cycles. *The American Economic Review,* Vol. 30, No. 2, Part 1 (June 1940), 257–271.

3. Special Issue of *Entrepreneurship Theory and Practice*: "Sector Studies in Entrepreneurship: Toward a Deeper Understanding of Industry-Specific Determinants, Processes, and Outcomes of Entrepreneurial Phenomena." http://www .babson.edu/Academics/centers/blank-center/global-research/step/Documents/ CFP%20Special%20Issue%20ETand%20P%20-%20Sector%20studies%20 in%20entrepreneurship.pdF.

4. Lélé, Sharachchandra M. Sustainable Development: A Critical Review. *World Development,* Vol. 19, No. 6 (June 1991), 607–621.

5. Tata Center for Technology + Design. http://tatacenter.mit.edu/.

6. http://www.renewableenergyworld.com/articles/2014/03/is-climate-cha nge-talk-a-distraction-from-what-really-matters.html, March 2014.

10. WRAPPING UP: MICROGRIDS EVERYWHERE

1. Ambachtsheer, Jane. December 4, 2015. The Future Makers: Long Term Investors as Climate Change 'Cops'. http://www.brinknews.com/the-future-ma kers-long-term-investors-as-climate-change-cops/.

2. Nelder, Chris, and Dyson, Mark. 2016. Nevada, Previously a Solar Leader, Shutters Its Residential Rooftop Market. http://blog.rmi.org/blog_2016_01_15_ nevada_shutters_its_residential_rooftop_market.

3. Bhave, Mahesh P. 2014. The Grid Is Coming? The Grid Is Going!. http:// www.renewableenergyworld.com/articles/2014/09/the-grid-is-coming-the-grid-is-going.html.

4. COP 21, Conference of Parties, Also Known as the 2015 Paris Climate Conference, of the UN Framework on Climate Change (UNFCCC). http://www.cop 21paris.org/about/cop21.

5. Tukaram said, "Though smaller than an atom, I yet encompass the entire skies." http://tukaram.com/english/english.htm See the YouTube video, https:// www.youtube.com/watch?v=9bDkmNBZKJ8.

6. Millay, Edna St. Vincent (1892–1950). *Renascence and Other Poems*. 1917.
http://www.bartleby.com/131/1.html.

> *The sky, I thought, is not so grand;*
> *I 'most could touch it with my hand!*
> *And reaching up my hand to try,*
> *I screamed to feel it touch the sky.*
> *I screamed, and—lo!—Infinity*
> *Came down and settled over me.*

7. David G. Victor, Professor, School of Global Policy and Strategy, UC San
Diego. Victor, David G. 2011. *Global Warming Gridlock: Creating More Effective
Strategies for Protecting the Planet*, Cambridge University Press.

8. Subramanian, Arvind. August 2, 2012, Can India's Power Problems Be
Solved? Peterson Institute. http://www.piie.com/blogs/realtime/?p=3051.

9. McPherson, Guy. http://guymcpherson.com/.

APPENDIX I

1. See http://www.microgridinstitute.org/our-team.html and http://microgrid
knowledge.com/.

Bibliography

Abaravicius, Juozas, Sernhed, Kerstin, and Pyrko, Jurek, "More or Less about Data: Analyzing Load Demand in Residential Houses," ACEEE Summer Study on Energy Efficiency in Buildings, 2006.

Abu-Sharkh, S., Arnold, R. J., Kohler, J., Li, R., Markvart, T., et al., "Can Microgrids Make a Major Contribution to UK Energy Supply?," *Renewable and Sustainable Energy Reviews,* 2006, vol. 10, no. 2, 78–127.

Addepalli, Raj, Presentation, Consumer & Utility Rights & Obligations (National Association of Regulatory Utility Commissioners, June 2007), available at www.narucpartnerships.org/Documents/Raj_Addepalli_Consumer_Protections_in_NY.pdf.

Advanced Microgrid Solutions, http://advmicrogrid.com/.

Aggarwal, Sonia, and Burgess, Eddie, "New Regulatory Models: Utility of the Future Centre," Arizona State University, 2014.

Alegria, Eduardo, Brown, Tim, Minear, Erin, and Lasseter, Robert H., "CERTS Microgrid Demonstration with Large-Scale Energy Storage and Renewable Generation," *IEEE Transactions on Smart Grid,* 2014, vol. 5, no. 2, 937–943.

Al-Khalili, Jim. Shock and Awe: The Story of Electricity, Part 1, 2, 3. BBC Horizon, http://www.bbc.co.uk/programmes/p00kjq6d/episodes/guide.

Ambachtsheer, Jane, "The Future Makers: Long Term Investors as Climate Change 'Cops'," December 4, 2015, http://www.brinknews.com/the-future-makers-long-term-investors-as-climate-change-cops/.

Annual Report: The Transforming Energy Economy, Joint Institute for Strategic Energy Analysis, 2013.

Antholis, W. J., and Talbott, S., *Fast Forward: Ethics and Politics in the Age of Global Warming,* Washington DC: Brookings Institution, 2010.

Bairiganjan, Sreyamsa, Cheung, Ray, Delio, Ella Aglipay, Fuente, David, Lall, Saurabh, and Singh, Santosh, "Power to the People: Investing in Clean Energy for the Base of the Pyramid in India," Centre for Development Finance—World Resources Institute, 2010.

Bajaj, Vikas, "In India, Anxiety over the Slow Pace of Innovation," *New York Times*, December 8, 2009.

Barnhart, Charles J., Dale, Michael, Brandt, Adam R., and Benson, Sally M., "The Energetic Implications of Curtailing Versus Storing Solar- and Wind-Generated Electricity," *Energy Environmental Science*, August 28, 2013.

Baron, David P., "Integrated Strategy: Market and Nonmarket Components," *California Management Review*, 1995, vol. 37, no. 2.

Barringer, Felicity, "New Technology Inspires a Rethinking of Light," *New York Times*, April 24, 2013.

Bazilian, Morgan, and Pielke, Roger Jr, "Making Energy Access Meaningful, Issues in Science and Technology," 2013.

Beckman, Karel, "Anil Srivastava, CEO Leclanché, Europe's Battery Leader: 'Public Transport Should Take the Lead in Electrification,'" November 5, 2015.

Bell, S., and Morse, *Sustainability Indicators: Measuring the Immeasurable?* 2nd ed., London: Earthscan, 2008.

Berger, Warren. The 5 Questions Every Company Should Ask Itself, February 4, 2013, http://www.fastcodesign.com/1671756/the-5-questions-every-company-should-ask-itself.

Bessette, Douglas L., Arvai, Joseph, and Campbell-Arvai, Victoria, "Decision Support Framework for Developing Regional Energy Strategies," American Chemical Society, 2014.

Bhugra, Nikhil, and Detroja, Ketan P., "Sliding Mode Control Based Power Balancing for Grid Connected PV System," IEEE Multi-conference on Systems and Control, 2013.

Binz, Ron, Sedano, Richard, Furey, Denise, and Mullen, Dan, "Practicing Risk-Aware Electricity Regulation: What Every State Regulator Needs to Know How State Regulatory Policies Can Recognize and Address the Risk in Electric Utility Resource Selection Highest Composite Risk Lowest," A Ceres Report, 2012.

Bonardi, Jean-Philippe, and Keim, Gerald D., "Corporate Political Strategies for Widely Salient Issues," *Academy of Management Review*, 2005, vol. 30, no. 3, 555–576.

Bony, Lionel, Doig, Stephen, Hart, Chris, Maurer, Eric, and Newman, Sam, "Achieving Low-Cost Solar PV: Industry Workshop Recommendations for Near-Term Balance of System Cost Reductions," Rocky Mountain Institute, 2010.

Borenstein, Severin, and Bushnell, James, "The U.S Electricity Industry after 20 Years of Restructuring," Energy Institute at Haas, 2014.

Boulder Municipalization Study—Issue Paper #1: What You Should Know about Boulder's Proposed Rates, Xcel Energy Inc., 2013.

Boulder Municipalization Study—Issue Paper #2: What You Should Know about Boulder's Carbon Tax Assumption, Xcel Energy Inc., 2013.

Boulder Municipalization Study—Issue Paper #3: What You Should Know about Boulder's Wind Cost Assumption, Xcel Energy Inc., 2013.

Boulder Municipalization Study—Issue #5: Boulder's New Study Shows Coal Needed and Most Scenarios Not Financially Feasible, Xcel Energy Inc., 2013.

Boulder Municipalization Study—Issue #6: Lessons Learned from Other Municipalities, Xcel Energy Inc., 2013.

Bourgeois, Thomas, Gerow, Jordan, Litz, Franz, and Martin, Nicholas, "Community Microgrids: Smarter, Cleaner, Greener, Pace Energy and Climate Centre," Pace Law School and Pace University, 2013.

Branker, K., Pathak, M.J.M., and Pearce, J.M., "A Review of Solar Photovoltaic Levelized Cost of Electricity, Renewable & Sustainable Energy," *Renewable and Sustainable Energy Reviews,* 2011, vol. 15, no. 9, 4470–4482, http://dx.doi.org/10.1016/j.rser.2011.07.104.

Breidenbach, Michelle, "As Syracuse Considers Ultra-High-Speed Internet, We Called the Mayor of "Gig City" for Answers," December 10, 2014, http://www.syracuse.com/news/index.ssf/2014/12/as_syracuse_considers_ultra-high_speed_internet_we_called_the_mayor_of_gig_city.html.

Brodkin, Jon, "Comcast Brings Fiber to City That It Sued 7 Years Ago to Stop Fiber Rollout," April 30, 2015, http://arstechnica.com/business/2015/04/comcast-brings-fiber-to-city-that-it-sued-7-years-ago-to-stop-fiber-rollout/.

Bronin, Sara C., and Mc Cary, Paul R., "Peaceful Coexistence," *Public Utilities Fortnightly,* 2013.

Brown, Ashley, and Lund, Louisa, "Distributed Generation: How Green? How Efficient? How Well Priced?" *The Electricity Journal,* 2013, vol. 26, no. 3, 28–34.

Browning, Kathryn C., "Electric Municipalization in the City of Boulder: Successful," CMC Senior Theses, 2013.

Burr, M., "Economy of Small," *Public Utilities Fortnightly,* May 2013.

Bushnell, James, Hobbs, Benjamin F., and Wolak, Frank A., "When It Comes to Demand Response, Is FERC Its Own Worst Enemy?" Centre for the Study of Energy Markets (CSEM) Working Paper Series, 2009.

Caldecott, Ben, and Mc Daniels, Jeremy, "Implications for European Capacity Mechanisms," Energy Markets and Climate Policy Working Paper, Stranded Assets Programme Working Paper, 2014.

Campoccia, A., Dusonchet, L., Telaretti, E., and Zizzo, G., "Comparative Analysis of Different Supporting Measures for the Production of Electrical Energy by Solar PV and Wind Systems: Four Representative European Cases," *Solar Energy,* 2009, vol. 83, 287–297.

Carl, Jeremy, Grueneich, Dian, Fedor, David, and Goldenberg, Cara, "An Energy Policy Essay: Renewable and Distributed Power in California Simplifying the Regulatory Maze—Making the Path for the Future," Hoover Institution Stanford University, 2013.

CBS News, February 28, 2013, http://www.cbsnews.com/videos/which-city-has-the-fastest-internet-in-the-nation/.

Central Electricity Regulatory Commission (CERC), http://www.cercind.gov.in/.

"Chattanooga's Gig: How One City's Super-Fast Internet Is Driving a Tech Boom," *The Guardian*, August 30, 2014, http://www.theguardian.com/world/2014/aug/30/chattanooga-gig-high-speed-internet-tech-boom.

Chowdhury, S., Chowdhury, S. P., and Crossley, P., Microgrids and Active Distribution Networks, Institution of Engineering and Technology: London, United Kingdom, 2009.

Chris, Marnay, "Providing Energy Services Locally," *A Google Tech Talk*, March 25, 2009, http://www.youtube.com/watch?v=3XuCJBvq6Sk.

Chris, Marnay, Hiroshi, Asano, Stavaros, Papathanassiou, and Goran, Strbac, "Policy Making for Microgrids: Economic and Regulatory Issues of Microgrid Implementation," *IEEE Power & Energy Magazine*, May/June 2008.

Chuang, Angela, Dollen, Don von, Mc Granaghan, Mark, and Mamo, Xavier, "Public Interest Energy Research (pier) Program Final Project Report: California Utility Vision and Roadmap for the Smart Grid of 2020," Electric Power Research Institute, 2011.

"Cisco CEO Pegs Internet of Things as $19 Trillion Market," http://www.bloomberg.com/news/articles/2014-01-08/cisco-ceo-pegs-internet-of-things-as-19-trillion-market.

Claremont Colleges Scholarship @ Claremont, "Greening or path to bankruptcy," http://scholarship.claremont.edu/cmc_theses/562.

Community Choice Aggregation, https://en.wikipedia.org/wiki/Community_Choice_Aggregation

Community Power, http://www.communitypowermn.org/about.

Costello, Kenneth W., Burns, Robert E., and Hegazy, Youssef, "Overview of Issues Relating to the Retail Wheeling of Electricity," The National Regulatory Research Institute, 1994.

Cudahy, Richard D., "Retail Wheeling: Is This Revolution Necessary?," *Energy Law Journal*, 1994, vol. 15, no. 351.

Dale, Michael, and Benson, Sally M., "Energy Balance of the Global Photovoltaic (PV) Industry—Is the PV Industry a Net Electricity Producer?" American Chemical Society, 2013.

Daly, H., "Ecological Economics: The Concept of Scale and Its Relation to Allocation, Distribution, and Uneconomic Growth," In H. Daly, *Ecological Economics and Sustainable Development: Selected Essays of Herman Daly*, Cheltenham, UK: Edward Elgar, 2007, 82–103.

Daly, H., "Toward Some Operational Principles of Sustainable Development," *Ecological Economics*, 1990, vol. 2, 1–6.

Dan, Arvizu, Stanford University Presentation, Director, National Renewable Energy Laboratory, April 1, 2009, discussion on "Renewable Energy and the Economy."

Dangerman, A.T.C. Jérôme, and Schellnhuber, Hans Joachim, "Energy Systems Transformation," pnas, 2012, www.pnas.org/cgi/doi/10.1073/pnas.1219791110.

den Elzen, Michel G. J., and van Vuuren, Detlef P. "Implications of the International Reduction Pledges on Long-Term Energy System Changes and Costs

in China and India," *Energy Policy,* 2013, vol. 63, 1032–1041, http://dx.doi
.org/10.1016/j.enpol.2013.09.026.

Deo, Kishore Chandra V. "Rashtriya Gram Swaraj Yojana," Lok Sabha
Unstarred Question No. 1863, March 8, 2013, http://www.panchayat.gov.in/
documents/401/0/USQ%201863.pdf.

Deshmukh, Ranjit, Bharvirkar, Ranjit, Gambhir, Ashwin, and Phadke, Amol,
"Changing Sunshine: Analyzing the Dynamics of Solar Electricity Policies in the
Global Context," *Renewable and Sustainable Energy Reviews Journal,* 2012, vol. 16.

Deshmukh, Ranjit, Pablo, Juan Carvallo, and Gambhir, Ashwin, "Sustainable
Development of Renewable Energy Mini—Grids for Energy Access: A Framework for Policy Design," 2013.

Di Lorenzo, Thomas J., "The Myth of Natural Monopoly," *Review of Austrian
Economics,* 1996, vol. 9, no. 2, 43–58.

Dubash, Navroz K., Raghunandan, D., Sant, Girish, and Sreenivas, Ashok, "Indian
Climate Change Policy Exploring a Co-Benefits Based Approach," *Economic &
Political Weekly,* June 1, 2013, vol. 48, no. 22.

"EDF Envisions a New Electric Utility Business Model That Will Incorporate
Clean Technologies, More Customer Engagement in New York," July 18,
2014, https://www.edf.org/media/edf-envisions-new-electric-utility-business-
model-will-incorporate-clean-technologies-more.

Edge Model Executive Summary, Rocky Mountain Institute, 2013.

Electric Power Research Institute (EPRI) Inc., "The Integrated Grid Realizing the
Full Value of Central and Distributed Energy Resources," 2014.

Energy Efficiency Markets, LLC, "Think Microgrid a Discussion Guide for Policy-
makers, Regulators and End Users," 2014.

Farzan, Farnaz, Lahiri, Sudipta, Kleinberg, Michael, Gharieh, Kaveh, Farzan,
Farbod, and Jafari, Mohsen, "Microgrids for Fun and Profit," *IEEE Power and
Energy Magazine,* 2013.

Felder, Frank A., and Athawale, Rasika, "The Life and Death of the Utility
Death Spiral," *The Electricity Journal,* 2014, vol. 27, no. 6, 9–16. http://dx.doi
.org/10.1016/j.tej.2014.06.008.

Fox-Penner, Peter, *From ERG to the Smart Grid: One Illini's Journey,* Brattle
Group, 2013.

Frank, Charles R. Jr., *The Net Benefits of Low and No-Carbon Electricity Technologies Global Economy and Development,* Workspaper, 73, 2014.

Frankel, David, Ostrowski, Kenneth, and Pinner, Dickson, "The Disruptive
Potential of Solar Power," McKinsey and Company, 2014.

Fthenakis, Vasilis, "How Long Does It Take for Photovoltaicsto Produce the
Energy Used?" National Society of Professional Engineers, 2012.

Gambhir, Ashwin, Toro, Vishal, and Ganapathy, Mahalakshmi, "Decentralised
Renewable Energy (DRE) Micro-Grids in India: A Review of Recent Literature," *Prayas Energy Group,* 2012.

Gentile, Basilio, Simpson-Porco, John W., Dorfler, Florian, Zampieri, Sandro, and
Bullo, Francesco, *"On Reactive Power Flow and Voltage Stability in Microgrids,"*

American Control Conference (ACC) June 4–6, 2014, Portland, Oregon, USA, 2014.

Ghazipour, Masoud Shirvan, and Asghar, Ali Ghadimi, "Determining the Capacity of Combined Distribution Generation Resources in an Independent Distributed Network Considering the Uncertainty Behaviour of Load and Energy Resource," *Indian Journal of Science and Technology*, 2013, vol. 6, no. 12, 5533–5541.

Ghosh, Probir, "Global Leadership through Breakthrough SEI (Sustainable Energy Initiatives) Will India Forge a Breakthrough like the Cell Phone Revolution?" International Symposium on Bioenergy, 2010.

Green, Jessica F., "Order Out of Chaos: Public and Private Rules for Managing Carbon," The Massachusetts Institute of Technology, 2013.

Greenstone, Michael, "IGC Evidence Paper Energy Growth and Developments," IGC International Growth Centre, 2014.

Gupta, Rajat, Sankhey, Shirish, Dobbs, Richard, Woetzel, Jonathan, Madgavkar, Anu, and Hasyagar, Ashwin, "From Poverty to Empowerment: India's Imperative for Jobs, Growth, and Effective Basic Services," McKinsey Global Institute, 2014.

Halu, Arda, Scala, Antonio, Khiyam, Abdulaziz, and González, Marta C., "Data-Driven Modeling of Solar-Powered Urban Microgrids," January 15, 2016.

Hamilton, Katherine, "Proceeding on Motion of the Commission in Regard to Reforming the Energy Vision," 2014.

Hande, Harish, "National Solar Mission and Related Policy Issues," http://www.forumblog.org/socialentrepreneurs/2010/12/indian-solar-mission-anti-poor-and-anti-democracy.html.

Hannes, Berthold, and Abbott, Matt, *Distributed Energy: Disrupting the Utility Business Model*, Bain and Company, 2013.

Hargadon, A., "Technology Policy and Global Warming: Why New Innovation Models Are Needed," *Research Policy*, 2010, vol. 39, no. 8, 1024–1026.

Hart, S., "Beyond Greening: Strategies for a Sustainable World," *Harvard Business Review*, January–February 1997.

Hayek, F. A., "Why I Am Not a Conservative," in *The Constitution of Liberty*, Chicago: University of Chicago Press, 1960.

Hayes, Sara, Herndon, Garrett, Barret, James P., Mauer, Joanna, Molina, Maggie, Neubauer, Max, Trombley, Daniel, and Ungar, Lowell, "Change is in the Air: How States Can Harness Energy Efficiency to Strengthen the Economy and Reduce Pollution," American Council for an Energy-Efficient Economy, 2014.

Hernandez, Mari, "Solar Power to the People: The Rise of Rooftop Solar among the Middle Class," Center for American Progress, 2013.

Hirose, Keiichi, Shimakage, Toyonari, Reilly, James T., and Irie, Hiroshi, "The Sendai Microgrid: Operational Experience in the Aftermath of the Tohoku Earthquake: A Case Study," New Energy and Industrial Technology Development Organization, 2013.

http://www.panchayat.gov.in/documents/401/0/USQ%201863.pdf.

http://tukaram.com/english/english.htm. See the YouTube video, https://www.youtube.com/watch?v=9bDkmNBZKJ8.

Huberty, M., and Zysman, J., "An Energy System Transformation: Framing Research Choices for the Climate Challenge," *Research Policy*, 2010, vol. 39, no. 8, 1027–1029.

Hulme, Mike, "The Road from Copenhagen: The Experts' Views," Macmillan Publishers Limited, 2010.

Hunter, Lesley, "Renewable Energy in the 50 States: Western Region," American Council on Renewable Energy, 2013.

Hyams, Michael A. "Microgrids: An Assessment of the Value, Opportunities and Barriers to Deployment in New York State," Nyserda, 2010.

"Increasing Renewable Resources: How ISOs and RTOs Are Helping Meet This Public Policy Objective," IRC Council, 2007.

Jackson, T., "Prosperity without Growth: The Transition to a Sustainable Economy," Sustainable Development Commission, 2010.

James, Tong, and Wellingoff, Jon, "Solar for Everyone, Including Public Utilities," *Rooftop Parity*, Fortnightly, August 2014.

Jamison, Mark A., Berg, Sanford V., Gasmi, Farid, and Távara, José, "Annotated Reading List for a Body of Knowledge on the Regulation of Utility Infrastructure and Services," Public Utility Research Centre University of Florida, 2004.

Jerram, Lisa, Dehamna, Anissa, and Lawrence, Mackinnon, "The Fuel Cell and Hydrogen Industries: 10 Trends to Watch," Navigant Consulting, 2014.

John, Richard R., and Vailand, Theodore N., "The Civic Origins of Universal Service," *Business and Economic History*, Winter 1999, vol. 28, no. 2.

Johnson, L., Yeh, S., and Hope, C., "The Social Cost of Carbon: Implications for Modernizing Our Electricity System," *Journal of Environmental Studies and Sciences*, 2013, vol. 3, no. 4, 369–375, doi: 10.1007/s13412-013-0149-5.

Jones-Albertu, Rebecca, Feldman, David, Fu, Ran, Horowitz, Kelsey, and Woodhouse Michael, "Technology Advances Needed for Photovoltaics to Achieve Widespread Grid Price Parity," *Progress in Photovoltaics*, September 20, 2015, submitted.

Joskow, Paul L., and Sloan, Alfred P. Foundation and MIT1, "Comparing the Costs of Intermittent and Dispatchable Electricity Generating Technologies," 2010.

Kaggere, Niranjan. "No Entry to BESCOM in 30 Flat Building," *Bangalore Mirror*, April 18, 2015, http://www.bangaloremirror.com/bangalore/others/No-entry-to-Bescom-in-30-flat-bldg/articleshow/46962841.cms.

Kates, R., Parris, T., and Leiserowitz, A., "What Is Sustainable Development?" *Environment*, 2005, vol. 47, no. 3, 8–21.

Katsigiannis, Y. A., and Georgilakis, P. S., "Optimal Sizing of Small Isolated Hybrid Power Systems Using Tabu Search," *Journal of Optoelectronics and Advanced Materials*, May 2008, vol. 10, no. 5, 1241–1245.

Kaun, B., "Cost-Effectiveness of Energy Storage in California," Electric Power Research Institute, 2013.

Kellow, Aynsley, *Science and Public Policy the Virtuous Corruption of Virtual Environmental Science,* Edward Elgar Publishing Limited, 2007.

Khandelwal, Shubham, Bhugra, Nikhil, and Detroja, Ketan P., "Controlled Power Point Tracking for Power Balancing in PMSG Based Wind Energy Conversion System," Preprint Submitted to the 5th International Symposium on Advanced Control of Industrial Processes, 2014.

Kharvel, Ranjith Annepu, "Sustainable Solid Waste Management in India," Columbia University in the City of New York, 2012.

Kim, Bongjin, Prescott, John E., "De Regulatory Forms, Variations in the Speed of Governance Adaptation, and Firm Performance", *Academy of Management Review,* 2005, vol. 30, no.2, 414–425.

Kind, Peter, "Disruptive Challenges: Financial Implications and Strategic Responses to a Changing Retail Electric Business," Edison Electric Institute, 2013.

King, Douglas, "The Regulatory Environment for Interconnected Electric Power Micro-Grids: Insight from State Regulatory Officials," Carnegie Mellon Electricity Industry Center, Working Paper CEIC-05–08, 2006, www.cmu.edu/electricity.

King, Douglas, and Morgan, M. Granger, "Guidance for Drafting State Legislation to Facilitate the Growth of Independent Electric Power Microgrids," Carnegie Mellon Electricity Industry Center, 2005.

King, Michael, "Community Energy Planning, Development and Delivery," The International District Energy Association, 2012.

Kishore, Avinash, Shah, Tushaar, and Prabha, Nidhi Tewari, "Solar Irrigation Pumps Farmers' Experience and State Policy in Rajasthan," *Economic & Political Weekly,* March 8, 2014, vol. 49, no. 10.

Kooijman-van Dijk, Annemarije L., "The Power to Produce: The Role of Energy in Poverty Reduction through Small Scale Enterprises in the Indian Himalayas," Dissertation: University of Twente, 2008.

Kristov, Lorenzo, and Martini, Paul De, "21st Century Electric Distribution System Operations," 2014.

Kumagai, Jean, "The Smartest, Greenest Grid: What the Little Danish Island of Bornholm is Showing the World about the Future of Energy," IEEE Spectrum, 2013.

Kumaravel, S., and Ashok, S., "An Optimal Stand-alone Biomass/solar-pv/pico- hydel hybrid energy system for remote rural area electrification of isolated village in western-Ghats region of India," *International Journal of Green Energy,* 2012, vol. 9, no. 5, 398–408.

Kunneke, Rolf, and Fens, Theo, "Ownership Unbundling in Electricity Distribution: The Case of the Netherlands," *Energy Policy,* 2007, vol. 35, 1920–1930.

"Kuznets, Simon, "Schumpeter's Business Cycles," *American Economic Review,* June 1940, vol. 30, no. 2, 257–271.

Lacey, Stephen, "Here's What Utilities Really Think about Microgrids," Greentech Media, 2014, http://reneweconomy.com.au/2014/heres-utilities-really-think-microgrids-16811.

Lahiri, Sudipta, Olof, Bystrom, Richard, Fioravanti, Nellie, Tong, and DNV GL, "Microgrid Assessment and Recommendation(s) to Guide Future Investments," California Energy Commission, Publication Number CEC-500–2015–071, 2015.

Laird, F., and Stefes, C., "The Diverging Paths of German and United States policies for Renewable Energy: Sources of Difference," *Energy Policy*, 2009, vol. 37, 2619–2629.

Leiserowitz, Anthony, "Climate Change Risk Perception and Policy Preferences: The role of Affect, Imagery, and Values," *Climatic Change*, 2006, vol. 77, 45–72.

Léna, Grégoire, "Rural Electrification with PV Hybrid Systems: Overview and Recommendations for Further Deployment," IEA PVPS Task 9CLUB-ER, 2013.

Levi, Tillemann, "Revolution Now: The Future Arrives for Four Clean Energy Technologies," U.S. Department of Energy, 2013.

Liam, Robert Dohn, "The Business Case for Microgrids White Paper: The New Face of Energy Modernization," Siemens AG, 2011.

Lipton, Chad, "Microgrids Key to Bringing a Billion Out of the Dark," National Geographic, May 15, 2015, http://voices.nationalgeographic.com/2015/05/15/microgrids-key-to-bringing-a-billion-out-of-the-dark/.

Lovins, Amory B., Datta, E. Kyle, Feiler, Thomas, Rábago, Karl R., Swisher, Joel N., Lehmann, André, and Wicker, Ken, "Small Is Profitable: The Hidden Economic Benefits of Making Electrical Resources the Right Size," Snowmass, CO: Rocky Mountain Institute, 2002.

Lubin, D., and Esty, D., "The Sustainability Imperative," *Harvard Business Review*, May 2010.

Luthi, S., "Effective Deployment of Photovoltaics in the Mediterranean Countries: Balancing Policy Risk and Return," *Solar Energy*, 2010, vol. 84, 1059–1071.

Mahajan, Shruti Deorah, and Chandran-Wadia, Leena, "Solar Mini Grids for Rural Electrification: A Roadmap to 100% Energy Access for India @75," Observer Research Foundation Mumbai, 2013.

Marcus, William B., Ruszovan, Gregory, and Nahigian, Jeffrey A., "Economic and Demographic Factors Affecting California Residential Energy Use," JBS Energy Inc., 2002.

Markvart, Tom. "Microgrids: Power Systems for the 21st Century," *Emerging Technologies Issue*, September 24, 2005.

Marnay, Chris, "Optimal Microgrid Equipment Selection and Operation," Presentation at Microgrid World Forum, Irvine CA, Wed 13 Mar 2013.

Marnay, Chris, and Bailey, Owen C., "The Certs Microgrid and the Future of the Macrogrid," Environmental Energy Technologies Division, 2004.

Maron, Dina Fine, "Electric Vehicle Market Looks for a Recharge," *Scientific American*, April 26, 2013.

Marshall, J. D., and Toffel, M. W., "Framing the Elusive Concept of Sustainability: A Sustainability Hierarchy," *Environmental and Scientific Technology*, 2005, vol. 39, no. 3, 673–682.

Martin, Chris, Chediak, Mark, and Wells, Ken, "Why the US Power Grids Are Numbered," *BusinessWeek,* 2013.

Martin, Richard, "India's Energy Crisis," October 7, 2015, http://www.technology review.com/featuredstory/542091/indias-energy-crisis/.

Martin, Richard, "In India's Hot Summer, the Solar Market Overheats," July 24, 2015, http://www.technologyreview.com/view/539671/in-indias-hot-summer-the-solar-market-overheats/.

McDermott, Karl, "Cost of Service Regulation in the Investor-Owned Electric Utility Industry: A History of Adaptation," The Edison Electric Institute (EEI), 2012.

McPherson, Guy, http://guymcpherson.com/.

Messner, Dirk, Schellnhuber, John, Rahmstorf, Stefan, and Klingenfeld, Daniel, "The Budget Approach: A Framework for a Global Transformation toward a Low-Carbon Economy," AIP Publishing LLC, 2010, http://dx.doi.org/10.1063/1.3318695.

Meyer, Roland, "Vertical Economies of Scope in Electricity Supply—Analysing the Costs of Ownership Unbundling," School of Humanities and Social Sciences, 2011.

Millay, Edna St. Vincent (1892–1950), *Renascence and Other Poems,* 1917, http://www.bartleby.com/131/1.html.

MIT Lectures, e.g., http://mitworld.mit.edu/video/900, Selin, Noelle, and Holdren, John, *Energy and Climate Change,* http://mitworld.mit.edu/video/845.

Mizani, Shervin, and Yazdani, Amirnaser, "Optimal Design and Operation of a Grid-Connected Microgrid," IEEE Electrical Power and Energy Conference, 2009.

Moniz, J. Ernest, and Kenderdine, A. Melanie, "Meeting Energy Challenges: Technology and Policy," American Institute of Physics, 2002.

Moore, Geoffrey, *Crossing the Chasm: Marketing and Selling High-Tech Products to Mainstream Customers,* Harper Business Essentials, 1991.

Morgan, M.G., and Zerriffi, H., "The Regulatory Environment for Small Independent Micro-Grid Companies," *The Electricity Journal,* 2002, vol. 15, no. 9, 52–57.

Morris, G., Chad, Abbey, Joss, G., and Marnay, C., "A Framework for the Evaluation of the Cost and Benefits of Microgrids," Lawrence Berkeley National Laboratory, 2011.

Morris, Jesse (RMI), Calhoun, Koben (RMI), Goodman, Joseph, and Seif, Daniel (RMI), "Reducing Solar PV Soft Costs: A Focus on Installation Labor," Rocky Mountain Institute, 2013, www.rmi.org/ knowledge-centre/.

Mosca, Manuela, "On the Origins of the Concept of Natural Monopoly: Economies of Scale and Competition," *The European Journal of the History of Economic Thought,* 2008, vol. 15, no. 2, 317–353, http://www.tandfonline.com/loi/rejh20.

Mowery, D., Nelson, R., and Martin, B., "Technology Policy and Global Warming: Why New Policy Models Are Needed (or Why Putting New Wines in Old Bottles Won't Work)," *Research Policy,* 2010, vol. 39, no. 8, 1011–1023.

Narain, Sunita, Ramesh, R., Mehrotra, A., Kapur, Lalit, and Gnanamuthu, Antony, "Report of the Committee for Inspection of M/S Adani Port and SEZ Ltd, Mundra, Gujarat," Ministry of Environment and Forests, New Delhi, 2013.

Narayanaswamy, Balakrishnan, Garg, Vikas K., and Jayram, T. S., "Online Optimization for the Smart (Micro) Grid," E-Energy, 2012.

Nelder, Chris, and Dyson, Mark, "Nevada, Previously a Solar Leader, Shutters Its Residential Rooftop Market," January 15, 2016, http://blog.rmi.org/blog_2016_01_15_nevada_shutters_its_residential_rooftop_market.

Nelson, David, and Shrimali, Gireesh, "Finance Mechanisms for Lowering the Cost of Renewable Energy in Rapidly Developing Countries," Climate Policy Initiative, 2014.

Newcomb, James, Lacy, Virginia, and Hansen, Lena, "New Business Models for the Distribution Edge: The Transition from Value Chain to Value Constellation," Rocky Mountain Institute, 2013, www.rmi.org/new _business_models.

Newcomb, James, Lacy, Virginia, Hansen, Lena, and Bell, Mathias, "Distributed Energy Resources: Policy Implications of Decentralization," *The Electricity Journal*, 2013, vol. 26, no. 8, 65–87, http://dx.doi.org/10.1016/j.tej.2013.09.003.

Newton-Evans Research Company, "Newton-Evans Research Company's Market Trends Digest," 2014, http://www.newton-evans.com/newsletter_archive/mtd1q14.pdf.

Nidumolu, R., Prahalad, C., and Rangaswami, R., "Why Sustainability Is Now a Key Driver of Innovation," *Harvard Business Review*, September 2009.

Nordman, Bruce, "Nanogrids Evolving Our Electricity Systems from the Bottom Up."May 2011, http://nordman. lbl. gov/docs/nano.pdf.

Nordman, Bruce, Christensen, Ken, and Meier, Alan, "Think Globally, Distribute Power Locally: The Promise of Nanogrids," *IEEE Computer Society*, 2012.

O'Boyle, Todd, and Mitchell, Christopher, "Wilson's Greenlight Leads North Carolina in Fast Internet," December 5, 2012, http://www.muninetworks.org/reports/wilsons-greenlight-leads-north-carolina-fast-internet.

Ortiz, Carlos Eduardo, Rada, José Francisco Álvarez, Hernández, Edson, Lozada, Juan, Carbajal, Alejandro, and Altuve, Héctor J., "Protection, Control, Automation, and Integration for Off-Grid Solar-Powered Microgrids in Mexico," 40th Annual Western Protective Relay Conference, October 2013.

Paatero, Jukka V., and Lund, Peter D., "A Model for Generating Household Electricity Load Profiles," *International Journal of Energy Research*, 2006, vol. 30, no. 5, 273–290.

Parga, Sheoli, and Ghosh, Sudeshna Banerjee, "More Power to India, the Challenge of Electricity Distribution," International Bank for Reconstruction and Development, The World Bank, 2014.

Parks, Keith, Wan, Yih-Huei, Wiener, Gerry, and Liu, Yubao, "Wind Energy Forecasting: A Collaboration of the National Center for Atmospheric Research (NCAR) and Xcel Energy," National Renewable Energy Laboratory, 2011.

Patterson, Walt, "Beyond the Fire Age," January 2013, http://www.waltpatterson .org/beyondfire.pdf.

Paul, L., Lucas, Shukla, P.R., Wenying, Chen, Bas, J. van Ruijven, Subash, Dhar, Schnitzer, Daniel, Lounsbury, Deepa Shinde, Pablo, Juan Carvallo, Deshmukh, Ranjit, Apt, Jay, and Kammen, Daniel M., "Microgrids for Rural Electrification: A Critical Review of Best Practices Based on Seven Case Studies," The United Nations Foundation, 2014.

Pearson, Natalie Obiko, and Nagarajan, Ganesh, "Solar Water Pumps Wean Farmers from India's Archaic Grid," *Bloomberg*, 2014.

Peterman, Andrew, Kourula, Arno, and Levitt, Raymond, "Balancing Act: Government Roles in an Energy Conservation Network," *Research Policy*, 2014, vol. 43, no. 6, 1067–1082.

Photovoltaic Power Systems Programme Annual Report, "Implementing Agreement on Photovoltaic Power System," IEA International Energy Agency, 2012.

Powergrid Corporation of India, http://www.powergridindia.com/_layouts/PowerGrid/User/ContentPage.aspx?PId=151&LangID=english.

Public–Private Roundtables at the Fourth Clean Energy Ministerial. *Clean Energy Ministerial*, India, 2013, http://www.cleanenergyministerial.org/Portals/2/pdfs/CEM4_roundtables_report_web.pdf.

RailTel Corporation of India, http://www.railtelindia.com/index.php?option=com_content&view=article&id=119&Itemid=172.

Ran, S. Kim, and Horn A., "Regulation Policies Concerning Natural Monopolies in Developing and Transition Economies," United Nations Department of Economic and Social Affairs, 1999.

Rangarajan, Anand, "World Water and Power: Using Solar Energy to Solve Water and Power Problems in Developing Countries," Water Conditioning and Purification, 2005.

Redclift, M., "Sustainable Development: *An Oxymoron Comes of Age*," *Sustainable Development*, 2005, vol. 13, no. 4, 1987–2005, 212–227.

Reiche, D., and Bechberger, M., "Policy Differences in the Promotion of Renewable Energies in the EU Member States," *Energy Policy*, 2004, vol. 32, no. 7, 843–849.

Reiss, Peter C., and White, Matthew W., "Household Electricity Demand, revisited," 2002, http://web.stanford.edu/~preiss/demand.pdf.

Reiter, Harvey L., "Competition between Public and Private Distributors in a Restructured Power Industry," *Energy Law Journal*, 1998, vol. 19, 333.

Reiter, Harvey L., "The Contrasting Policies of the FCC and FERC Regarding the Importance of Open Transmission Networks in Downstream Competitive Markets," *Federal Communications Law Journal*, 2005, vol. 57, no. 2.

Renewable and Sustainable Energy Reviews, 2006, 78–127.

Report of the City of Boulder and Xcel Energy Community Task force, City of Boulder and Xcel Energy Community Taskforce, 2013.

Report of the World Commission on Environment and Development: Our Common Future. 1987, United Nations.

RET Screen International, *Clean Energy Project Analysis: RET Screen Engineering and Cases*, 3rd ed., 2005.

Rickover, H. G. Admiral, "Thoughts of a Man's Purpose in Life," Council on Religion and International Affairs, 1982.

Roach, Michael, "Community Power and Fleet Microgrids," *IEEE Electrification Magazine*, 2014.

Robert, Lasseter, et al., "Integration of Distributed Energy Resources: The CERTS MicroGrid Concept," LBNL-50829, Berkeley, 2002.

Rosenberg, Martin, "Here Come Microgrids," September 29, 2013, http://www .energybiz.com/article/13/09/here-come-microgrids.

Sagar, A., and van Der Zwaan, B., "Technological Innovation in the Energy Sector: R&D, deployment, and learning-by-doing," *Energy Policy*, 2006, vol. 36, no. 17, 2601–2608.

Saif, A., et al. "Multi-Objective Capacity Planning of a PV-Winddiesel-Battery Hybrid Power System," *IEEE International Energy Conference and Exhibition (EnergyCon)*, 2010, 217–222, copyright 2010 IEEE.

Sanden, B., "The Economic and Institutional Rationale of PV Subsidies," *Solar Energy*, 2005, 78, 137–146.

Sarma, E.A.S., "Myopia on Coal," *Economic & Political Weekly*, 2013, vol. 48, no. 44.

Schumacher, E. F., *Small Is Beautiful: Economics as If People Matters*, Harper and Row, 1973.

Seel, Joachim, Barbose, Galen L., and Wiser, Ryan H., "An Analysis of Residential PV System Price Differences between the United States and Germany," *Energy Policy*, 2014, vol. 69, 216–226.

Sharachchandra, M. Lélé, "Sustainable Development: A Critical Review," *World Development*, June 1991, vol. 19, no. 6, 607–621.

Sharma, Shankar, "Nuclear Power in the Context of Global Warming," *Economic & Political Weekly*, 2014, 2013, 24, vol. 47, no. 17.

Sidak, J. Gregory, and Spulber, Daniel F., *Deregulatory Takings and Breach of the Regulatory Contract*, New York University Law Review, 1996, vol. 71, no. 4, 924–999.

Siddiqui, Afzal, Asano, H., Hatziargyriou, N., Hernandez, C., and Marnay, C., *Microgrids: Engineering and Economics*, SPIN Springer, May 2008.

Simpa Networks, http://simpanetworks.com/.

Sims, R., "Renewable Energy: Response to Climate Change," *Solar Energy*, 2004, vol. 78, 137–146.

Sinha, Sunanda, and Chandel, S.S., "Review of Recent Trends in Optimization Techniques for Solar Photovoltaic–Wind Based Hybrid Energy Systems," *Renewable and Sustainable Energy Reviews*, 2015, vol. 50, 755–769.

Smith, Aimee M., and Earl, Laura M., "Cost of Capital Application of San Diego Gas and Electric Company (U 902 M)," San Diego Gas and Electric Company, 2012.

Southern California Edison, http://www.edisoncarriersolutions.com/.

Special Issue of Entrepreneurship Theory and Practice, "Sector Studies in Entrepreneurship: toward a Deeper Understanding of Industry-Specific

Determinants, Processes and Outcomes of Entrepreneurial Phenomena," http://
www.babson.edu/Academics/centers/blank-center/global-research/step/
Documents/CFP%20Special%20Issue%20ETand%20P%20-%20Sector%20
studies%20in%20entrepreneurship.pdF.

Sreekumar, N., and Dixit, Shantanu, "Rajiv Gandhi Rural Electrification Program
Urgent Need for Mid-Course Correction," Discussion Paper by Prayas Energy
Group, 2011.

Stanton, Tom, "Are Smart Microgrids in Your Future? Exploring Challenges
and Opportunities for State Public Utility Regulators," National Regulatory
Research Institute, 2012.

Stewart, James B., "Problems at Volkswagen Start in the Boardroom," September 24,
2015, http://www.nytimes.com/2015/09/25/business/international/problems-
at-volkswagen-start-in-the-boardroom.html.

Su, Wencong, and Wang, Jianhui. "Energy Management Systems in Microgrid
Operations," *The Electricity Journal*, October 2012, vol. 25, no. 8, 45–60, http://
dx.doi.org/10.1016/j.tej.2012.09.010.

Subramanian, Arvind, "Can India's Power Problems Be Solved?" Peterson
Institute, August 2, 2012, http://www.piie.com/blogs/realtime/?p=3051.

Sudhakar, K., Premalatha, M., and Sudharshan, K., "Energy Balance and Exergy
Analysis of Large Scale Algal Biomass Production," The 2nd Korea—Indonesia
Workshop and International Symposium on Bio Energy from Biomass, 2012.

Summary Report: DOE Microgrid Workshop, Office of Electricity Delivery and
Energy Reliability Smart Grid R&D Program, 2012.

Sustainable Energy for All, http://www.se4all.org/.

Tata Center for Technology + Design, http://tatacenter.mit.edu/.

Tenenbaum, Bernard, Greacen, Chris, Siyambalapitiya, Tilak, and Knuckles,
James, "From the Bottom Up How Small Power Producers and Mini-Grids Can
Deliver Electrification and Renewable Energy in Africa," International Bank for
Reconstruction and Development/The World Bank, 2014.

"The Grid Is Coming? The Grid Is Going!," September 9, 2014, http://www
.renewableenergyworld.com/articles/2014/09/the-grid-is-coming-the-grid-is-
going.html.

Thirumurthy, N., Harrington, L., Martin, D., Thomas, L., Takpa, J., and Gergan,
R., "Opportunities and Challenges for Solar Minigrid Development in Rural
India," National Renewable Energy Laboratory, 2012.

Tillemann, "The Future Arrives for Four Clean Energy Technologies," U.S
Department of Energy, 2013.

Tongia, Rahul, and Wilson, Ernest J. III, "The Flip Side of Metcalfe's Law:
Multiple and Growing Costs of Network Exclusion," *International Journal of
Communication*, 2011, vol. 5, 2010.

Tongia, Rahul, Subrahmanian, Eswaran, and Arunachalam V. S., "Information
and Communication Technology for Sustainable Development: Defining a
Global Research Agenda," Allied Publishers Pvt. Ltd, 2005.

Tranp, Tony, Doğru, Mustafa F., Ozen, Ulas, and Christopher, Beck J., "Scheduling a Multi-Cable Electric Vehicle Charging Facility," Association for the Advancement of Artificial Intelligence, 2013.

Transactive Energy Workshop Proceedings, "The Grid Wise Architecture Council, Transportation Industry Review," American Council on Renewable Energy (ACORE), 2012, 2013.

Tweed, Katherine, "Comcast Picks NRG as Electricity Partner in Pennsylvania," February 3, 2014, http://www.greentechmedia.com/articles/read/comcast-picks-nrg-as-electricity-partner-in-pennsylvania.

Tweed, Katherine, "Where's My Microgrid?" April 12, 2013, http://www.greentechmedia.com/articles/read/wheres-my-microgrid.

Tweed, Katherine, "Why Cellular Towers in Developing Nations Are Making the Move to Solar Power," January 15, 2013, http://www.scientificamerican.com/article/cellular-towers-moving-to-solar-power/.

Urban, Robert A., and Bakshi, Bhavik R., "Techno-Ecological Synergy as a Path toward Sustainability of a North American Residential System," *Environmental Science and Technology,* 2013, vol. 47, no. 4, 1985–1993.

Vaclav, Smil, "Drivers of Environmental Change: Focus on Energy Transitions," Vancouver: University of British Columbia Library, 2011, http://hdl.handle.net/2429/36661.

Valeur, Henrik, "Alternatives to the Automobile in the Indian," *City Economic & Political Weekly,* 2013, vol. 48, no. 47, 22–25.

van den Bergh, Jeroen C.J.M., "Policies to Enhance Economic Feasibility of a Sustainable Energy Transition," Policy Challenges for a Transition to Sustainable Energy, 2013, www.pnas.org/cgi/doi/10.1073/pnas.1221894110.

Victor, David G., *Global Warming Gridlock,* Cambridge University Press, 2011.

Villarreal, Christopher, Erickson, David, and Zafar, Marzia, "Microgrids: A Regulatory Perspective," California Public Utilities Commission Policy & Planning Division, 2014.

Virani, Aarti, "In 'Powerless', India's Electricity Crisis Pits Maverick against the State," *New York Times,* April 25, 2013.

Wald, Matthew L., "In Two-Way Charging, Electric Cars Begin to Earn Money from the Grid," *New York Times,* April 25, 2013.

Weil, Jonathan, "Are There Cockroaches under Tesla's hood?" *Bloomberg,* 2013.

Wimmer, Nancy, *Green Energy for a Billion Poor,* MCRE, January 2012.

Wimmer, Nancy, "The Art of Rural Business," *Journal of Management for Global Sustainability,* 2013, vol. 2, 107–119.

Wiser, Ryan, Phadke, Amol, and Goldman, Charles, "Pursuing Energy efficiency as a hedge against carbon regulatory risks: Current resource planning practices in the west," University of Nebraska—Lincoln Digital Commons @ University of Nebraska, 2008, Lincoln, http://digitacommons.unl.edu/usdoepub/20.

World Bank, "Turn down the Heat: Why a 4°C Warmer World Must be Avoided," World Bank, Washington, DC, 2012.

The World Bank Group, Collaboration for Development, https://collaboration
.worldbank.org/groups/incubating-innovation-for-rural-electrification-
the-telecom-energy-initiative/blog/2015/05/22/microgrids-key-to-bringing-
a-billion-out-of-the-dark.

World Wildlife Fund, "Weathercocks and Signposts: The Environment Movement at a Crossroads," Washington, DC, 2012, April 1, 2008.

Wu, Tim, "Wireless Carterfone," *International Journal of Communication,* 2007,
vol. 1, 389–426.

Wydick, Bruce, *Games in Economic Development,* Cambridge University Press, 2008.

Zakariazadeh, Alireza, Jadid, Shahram, and Siano, Pierluigi, "Smart Microgrid
Energy and Reserve Scheduling with Demand Response Using Stochastic Optimization," *Electrical Power and Energy Systems,* 2014, vol. 63, 523–533.

Zhen, Cheng, and Kammen, Daniel M., "An Innovation-Focused Roadmap
for a Sustainable Global Photovoltaic Industry," *Energy Policy,* 2014, vol. 67,
159–169.

VIDEOS

A Smart Grid for Intelligent Energy Use, http://www.youtube.com/watch?v=
YrcqA_cqRD8&NR=1.

Charlie Rose with Richard Branson and Vinod Khosla, http://video.google
.com/videoplay?docid=-8446023559190691675&hl=en#docid=-81902897
94591872373.

"Convergence of Electrical and Telecommunications Infrastructure," http://www
.youtube.com/watch?v=zB4-mBQPd7k&feature=related.

Gopalakrishnan, Kris, "Infosys on Smart Grid and More," http://www.cleanskies
.tv/videos/kris-gopalakrishan-discusses-infosys-and-technology-energy-
industry.html.

"National Public Radio," http://www.npr.org/templates/story/story.php?story
Id=110997398.

Patterson, Walt, "Smart Energy," http://www.youtube.com/watch?v=s1UW7d
C3Dhc and http://waltpatterson.org/.

"Renewable Energy and the Economy," http://www.youtube.com/watch?v=Fc01
HalhoNc&feature=player_embedded#at=2257.

Smil, Vaclav, "Drivers of Environmental Change: Focus on Energy Transitions,"
http://www.youtube.com/watch?v=nJxmlNyu4sE.

Smil, Vaclav, on Energy Transitions, http://www.youtube.com/watch?v=ZyET8
FAYJW8.

Talbott, Strobe, "Idaho Public Radio," http://video.idahoptv.org/video/1694
332485/.

Index

ABOUT THE AUTHOR

Mahesh P. Bhave is a visiting professor of strategy, Indian Institute of Management (IIM), Kozhikode, Kerala, India, for the past four plus years. Before that, he was the founder of a start-up in San Diego and Silicon Valley. Earlier, Mahesh worked at senior positions—director, vice president—in new business development, corporate strategy, and product management at Citizens Utilities, Sprint, Hughes Network Systems, and start-ups. Mahesh is a chemical engineer from Indian Institute of Technology (IIT), New Delhi, and has a master's in public administration and PhD in interdisciplinary social sciences from the Maxwell School, Syracuse University, Syracuse, New York. Mahesh is a U.S. citizen and lives with his wife and two sons in San Diego, California; he travels to India several times a year to teach at IIM.